Negotiating Secular and Ecclesiastical Power:
Western Europe in the Central Middle Ages

INTERNATIONAL MEDIEVAL RESEARCH:

Selected Proceedings
of the International Medieval Congress
University of Leeds

VOLUME 6

EDITORIAL BOARD

Axel E.W. Müller, Alan V. Murray, Ian N. Wood
with the assistance of the IMC Programming Committee

EDITORIAL ASSISTANTS

Amanda Banton
Elizabeth Wall

NEGOTIATING SECULAR AND ECCLESIASTICAL POWER

WESTERN EUROPE IN THE CENTRAL MIDDLE AGES

Edited by

Arnoud-Jan A. Bijsterveld,
Henk Teunis,
and Andrew Wareham

INTERNATIONAL MEDIEVAL RESEARCH

6

BREPOLS
Turnhout, Belgium
1999

© BREPOLS 1999
Printed in the European Union on acid-free paper.
D/1999/0095/47
ISBN 2-503-50872-3
All rights reserved.
No part of this publication may be reproduced, stored in a retrieval system or transmitted,
in any form or by any means, electronic, mechanical, photocopying, recording or
otherwise, without the prior permission of the publisher.

Contents

List of Illustrations and Maps vii

Preface ix
        Ludo J.R. Milis

Introduction xi
        Arnoud-Jan A. Bijsterveld, Henk Teunis, &
        Andrew Wareham

Notes on Contributors xv

List of Abbreviations xix

Negotiating Secular and Ecclesiastical Power in the Central
Middle Ages: A Historiographical Introduction 1
        Henk Teunis

PART ONE. TEXTS AS TOOLS OF POWER

The Political Use of Piety in Episcopal and Comital Charters of
the Eleventh and Twelfth Centuries 19
        Benoît-Michel Tock

The Crisis of Episcopal Authority in Guibert of Nogent's
Monodiae 37
        Trudy Lemmers

Relics as Tools of Power: The Eleventh-Century *Inventio* of St
Bertin's Relics and the Assertion of Abbot Bovo's Authority 51
    Karine Ugé

Monastic Freedom vs. Episcopal and Aristocratic Power in the
Twelfth Century: Context and Analysis of the *De libertate
Beccensis* 73
    Julie Potter

PART TWO. LAND AND KINSHIP

Bishops as Contenders for Power in Late Anglo-Saxon England:
The Bishopric of East Anglia and the Regional Aristocracy 89
    Christine Senecal

Two Models of Marriage: Kinship and the Social Order in
England and Normandy 107
    Andrew Wareham

Forging Unity between Monks and Laity in Anglo-Norman
England: The Fraternity of Ramsey Abbey 133
    Hirokazu Tsurushima

PART THREE. CONFLICT AND AFFIRMATION

Parchment and Power in Abbey and Cathedral: Chartres,
Sherborne and Vézelay, c. 1000–1175 149
    John O. Ward

Conflict and Compromise: The Premonstratensians of Ninove
(Flanders) and the Laity in the Twelfth Century 167
    Arnoud-Jan A. Bijsterveld

Index of Persons 185

Index of Places 191

Thematic Index 195

List of Illustrations and Maps

Senecal

    Map 1: The Commended Freemen, Estates and Soke of the Bishopric of East Anglia in 1066 92

    Map 2: The Commended Freemen, Estates and Soke of the Archbishop Stigand's Anglian Holdings in 1066 93

    Map 3: The Commended Freemen, Estates, and Soke of East Anglia's Monastic Communities in 1066 98

    Map 4: The Commended Freemen, Estates, and Soke of the Wealthiest Aristocrats in East Anglia in 1066 99

Wareham

    Map 1: Marriages of Ealdorman Uhtred's Kin 110

    Table 1: Ealdorman Uhtred's Family and Kin 111

    Map 2: Marriages of FitzOsbern and Tosny Families 118

    Table 2: FitzOsbern and Tosny Family Trees 119

Tsurushima

    Map: Laymen, Priests and a Parish Gild as Members of the Fraternity of Ramsey Abbey 143

Ward

>Plate 1: The Sherborne Illumination of St John: BL Add. MS 46,487 152

>Plate 2: The Illumination of Fulbert of Chartres: Chartres, Bibliothèque Municipale, MS nouv. acq. 4 154

>Plate 3: Facsimile of Chartres, Bibliothèque Municipale, MS nouv. acq. 4 155

>Plate 4: The Auxerre Illumination of Girart and Bertha of Roussillon: Auxerre, Bibliothèque Municipale, MS 227, f. 22 158

Bijsterveld

>Plate: Manuscript of the *Liber miraculorum* and the *De fundatione Ninivensis abbatie*: New York, Union Theological Seminary, MS 11, f. 22^r 170

Preface

LUDO J.R. MILIS

The study of power relationships is rooted in the deeper sense of historical investigation at large. History, as the sum of acts past and present, is a continuous succession of evaluations, decision-making and achieved factual behaviour. More precisely defined, it stands for interplay and interaction.

For far too long, institutional history, legal history, and *histoire événementielle* have tried to monopolize power relationships and to encapsulate them in rather narrow explanatory schemes. Instead, they were begging for a broader and more encompassing approach. This enrichment could proceed from an interdisciplinary breakthrough. For several decades now, sociology, anthropology, political studies, and even aetiology have made historians see the primary evidence transmitted from the past in a new way, in which the structure of what has happened is emphasized to the detriment of the mere description of facts. Facts have increasingly lost their relevance for the reconstruction of past (and present) behaviour. Broader disciplines selected facts out of an unlimited reservoir to legitimize their own validity and at the same time to manage the endlessness of the documentation. In other words, historians, and among them medievalists, needed to deal in an unprecedented way with the past they had invented as the *magistra vitae* and protected as their very own intellectual hunting grounds. We all know how, as a result of this type of change, historiography became fragmented. A panoply of schools, a spectrum of approaches, and a proliferation of publications generated a disenchanting number of unquestionable conclusions.

In this sense I welcome the book *Negotiating Secular and Ecclesiastical Power: Western Europe in the Central Middle Ages*. Certainly, its scope is not to offer a wide range of definitive explanatory schemes, but it shows how medievalists should try (and indeed do try) to return to the close reading of their documents. Such a meticulous analysis (in colloquial language I would use the word 'peeling') needs, and at the same time suggests, an elaborated set of questions. Applied to different types of primary evidence, all intrinsically fragmented and mutually incoherent, results may be compared, put together, and eventually synthesized. This book, composed around three major themes ('Texts as Tools of Power', 'Land and Kinship', and 'Conflict and Affirmation'), constitutes a nice example of how medievalists can reshape their discipline into a more responsive one.

Introduction

This volume contains ten studies dealing with the interaction of secular and ecclesiastical power in the Central Middle Ages. The study of the relationships between church and state in the Middle Ages, both at the highest level, between popes and rulers, and at a lower level, between bishops and barons, emerged during the nineteenth century. However, historiography on medieval power relationships was shaped by nineteenth- and twentieth-century positivist institutional and legal history, which was in turn moulded by contemporary political concerns. The call for the separation of church and state in some western European nations, and their close collaboration in others, have often resulted in anachronistic views of the medieval interplay between secular and ecclesiastical power, generally stressing their opposition and contradiction. Although events such as the Investiture Contest and the Fourth Lateran Council still occupy a central place in our understanding of the Middle Ages, they are no longer regarded as the *fons et origo* of the full range of relationships between spiritual and temporal power.

In contrast, in this volume the focus is on the interdependence of secular and ecclesiastical power and on the ways both secular rulers, kings, counts and other lords, and ecclesiastical authorities and institutions continuously interacted, trying to affirm the relationships between them. Norms and interests were partly shared, and partly not, which entailed negotiations on a vast array of issues. Ecclesiastical leaders defended their dignity and property by negotiating their way through such issues. Such complexities may cause some puzzlement to modern readers, but it was an essential means through which the higher clergy protected their position. Explaining how negotiations between the clergy and the laity differentiated between secular and ecclesiastical power, while at the same time affirming shared values, is not an easy task, given the fragmentary nature of the evidence, but is an important issue. For several years the contributors to this volume have been exchanging ideas, viewpoints, and papers at the Leeds International Medieval Congress on this theme. In 1997 it seemed a good moment to present this work in a more formal form.

Besides the theme, what links the papers in this volume is also a shared methodological approach. Nowadays, as a result of an interdisciplinary breakthrough in historiography, the focus is more on the structure of what has happened than on the mere description of facts. To achieve a more structural and contextualised evaluation of historical facts, historians have returned to close reading of their primary sources and to the conceptual analysis of social mechanisms such as network building, gift exchange, and dispute settlement. More attention is being paid to the role played by landed property and kinship (both consanguinity and spiritual kinship) in structuring society as a whole.

This selection of a historiographical introduction and nine case studies from England, northern France and the Low Countries allows for a subtle comparison of secular and ecclesiastical links and social interactions in a series of regional and local contexts in the Central Middle Ages. Four essays demonstrate how texts (charters, autobiography, hagiography, and historiography) were used to define relations between ecclesiastical and lay powers. Three further essays focus upon how land and kinship (through marriage and spiritual fraternity) defined the social relations between and within the laity and the clergy. The final two essays concentrate upon the solution of conflicts between ecclesiastical institutions and the outer world. It is hoped that the reader may find stimulating answers to questions regarding the interconnection of secular and ecclesiastical power. This collection of papers suggests that, instead of underlining hostility, more attention should be given to a wider range of relationships between these powers. It is shown that the key process was negotiation, resulting in the affirmation of shared values. Instead of assuming vertical lines of command on opposing sides, placing church and laity in conflict, there seems to have been a series of horizontal negotiations over the use of spiritual and worldly power and wealth. These contributed to the creation of medieval Europe's social values. This tradition of accommodation between laity and clergy is a theme with strong resonances up to the present day.

Bringing together papers from four continents has only been made possible by the goodwill of all contributors (and through the blessings of

Introduction

e-mail). Amanda Banton, Simon Forde, Hans Harbers, Christopher Holdsworth, and Ian Wareham provided helpful comments and advice, and through their kindness ensured that problems and doubts were quickly resolved. Our greatest debt is to the International Medieval Congress, which brought us together. Our focus has been upon western Europe in the Central Middle Ages, but we hope that in future years scholars working on similar themes relating to eastern Europe and the Mediterranean, and perhaps also to the Islamic world, will join our sessions and provide us with new perspectives on secular and ecclesiastical power at future Leeds congresses.[1]

Leuven, Utrecht, and London, 16 April 1999
Arnoud-Jan A. Bijsterveld
Henk Teunis
Andrew Wareham

---

[1] A note on placenames: in this volume the modern indigenous form is used for all places that do not have a generally received English form: thus, Leuven, not Louvain; Brugge, not Bruges; Veurne, not Furnes; etc. Cross-references are found in the Index of Places.

Notes on Contributors

Arnoud-Jan A. Bijsterveld (b. 1962) held a postdoctoral research fellowship with the Netherlands Organization for Scientific Research (NWO) at the Vrije Universiteit in Amsterdam (The Netherlands) from 1995 to 1999. Currently he is a research fellow at the Katholieke Universiteit Leuven (Belgium). In 1993 he defended his dissertation, a prosopographical study of the parish priests in fifteenth- and sixteenth-century North Brabant. He works on the formation of power through gift exchange and dispute settlement in the Meuse-Demer-Scheldt Area, c. 900–1200, on which he published several articles, such as 'Gift exchange, landed property, and eternity. The foundation and endowment of the Premonstratensian priory of Postel (1128/1138–1179)' in *Land and Ancestors: Cultural Dynamics in the Urnfield Period and the Middle Ages in the Southern Netherlands*, eds. F. Theuws and N. Roymans (Amsterdam, 1999), pp. 309–48.

Trudy Lemmers (b. 1958) worked as a research assistant at the Katholieke Universiteit in Nijmegen (The Netherlands) from 1995 to 1999. In 1998 she defended her dissertation on the structure and meaning of the three books of Guibert of Nogent's *Monodiae*. This dissertation was published as *Guiberts van Nogents Monodiae. Een twaalfde-eeuwse visie op kerkelijk leiderschap* (Hilversum, 1998). She currently works as a quality manager in a general hospital and as an independent scholar.

Ludo J.R. Milis (b. 1940) is professor of Cultural and Religious History of the Middle Ages at the University of Gent (Belgium). He is the author of *Angelic Monks and Earthly Men: Monasticism and its Meaning to Medieval Society* (Woodbridge, 1992), and editor of *The Pagan Middle Ages* (Woodbridge and Rochester, 1998).

Julie A. Potter (b. 1968) is a postdoctoral student at Cambridge University (UK). She is currently working on her dissertation on the friendship network of the abbey of Le Bec-Hellouin, 1034–1204. She has previously published an article on the *Vita Gundulfi* in its historical context in *The Haskins Society Journal. Studies in Medieval History* 7 (1995), 89–100.

Christine Senecal (b. 1970) is writing her dissertation at Boston College (USA) on regional identity in late Anglo-Saxon England. She has worked on the questions of landholding patterns of England's tenth- and eleventh-century elite, and defining the English thegnage.

Henk Teunis (b. 1940) holds a teaching and research position at Utrecht University (The Netherlands). His major fields of interest are in medieval historiography and in church-state relations in the Angevin area. He recently published articles on Suger, Benoît of Saint-Maur and Marbod of Rennes.

Benoît-Michel Tock (b. 1963) has lectured as a 'maître de conférences' at Université Marc Bloch in Strasbourg (France) since 1992; also, he has been a 'chargé de cours invité' at the Facultés Universitaires Saint-Louis in Brussels (Belgium) since 1990. After having defended his dissertation on the chancery of the bishops of Arras (published Louvain-la-Neuve, 1991), he co-edited the volume *Diplomatique médiévale* in the series 'Atelier du médiéviste' (Turnhout, 1993). He currently works on the links between charters, law, and power in the Central Middle Ages.

Hirokazu Tsurushima (b. 1952) is a professor at Kumamoto University (Japan). He is the author of 'The Fraternity of Rochester Cathedral Priory about 1100', *Anglo-Norman Studies* 14 (1992), 313–37. He currently works on the unification of societies in England immediately after the Norman Conquest.

Karine Ugé (b. 1969) is a doctoral student at Boston College (USA), working on monastic assertion of identity and authority through the production of narrative texts in northern France from the ninth to the twelfth century. She recently published 'Creating a Useable Past in the Tenth Century: Folcuin's *Gesta* and the Crises at Saint-Bertin', *Studi Medievali* 37 (1996), 887–903.

Contributors

John O. Ward (b. 1940) has lectured in Medieval and Renaissance History at the University of Sydney (Australia) since 1967. His major field of interest is in Ciceronian rhetoric in the Middle Ages, on which he has published extensively (see his *Ciceronian Rhetoric in Treatise, Scholion and Commentary*, Typologie des sources du moyen âge occidental 58 (Turnhout, 1995)). With John Scott he has published a fully annotated translation of the twelfth-century Vézelay Chronicle, and in connection with that has been working lately on the role of the monastic memorial volumes in the process of dispute resolution in the Central Middle Ages.

Andrew Wareham (b. 1965) completed his Ph.D. on *The Aristocracy of East Anglia c. 930–1154* at the University of Birmingham in 1992. He has held teaching positions at the University of Manchester and Somerville College, Oxford, and since 1995 has worked at the Institute of Historical Research, University of London. He is the co-editor of the *Victoria County History of Cambridgeshire* volume 10 (forthcoming, Oxford), and is also responsible for the preparation of other county volumes at the VCH central office. He has published articles on St Oswald's family and kin, the rebellions of the Bigod family, and most recently on 'Piety and the Emergence of the Patrilinear Family in Pre-Conquest England' (*Early Medieval Europe*, forthcoming).

List of Abbreviations

AA.SS.	*Acta Sanctorum* etc., eds. Société des Bollandistes, 114 vols. (Brussels, 1643–1996).
Anglo-Saxon Wills, ed. Whitelock	*Anglo-Saxon Wills*, ed. D. Whitelock (Cambridge, 1932) [cited by will number].
Anglo-Saxon Writs, ed. Harmer	*Anglo-Saxon Writs*, ed. F. E. Harmer (London, 1952) [cited by writ number].
ANS	*Anglo-Norman Studies* (formerly *Proceedings of the Battle Conference on Anglo-Norman Studies*)
ASE	*Anglo-Saxon England*
BAR	British Archeological Reports
BL	British Library (London)
BN	Bibliothèque Nationale (Paris)
CCCM	Corpus Christianorum, Continuatio Mediaevalis
DB	*Domesday Book, seu liber censualis Wilhelmi primi regis Angliae*, ed. A. Farley, 2 vols. (London, 1783).
EHR	*English Historical Review*
MGH DD	*Monumenta Germaniae Historica. Diplomata*
MGH SS	*Monumenta Germaniae Historica. Scriptores*
MGH SS Rer. Mer.	*Monumenta Germaniae Historica. Scriptores Rerum Merovingicarum*
MS	manuscript
Orderic, Ecclesiastical History, ed. Chibnall	Ordericus Vitalis, *Historia Æcclesiastica*, ed. and transl. M. Chibnall, 6 vols. (Oxford, 1969–80).

PL	*Patrologia latina cursus completa*, ed. J.-P. Migne, 221 vols. (Paris, 1844–64).
TRHS	*Transactions of the Royal Historical Society*
VCH	*Victoria County Histories of England* (London, 1899-) [fourteen county sets are complete].

Negotiating Secular and Ecclesiastical Power in the Central Middle Ages: A Historiographical Introduction

HENK TEUNIS

The study of the relationships between church and state, both at the highest level, between popes and rulers, and at a lower level, between bishops and barons, emerged during the nineteenth century.[1] The great German, French, and English historians had very different perspectives upon this issue. Historical questions nowadays are increasingly influenced by the debates on literary theory, social anthropology, sociology, psychology, and economics, to name only the most obvious ones. Their methodologies inform and invigorate historical research, but the questions raised by the nineteenth-century scholars who established medieval history as an academic discipline, are in a broader sense still of importance today. In this article the national differences in the historiography of secular and ecclesiastical relations are described. Also, some of the results of more recent work in both Europe and the United States are analyzed in order to develop an overview of current perceptions of those issues, and how they have changed since the late nineteenth century.

Germany

H. Bresslau, in his volume of the *Jahrbücher des deutschen Reiches* which deals with the government of Emperor Conrad II (1024–39), published in

---

[1] The author wishes to thank Christopher Holdsworth for reading and commenting on an earlier version. The author also apologizes for not having been able to refer to English translations of some of the works cited.

1884, wrote that the emperor strengthened the power of the crown inside and outside the Reich, that he raised the prestige of the German name, and advanced the material interests of the German nation.[2] As a result of following moderate policies, internal revolts were averted. He settled the border problems with Poland to his own advantage. He avoided difficulties with the French barons by maintaining an alliance with the French King Henry I. He created order out of chaos in Italy. His rule over the church was at no stage endangered. He presided over the synods that he convoked. He adopted a benevolent attitude towards the reform of monasteries in Bavaria and Lotharingia, while not actually encouraging it. He can be regarded as a stable ruler without inner devotion. It is therefore hardly surprising that he did not realize what was going on in Lotharingia. There the 'romanization of the German church' was prepared before his eyes.[3] The Cluniac party (as Bresslau called the movement) was at this time still free from the Gregorian inclinations, but this party nevertheless was preparing the ground for a development which in time would become highly dangerous to the German empire. This party 'through its tight organization, its hierarchical approach and its uncompromising emphasis on obedience' represented the core principles of the organized church.[4] Conrad was not aware of this danger, and cannot in the least be blamed for it.

There was, in Bresslau's view, a fundamental antithesis between the principle of the organization of the German empire and the principles of the Roman church. The German empire was an assembly of lords under the unchallenged direction of a king (at least in principle); the second body was marked by the notions of hierarchy and obedience. These two sets of ideas were incompatible. The second represented a danger to the first.

Bresslau belonged to the circle around G. Waitz that edited the *Neues Archiv* and published the *Monumenta Germaniae Historica*.[5] The historians of this circle can be seen as belonging to the Protestant middle-class which at the end of the nineteenth century controlled German cultural life. Its members also occupied the higher ranks of the civil service and were

---

[2] H. Bresslau, *Jahrbücher des deutschen Reiches unter Konrad II.*, 2 vols. (Leipzig, 1879–84), II, 382.

[3] Bresslau, *Jahrbücher*, II, 420: 'Romanisierung der deutschen Kirche'.

[4] Ibid.: 'in ihrer straffen Organisation, in ihrer hierarchischen Gesinnung, in ihrer schroffen Betonung des Prinzips des Gehorsams'.

[5] P. Kehr, 'Harry Bresslau', *Neues Archiv* 47 (1928), pp. 251–66; D. Knowles, 'The Monumenta Germaniae Historica', in *Great Historical Enterprises* (London, 1963), pp. 65–97.

bound up with political nationalism. They believed that they had taken over the leadership of the nation and incorporated the values of the future—even though the policies of Bismarck, who forged German unity without them, were disappointing. 'The liberals were motivated by genuine conviction when they contested the privilege that the Catholic Church had inherited within the modern secular state: the *Kulturkampf* was not a mere tactical exercise'.[6] Bresslau's description of Conrad II's reign was saturated with this conviction. In the next volumes of the *Jahrbücher des deutschen Reiches* it is always present in the background and sometimes made explicit.

In the reign of the Emperor Henry III (1039–56) the situation changed, according to E. Steindorff. Henry III himself was genuinely devout, he argues, and wanted to establish an enduring peace, like Charlemagne, in accordance with the ecclesiastical-monarchical spirit, that is, a government of the realm with the clergy dependent upon the pope, and the pope in turn dependent upon the emperor.[7] Wars outside the empire and revolts within kept Henry III from realizing this ideal. Whereas the emperor gave all his attention to the re-establishment of peace, papal power developed in Rome unhampered by the emperor's intervention. This was especially the case in the reign of Pope Leo IX, installed by Henry III himself. The church hierarchy in this way had the opportunity to develop a self-consciousness, such as had not been possible for centuries. This does not mean, according to Steindorff, that the empire had already been damaged in Henry III's time. Bishops and abbots were still true pillars of order and unity, but the reign of Henry III can justly be characterized as an interim period, standing between the reign of Conrad II, when the nation and the empire were so powerful, and the reign of Henry IV, when the 'decline of the Empire, of the Dynasty and of the Nation by the influence of the church hierarchy' became visible.[8]

The ambitions of Gregory VII became, as G. Meyer von Knonau argues, apparent soon after his controversial election.[9] He wanted to organize a military expedition to the East with the help of the German King Henry IV.

---

[6] W.J. Mommsen, *Imperial Germany 1867–1918: Politics, Culture and Society in an Authoritarian State* (London, 1996), p. 122.

[7] E. Steindorff, *Jahrbücher des deutschen Reiches unter Heinrich III.*, 2 vols. (Leipzig, 1874–81), II, 442.

[8] Steindorff, *Jahrbücher*, II, 367: 'vornehmlich durch hierarchische Einflüsse herbeigeführten Zerfall des Reiches, der Dynastie und der Nation'.

[9] G. Meyer von Knonau, *Jahrbücher des deutschen Reiches unter Heinrich IV. und Heinrich V.*, 7 vols. (Leipzig, 1890–1909), II, 442.

In fact he wanted to turn things upside down. He used synods as his instrument to advance his plans and principles 'ever more expansively', reaching its climax in the first excommunication of Henry IV in 1076.[10] The emperor's humiliation at Canossa was colossal: after having abandoned all royal insignia, he stayed for three days before the gates of Mathilda's castle.[11] When Henry IV seemed to be recovering his power, Gregory showed his true intentions by the second excommunication: he called upon Peter and Paul directly in his letters and indicated in this way he believed he had the authority to control all affairs on earth 'without any limitation'.[12] He wanted to rule the world from Rome, and Henry was excommunicated because he did not obey.

In the volumes of the *Jahrbücher* an image of the relations between ecclesiastical and secular power was created that has had a lasting effect in the twentieth century. It is the idea which presupposes the incompatibility of the two principles on which church and state were built. This line of thought underlies the book that has perhaps been the most influential in the German-speaking world: the *Kirchengeschichte Deutschlands* by K. Hauck.[13] It is also dominant in G. Tellenbach's thinking, who points to hierarchization and clericalization as the central characteristics of the Gregorian reformation.[14]

France

A counterpart of this concept, created in Germany between 1870 and 1890, was developed in France. It has been described most fully in the works of A. Fliche.[15] His books were published somewhat later than the *Jahrbücher*, but his ideas had their roots in the same period. Fliche, unlike his German predecessors, came from a wealthy Catholic family. His father was a

---

[10] Meyer von Knonau, *Jahrbücher*, II, 548: 'auf immer großartiger Weise'.

[11] Meyer von Knonau, *Jahrbücher*, II, 759.

[12] Meyer von Knonau, *Jahrbücher*, III, 257: 'ohne Einschränkung'.

[13] K. Hauck, *Kirchengeschichte Deutschlands* (Leipzig, 1896), siebentes Buch: 'Das Übergewicht des Königtums in der Kirche und der Bruch desselben durch Rom (1002–1122)'!

[14] G. Tellenbach, *Libertas, Kirche und Weltordnung im Zeitalter des Investiturstreites* (Leipzig, 1936); idem, *Die westliche Kirche vom 10. bis zum 12. Jahrhundert* (Göttingen, 1988).

[15] A. Fliche, *La Réforme grégorienne*, 3 vols. (Louvain, 1924–37).

supporter of Pope Leo XIII and of his policy of rallying to the Republic. These Catholics wanted a dialogue with science, with the government, and with the people. Fliche's father, consistent with the ideas promoted in his circles, founded a charity.[16] This was 'a programme for clerical action: priests were to establish and control such *oeuvres*, and laymen were seen as the objects of action'. They 'presented the revolutionary idea and the Christian idea as irreconcilable'.[17]

Action by the clergy and above all by the pope in order to save the church and Christian life, was, according to Fliche, more urgently needed in the eleventh century than ever before. From the very beginnings, when the Christians left the catacombs, they had chosen their bishops. This principle of church organization had been laid down in canon law and had been maintained in the following centuries. The violations of this principle were always numerous but were usurpations of an ecclesiastical right. This right, Fliche notes, is indispensable to a good functioning of the church.[18] In the tenth century, during the fragmentation of the Carolingian empire, it became apparent what happened if violations occurred frequently. Simony and nicolaism, that is to say, thirst for money and lasciviousness, became dominant in clerical life: 'bishops and priests visit taverns and places of debauchery'.[19]

In Fliche's work the church occupies the central place. The church was first-born, the principles of its organization were fixed early. Lay power continually threatens the church, because laymen are essentially concerned with naked power. They unscrupulously usurp ecclesiastical rights in order to extend their power and violate the core principles of the church's organization on earth. The church had already fallen victim to this reprehensible behaviour in the Merovingian era, but did even more so in the tenth century. The strains between church and state, always present, became untenable.

The monks of Cluny in Fliche's view were not the revolutionaries Bresslau considered them to be, but monks who maintained a pure religious

---

[16] J.R. Palanque, 'Notice sur la vie et les travaux de M. Augustin Fliche', *Comptes rendus des séances de l'année 1974 de l'Académie des Inscriptions et Belles-Lettres*, pp. 238–49.

[17] R. Gibson, *A Social History of French Catholicism (1789–1914)* (London and New York, 1989), pp. 99–100.

[18] A. Fliche, *Études sur la polémique religieuse à l'époque de Grégoire VII: Les prégrégoriens* (Paris, 1916), p. 3.

[19] A. Fliche, *La querelle des investitures* (Paris, 1946) p. 22: 'évêques et prêtres fréquentent la taverne et les lieux de débauche'.

life without intervention from outside.[20] Reform of the church was not in their programme. It was rather bishops who came from the Cluniac monasteries, or were under their influence, who developed such a programme, namely Rather of Verona, Atto of Vercelli, Peter Damian and Humbert of Moyenmoutier. Humbert especially offered clearly expressed views on lay investiture as he believed it was the 'cause and basis' of simony. He did not go so far in his reasoning as to argue in favour of abolishing lay investiture itself, but he did see that reform of the church could only be realized under the guidance of the Holy See. He also saw that strengthening of the hierarchy through centralization was necessary and that the reform of the church could not be successful without 'a more clear-cut subordination of the temporal power to the ecclesiastical'.[21]

The image Fliche sketched is the exact counterpart of the images of the emperors and popes in the pages of the *Jahrbücher*—but the antithesis between secular and ecclesiastical power is there all the same. Pope Gregory VII in Fliche's eyes was not a man eager for power, who aimed at controlling the world, as Meyer von Knonau had argued. He was, instead, a saint, with a mystical kind of piety, who wanted to subordinate himself totally to the divine will.[22] The primacy of the church of Rome was divinely ordained. With this authority Gregory VII wanted to bring about the reform of the church through the agency of letters and legates and, when this appeared to be insufficient, by prohibition of lay investiture. This was not at all a manifestation of his wish to dominate the world, but was necessary for the reform of the church. In Germany there was, in Fliche's view, an emperor who aimed at world domination and who wanted to rule over the church. Therefore, two concepts of the organization of the Christian world clashed. Henry IV was the protagonist, taking up the attack at Worms against papal power and the pope's response was deposition and excommunication: 'un cas particulier du conflit entre deux doctrines'.[23] Gregory could not act otherwise, but he was more sad than angry. He was prepared to forgive, which he did at Canossa. But when Henry IV, even after Canossa, did not recognize Gregory's authority, a second excommunication was inevitable.

---

[20] Fliche, *La Réforme grégorienne*, I, 265.

[21] Fliche, *La Réforme grégorienne*, I, 265: 'une subordination plus étroite du pouvoir temporel au pouvoir spirituel'.

[22] Fliche, *La Réforme grégorienne*, II, 90.

[23] Fliche, *La querelle*, p. 70.

In France this ultramontane view did not disappear when the *Annales* historians became influential. The idea that morals of the clergy before the reformation were low and that a change in this respect was brought about by the Gregorian reform, became the main theme in a highly influential handbook by E. Amann and A. Dumas.[24] A new conception of the nature of the church reform of the eleventh and twelfth centuries (if there was such a thing) was not formulated in France. In 1960, A. Chédeville, author of one of the famous regional monographs,[25] was still able to begin an article with the following sentence: 'The destiny of the Gregorian reformation was to allow the church to develop a purity and a sanctity which centuries of invasions and anarchy had undermined, and had as its first objectives, the aim of ending the influence of the laity.'[26] Fliche's concept was still influential in the 1960s. The French authors in the yearly *Studi Gregoriani* contributed much detailed research, but there were no new impulses in the field of secular and ecclesiastical relationships.[27] Many historians started to direct their attention away from ecclesiastical history, towards religious history.[28]

England

In English historiography the dichotomy between a clerical principle on the one hand, and lay power on the other has been absent.[29] At the end of the nineteenth century W. Stubbs (1825–1901) and F.W. Maitland (1850–1906) formulated opinions on the theme of ecclesiastical and secular power in the eleventh and twelfth centuries. They articulated their thinking in their

---

[24] E. Amann and A. Dumas, *L'Église au pouvoir des laïques (888–1057)*, Histoire de l'Église depuis les origines jusqu'à nos jours, VII (Paris, 1940).

[25] A. Chédevile, *Chartres et ses campagnes* (Paris, 1973).

[26] A. Chédeville, 'Les restitutions d'églises en faveur de l'abbaye de Saint-Vincent du Mans', *Cahiers de Civilisation Mediévale* 3 (1960), 200–17: 'La réforme grégorienne destinée à rendre à l'Eglise une pureté et une sainteté que des siècles d'invasions et d'anarchie avaient dangereusement altérées, eut pour premier but de débarrasser celle-ci de l'emprise des laïques.'

[27] *Studi Gregoriani* (Rome, 1947–).

[28] A. Vauchez, 'Les nouvelles orientations de l'histoire religieuse de la France médiévale (avant le XIVe siècle)', *Studi Medievali* 21 (1980), 839–54.

[29] With the great exception of W. Ullmann, especially his *The Growth of Papal Government in the Middle Ages* (London, 1955).

accounts of the conflict between Archbishop Anselm and the Kings William II and Henry I. In Stubbs's history there are two presuppositions: in the first place, this conflict has to be placed in the context of the formation of the English constitution; secondly, the conflict actually originated in Roman influence, which was not helpful to the English church. We need to know that Stubbs himself lived through the period of the re-installation of the Catholic hierarchy and the Ecclesiastical Titles Act of 1851, which prohibited the assumption of territorial titles by the Roman prelacy. Stubbs himself became a bishop in the Anglican Church in 1884.[30] Still his description of the conflict between Anselm and Henry I is not marked by a dichotomy. It was, according to him, a matter of politics and compromise. Ranulf Flambard, bishop of Durham and opponent of Archbishops Lanfranc and Anselm, 'saw no other difference between an ecclesiastical and a lay fief than the superior facilities which the first gave for extortion'.[31] Through skilful political management his early clashes with the archbishops of Canterbury did not lead to serious damage. When, however, Anselm came under the influence of Rome, the conflict escalated. The result of the controversy had positive aspects. Stubbs comments: 'The political consequences of the struggle [...] were to draw the clergy and people more closely together, and to force on the king the conviction that [...] there were regions of life and thought in which he must allow the existence of liberty.'[32]

Maitland, contradicting Stubbs, accepted that in the eleventh and twelfth centuries the English church was not independent of the church of Rome. There was after all only one canon law. Maitland's position was that the English bishops applied this law as far as the state permitted it.[33] It was the task of William the Conqueror to set the limits, but he left many questions open. During the first half of the twelfth century the claims of the church were growing, and the duty of asserting them also passed into hands of men representing both church and secular leaders. They were not only

---

[30] H. Cam, 'Stubbs Seventy Years After', in *Law-Finders and Law-Makers* (London, 1962), pp. 188–211.

[31] W. Stubbs, *The Constitutional History of England* (Oxford, 1891), I, 325.

[32] Stubbs, *The Constitutional History*, I, 342.

[33] F.W. Maitland, *Roman Canon Law in the Church of England* (London, 1898), p. 52; cf. S.F.C. Milsom, 'Maitland and the Grand Assize', *The Haskins Society Journal. Studies in Medieval History* 7, eds. C.P. Lewis and E. Cownie (Woodbridge, 1997), 151–77.

theologians but also expert lawyers skilled in the art of compromise.[34]

Canon law also plays a crucial role in the work of Z.N. Brooke. According to him, problems arose in the eleventh century, in large part because of 'the new canonical collections in which the rising generation was being trained'.[35] A clearer understanding of canon law was brought to England by Lanfranc. The idea of a centralized church directly controlled by the pope was unacceptable to William the Conqueror. This was a cause of the troubles between Henry I and Anselm, who wanted to obey the pope. According to Brooke, the power over the English Church was at stake: the pope and the king both wanted to control it. The election of bishops was the central issue. It was an institutional-political problem which would with some difficulties be solved by Henry I. King Henry remained in control as the bishops were his nominees. It was, in Brooke's view, not a contested church reform which was going on, with the church representing one principle while the state or lay power represented another, but an institutional-political problem between the king and the pope, both of whom led expanding organizations.

R.W. Southern too discusses the investiture dispute which occurred during Anselm's archiepiscopate. In Southern's view, the investiture dispute was only the beginning of a 'great social and ecclesiastical revolution [...]. From the papal summit down to the holders of parochial benefices, the clergy became a force capable of laying down and imposing on the world at large the fundamental rules, not only of ecclesiastical discipline, but also of lay behaviour.'[36] This revolution produced a highly integrated and purposeful western European society; it was a long process, initiated by the leading figures of the investiture dispute, who were not conscious of the fact that they were entering a new phase in European history. The first step was indeed to bring the most important ecclesiastical appointments under clerical control. An important process was underlying this dispute, but in itself it was not a question of principle: 'Everyone agreed that investiture by lay rulers conferred no spiritual power'.[37] There were extreme Gregorians who perhaps wanted to abolish all homage for church land, but they

---

[34] F. Pollock and F.W. Maitland, *The History of English Law Before the Time of Edward I*, 2 vols. (Cambridge, 1911; first edition Cambridge, 1898), I, 75, 124.

[35] Z.N. Brooke, *The English Church and the Papacy from the Conquest to the Reign of John* (Cambridge, 1952; first edition 1931), p. 43.

[36] R.W. Southern, *Saint Anselm: A Portrait in a Landscape* (Cambridge, 1990), p. 233.

[37] Southern, *Saint Anselm*, p. 283.

were few. The period of Hildebrandine reform, when some hoped to gain full victory, was only a temporary episode. A properly functioning church was possible without extremism. Anselm was dragged into this controversy. He came from a monastically oriented world and Southern maintains he found the new claims confusing. Southern may be right on Anselm. His hypothesis of a new phase in European history in which the foundations of society and culture were replaced and reshaped by clerical rules is his main theme and not to be discussed here. Generally speaking, controversy, not antagonism, was, according to Stubbs, Maitland, Brooke, and Southern, characteristic of the interaction between ecclesiastical and secular power in the eleventh and twelfth centuries. It focused upon juridical and administrative issues.

This intellectual position was contested for the first time in the English-speaking world in the work of S. Vaughn. She argues that Anselm inherited the Canterbury idea of co-rule: king and archbishop ought to rule the kingdom together without the subordination of one to the other. For Anselm the king was his protector and lord. He himself ought to have the highest authority in spiritual matters and church affairs, which the king should recognize. 'The former rules by secular justice and sovereignty (*imperio*), the latter by divine doctrine and authority (*magisterio*).'[38] The 'unity of church and state' had already been an ecclesiastical ideology for a long time.[39] For Anselm, consequently, there was no problem at all in giving King Henry a great deal of influence in such matters as appointments of bishops. One has to be aware, according to Vaughn, that in Henry I's view and in the view of his intimate advisers, Henry's and Anselm's roles were complementary. The king 'has to seek after the safety of the kingdom and of the church of God as a divinely commissioned steward'.[40] The king had a justifiable purpose in his reign which was acknowledged by the primate of Canterbury. Anselm and Henry's chief adviser Robert of Meulan 'were of one mind in their desire for a united and well-governed Anglo-Norman realm, ruled by an able peace-keeping king who was prepared to protect the church, curb violence and bring order to his dominions.'[41] There was a

---

[38] S.N. Vaughn, *Anselm of Bec and Robert of Meulan: The Innocence of the Dove and the Wisdom of the Serpent* (Los Angeles, 1987), p. 151.

[39] P. Leupen, *Gods stad op aarde: Eenheid van kerk en staat in het eerste millennium na Christus: Een kerkelijke ideologie* (Amsterdam, 1996).

[40] Vaughn, *Anselm*, p. 166.

[41] Vaughn, *Anselm*, p. 311.

basic agreement about the role each had to play and therefore a solution to the problems of their time was possible. In Vaughn's view there was no difference of principle, nor a dispute about power over the church between the protagonists, but recognition by both Anselm and King Henry of each other's position. This argument represents a break with the preceding German, French, and English viewpoints. There was in fact diversity, not incompatibility or opposition.

Bloch and Duby

In the groups of ideas discussed so far (apart from S. Vaughn's) the tie with national—i.e. German, French, and English—history cannot be denied. M. Bloch (1886–1944), however, differs.[42] He is not concerned with the church and its place in national politics or history, but with the relationship between society and religion as part of his wider interest in conditions of life and society's ideas about them. This frame of thought was not provided by national history. Its intellectual roots lay with Fustel de Coulanges and Durkheim. Bloch did not merely apply their concepts to eleventh- and twelfth-century history. He is in my opinion the first historian who in an impressive way placed the many facets which are inherent to each historical development in a concrete setting, in his case, *la société féodale*. Historical development is not determined by politics, or religion, war, societal institutions, or discrete groups separately, but by the subtly layered interplay of these and other forces. It is the task of the historian to study and to describe those interconnections.

Bloch maintains that religion is one of the forces indispensable to the development of eleventh- and twelfth-century society. For contemporaries reality was a mask behind which the Almighty reigned together with saints, angels, and devils. After all, reality provided little assurance: wars, disease, hunger, and violence determined the shape of life. Religion was a refuge and comfort. This was important for the functioning of society as a whole, because this attitude of looking for protection enabled men to build a system of social relations based on interdependence and subordination— peasant and lord, monk and abbot, vassal and lord: in short, feudal relations. According to Bloch, the church was part of this feudal pattern. The Christian religion, which originated in an age before the feudal period, and its institutions endured and found protectors because powerful people

---

[42] M. Bloch, *La société féodale* (Paris, 1968; first edition, 1939).

wanted to be prayed for. Here secular social habits crept in, because the protector and donor, the layman, required the fidelity of the clerical recipient of the gift. In his turn the cleric required the same of a subordinate who was appointed to office. Here the danger of neglecting the spiritual for the material became very real.[43] An office was wanted because of its material benefits. The Gregorian reform attempted to counteract this. It was typical for the situation that the pope who gave a strong impetus to it, Leo IX, owed his papal office to his qualities as a military commander.[44] The intended separation of the spiritual and the material misfired. In the lower ranks of society lords simply remained in control. The introduction of the principle of free election did not bring about the desired changes: clerics never agreed among themselves, and appointments had to be decided by lay rulers.

For Bloch the history of the Roman or European church is not very important. Institutionally interaction between ecclesiastical and secular power was unproblematic in the feudal period. There was no dichotomy or administrative problem. The 'représentations mentales' are much more important: they are the breeding ground for cultural activities such as writing, comfort, and social relations in the shape of interdependence.

Duby also is not interested in institutional or political problems. He started his career as a social and economic historian, but turned toward religious 'représentations' with *Le temps des cathédrales*.[45] Religion was of the utmost importance in the eleventh and twelfth centuries because it gave form and substance to the conceptual universe essential to the functioning of society. The idea of the three orders came to the fore by way of the bishops Adalbero of Laon and Gerald of Cambrai. Then it passed to monks, episcopal schools, and princely advisers. This enabled it to be of lasting influence in constructing society after 1200.[46] For Duby religion is important because of the concepts it generates.

As a societal group the clerics were a part of the dominant class. Duby speaks about 'complicité structurelle'.[47] Clerics and laymen were competitors in an economic sense, but they were united in their efforts to maintain a division in society between those who worked and those who did not

---

[43] Bloch, *La société féodale*, p. 485.

[44] Bloch, *La société féodale*, p. 486.

[45] G. Duby, *Le temps des cathédrales* (Paris, 1976; first edition Genève, 1966–67).

[46] G. Duby, *Les trois ordres ou l'imaginaire du féodalisme* (Paris, 1978).

[47] Duby, *Les trois ordres*, p. 199.

work. The church had a role to play in ensuring that common people remained submissive. Neither Bloch's work nor Duby's assigns an important role to the church or to ecclesiastical institutions in feudal society. No wonder that in regional monographs, whenever phenomena like tithes or episcopal elections are discussed, the spirit of Fliche seems all of a sudden to be alive.[48]

The Gregorian reform was, according to Duby, an attempt to push the clerics into the first rank of society.[49] Its leaders wanted to separate as sharply as possible the spiritual and the temporal, and consequently to divide God's people into two groups, the laymen and the clerics, in such a way that in their interrelations the position of the clerics was strengthened. Relations, however, did not change significantly. With the landowners the clerics constituted the upper stratum of society which kept the workers down. The Gregorian reform had not been of real importance.

Duby's work took shape in the period in which the *histoire des mentalités* was propagated in France and to a certain extent outside it. It was the same period in which religious history came to be preferred over church history. Rome and the reforms originating from Rome were no longer the central issue. Whether one was willing to compromise with the reforms or to oppose them with various degrees of emphasis, was no longer the key issue. The reformation generated by Rome was no longer regarded as the central phenomenon to be studied, and it is most unlikely that it will regain its centrality in the next few generations of scholarship. There were many bishoprics and monasteries of seminal importance in the development of religious representations, which were renewed during the eleventh and twelfth centuries. Bloch, Duby, and the French regional historians, however, did not develop a theory on the meaning and role of these institutions. That work was to be done by a number of mainly American medievalists.

---

[48] For example, G. Devailly, *Le Burgh du Xe siècle au milieu du XIIIe* (Paris and La Haye, 1973), p. 248: 'Que l'Eglise de Bourges soit en grande partie tombée aux mains des laïcs n'était pas un fait exceptionnel au milieu du XIe siècle. Il en était de même pour l'ensemble des diocèses de la chrétienté occidentale, et le mal était peut-être encore plus grand dans des régions comme la Germanie ou l'Italie que dans le centre de la France. Nommés par des laïcs, soumis à leur pression constante, privés de l'essentiel de leurs ressources canoniques, les détenteurs d'églises paroissiales étaient fatalement amenés à pratiquer la simonie.'

[49] Duby, *Les trois ordres*, p. 243.

American Historians

One theme of American medieval studies in the late twentieth century is a focus upon the monasteries and the world around them.[50] The objects of these studies are small-scale. They all assume that the main elements in the pattern of behaviour they find are interconnected: conceptions of property, transfer of property, family relations, sense of justice, and religion. In other words, the anthropologization of history writing seems to have been accomplished. In this respect these authors follow Marc Bloch. The question remains, however, how the connections between the elements of the behaviourial pattern they describe can best be understood.

First I want to discuss B.H. Rosenwein's position.[51] She found that in Burgundy (909–1049) there was more or less continuous interaction between the monasteries of Cluny and laymen by way of gifts, which were given, then reclaimed, and later given again. This give-and-take created social relations which were redefined when circumstances changed. In this way all laymen-donors had a bond with St Peter, which was their common denominator. This give-and-take was the local 'social glue'. In Rosenwein's view it is evident that in the circumstances of the time such bonds, forged by religion, were needed. Society was fragmented and dislocated.[52] She attributes the main integrating role in the region to the monastery of Cluny in accord with a deeply felt societal need.

There definitely were rules, norms, and prescriptions in lay society about what was right and wrong. This is part of S.D. White's argument.[53] The monasteries believed that laymen ought to give and that it was unjust to take away without permission what was donated. Heads of families who wished to make donations could be confronted with statements from the eldest son that this was inappropriate, because the gift was part of the inalienable family patrimony. Not making donations from the patrimony was an accepted norm too. The two norms could clash. The continuous disputes in terms of the application of norms sometimes made society dangerous and unstable. The purpose of giving was to try and avert these

---

[50] Here, as before, I mention publications only in order to demonstrate intellectual positions.

[51] B.H. Rosenwein, *To Be the Neighbor of Saint Peter: The Social Meaning of Cluny's Property 909–1049* (Ithaca and London, 1989).

[52] Rosenwein, *To Be the Neighbor*, p. 202.

[53] S.D. White, *Custom, Kinship, and Gifts to Saints: The* Laudatio Parentum *in Western France, 1050–1150* (Chapel Hill and London, 1988).

dangers. To give was to create relationships. To give and to repeat the act of giving continuously was a way of overcoming the dangers which continuously arose. The results could never be completely satisfactory. The act of giving to a monastery or saint is not the manifestation of universal religious consensus which created the bonds needed, but a social technique intended to cope with the threatening chaos. This technique was at everyone's disposal. But even gifts to monasteries did not guarantee anything. Nobody knew what would happen in the future and if unfortunately the gift did not remain in the monastery's possession, this would mean the end of the saint's favour. Chaos in White's perspective was not caused by lack of a central administration or lack of social cohesion, but by conflicting norms. Society, however, had an antidote: to give and redefine relations continuously. There is no problem-solving religion, but the members of society themselves create a counterbalancing technique in order to maintain a somewhat unstable equilibrium.

Conclusion

The historiographical development of the relationship between secular and ecclesiastical power has moved radically since the late nineteenth century. It can no longer be argued that the medieval mental framework was taken up by the great struggles between Rome and lay rulers, but neither can we assume that local communities were islands of cohesion in a wider world of chaos and conflict. The founding fathers of medieval history, despite their differing national perspectives, raised an interesting theme, worthy of further study. What were the motives of churchmen and laymen in writing history, in engaging in many other activities, and in resolving conflicts? The interplay between bishops and counts, abbots and barons, clerics and knights, and townsmen and merchants with prelates was as much a part of that interrelationship as the dialogue between popes and monarchs.

The selection of nine case studies from England, northern France, and the Low Countries enables a more subtle comparison of secular and ecclesiastical links. Some of the essays in this volume demonstrate how texts were used as weapons by ecclesiastical authorities in defining their relationships with lay powers; others focus upon how land and kinship were used to define the social relations between the laity and the clergy; and the final two essays concentrate upon the solution of conflicts. It is hoped that the reader may find stimulating answers to the question of the interaction between secular and ecclesiastical power, the perception of which is moving away from either contradiction or integration, towards differentiation through negotiation and affirmation.

Part One

Texts as Tools of Power

———

The Political Use of Piety in Episcopal and Comital Charters of the Eleventh and Twelfth Centuries

BENOÎT-MICHEL TOCK

Most medieval charters are political texts, because they give notice of a decision taken by a powerful man (a king, a bishop, a count, and so forth). They are also judicial texts, because they give to that decision a juridical protection. Finally they are pious texts, because their beneficiaries are often churches, and the motivation behind the acts is religious. We cannot clearly distinguish the pious substance, the juridical form, and the political purpose. Piety in charters can be used as a political tool: by bringing the king, the count, or the bishop close to God, piety reaffirms the foundations of a power which, like every power in the Middle Ages, stems from God.

A well-known example is that of Charlemagne. The first authentic Frankish royal diploma containing a verbal invocation is dated to the 29th of May 801.[1] The imperial coronation changed the nature of Charlemagne's power: as an emperor, he could do more than as a king, both in his relations with the pope and in legal matters.[2] Is this invocation a sign of

---

[1] *Die Urkunden Pippins, Karlmanns und Karls des Grossen*, ed. E. Mühlbacher, *MGH DD Karolinorum I* (Hannover, 1906), pp. 265–66, no. 197. See R.-H. Bautier, 'La chancellerie et les actes royaux dans les royaumes carolingiens', *Bibliothèque de l'Ecole des Chartes* 142 (1984), pp. 5–80 at p. 43 (reprinted in idem, *Chartes, sceaux et chancelleries. Etudes de diplomatique et de sigillographie médiévales*, 2 vols. (Paris, 1990), II, 461–536 at p. 499). From that diploma, the year of reign is said to be 'Christo propitio', 'with Christ's mercy'.

[2] Charlemagne was also the first Frankish king to add the formula 'Dei gratia' to his

piety? Certainly, but it is primarily a sign of power, a sign of a more religious power. The text of this invocation was important too: the Frankish chancery chose the Byzantine invocation ('In nomine patris et filii et spiritus sancti', 'In the name of the Father and the Son and the Holy Ghost'). Louis the Pious, however, changed this formula into 'In nomine Dei et salvatoris nostri Iesu Christi', 'In the name of God and our Redeemer, Jesus Christ', perhaps to appease the Byzantine hostility, but more probably, because the unity of the Empire was reflected by the oneness of God more than by the Holy Trinity, and was personified by Christ.[3] As this example shows, piety could be used for political purposes in the construction and the defence of lay power. This political use of piety will be studied here. Whether someone really was pious or not is not the matter here, as our concern is with the practical aspects of piety.[4] What follows is an attempt to make an inventory of the charter material from northern France and Lower Lotharingia containing pious formulas and of the questions which can be posed regarding the political use of piety in charters, especially in the invocation, the *intitulatio*, and the *sanctio*.

In this article I will not study charters issued by popes, emperors, and kings, but rather what the nineteenth century called the 'lower chanceries', of bishops and princes. Of course counts and dukes were not kings: they were not anointed and had no book like the *De institutione regia* of Jonas of Orleans dedicated to them, but their power too came from God. To give just one example, from a charter of Baldwin V, count of Hainault, for Vicoigne abbey, of 1187, which reads 'Ego Balduinus, Deo a quo omnis potestas permittente, Hainoensium comes', 'I, Baldwin, with the permission of God, from whom all power comes, count of Hainault'.[5] Did these counts

---

intitulatio. C. Richter, *Der Sinn der Dei-gratia-Formel in den französischen und deutschen Dynastenurkunden bis zum Jahre 1000 untersucht mit besonderer Berücksichtigung der Geschichte dieser Formel von der paulinischen Zeit an* (Frankfurt, 1972), thinks that, until the end of the first Christian millennium, this is a merely pious, and not a political formula. I think it can be both.

[3] H. Fichtenau, 'Zur Geschichte der Invokationen und Devotionsformeln', in idem, *Beiträge zur Mediävistik*, 3 vols. (Stuttgart, 1975–86), II, 37–61 at pp. 41–42.

[4] Piety can also be used for rhetorical reasons. According to W. Grebe, 'Die Urkundenarengen des Kölner Erzbischofs Arnold von Wied (1151–1156)', *Annalen des historischen Vereins für den Niederrhein* 173 (1971), 205–09, Arnold II used quotations from the Bible less than his predecessor, Arnold I, not because this friend of Wibald of Stavelot and Anselm of Havelberg was not pious, but because he did not like rhetorical prolixity.

[5] *Actes et documents anciens intéressant la Belgique. Nouvelle série*, ed. Ch. Duvivier (Bruxelles, 1903), pp. 134–35, no. 65.

and dukes use piety to strengthen their power? Or did they need less religious help, because their power and authority went uncontested? Although bishops as actual representatives of religion did not need the type of religious assistance that counts hoped for, episcopal charters form a useful comparison with comital charters.

Many external signs of piety can be found in poems, saints' lives, art and architecture, and in political or personal acts such as the foundation of a church, the departure on crusade or pilgrimage, and so forth. Here, I study external signs of piety in charters. Charters are, with money, the main public medium of the Middle Ages.[6] Many parts of the charters contain signs of piety, first of all the symbolic invocation (the chrismon), and the verbal invocation with the formula 'In nomine sancte et indiuidue Trinitatis' ('In the name of the holy and undivided Trinity'). Secondly, there is the pious formula in the *intitulatio* ('Dei gratia', 'through God's grace'), or, in the same part, the formula of humility ('licet indignus', 'however unworthy'). Piety can also be found in the Christian address ('omnibus sancte ecclesie fidelibus', 'to all believers of the holy church'), in the preamble, in the *sanctio* (which can contain a threat of excommunication), in the *dispositio*, the motivation clause ('pro remissione peccatorum meorum', 'for the remission of my sins'), the request for prayers, and any insistence on religion ('ecclesia sanctissimi et beatissimi patris et domini nostri martyris Talis', 'the church of the holy and blessed father, our lord martyr N.' instead of 'ecclesia sancti Talis', 'the church of St N.'). The pious formula in the *intitulatio* is politically important because it shows the independence of the issuer's power and his submission to God. The *sanctio* of excommunication accords a great role to ecclesiastical power, the only one which can exclude someone from the community of Christians. In assessing the political use of piety, the invocation, the *intitulatio*, and the *sanctio* thus provide the most important evidence.

This article focuses on the charters of northern France (Picardy, Artois, Flanders, Normandy, and Champagne) and Lower Lotharingia from the eleventh and twelfth centuries. The eleventh century saw the birth of the comital and episcopal charters; the twelfth century was the age of the transformation of those charters into very common documents. However, since not all documents are easily available, we will focus on some institutions, the charters of which have been edited. We can complete our

---

[6] B.-M. Tock, 'Les textes diplomatiques, des médias au Moyen Age?', in *Le rôle des médias à travers l'histoire. Actes du VIIIe colloque Poznan-Strasbourg, mai 1994* (Poznan, 1995), pp. 61–84.

sample by using two collections of charters, namely the database *Original Charters before 1121 Conserved in France*, organized by Artem, at Nancy,[7] which includes texts and photographs of all those original charters, and the CD-ROM *Thesaurus Diplomaticus* and its collection of 'Belgian' charters.[8]

A problem arises concerning the authorship of these charters. Although a few twelfth-century comital charters were drafted by comital chanceries, most were written in monastic scriptoria. The problem is that, as a result, these charters express monastic or clerical perceptions of power rather than comital attitudes towards power. Episcopal chanceries came into being earlier, but until the end of the twelfth century we find some charters having been prepared by their recipients. These charters are not dealt with here, as they primarily show how pious the count, or the bishop, was presumed to be. Unfortunately, it is not easy to see whether a charter was written by a comital or episcopal chancery, as detailed studies are not available.

The Invocation

In the charters of the counts of Flanders, the use of an invocation, which had been decreasing since the mid-twelfth century, ends in 1191, at least in all of the charters drafted by the chancery.[9] At the same time, the comital chancery became more active and drafted more than 60% of the comital charters. During the two first decades of the principate of Count Thierry of Alsace (until 1147), about 75 to 80% of the comital charters have an invocation; from 1148 to 1168, about 60% of the comital charters have one.[10] From 1191 to 1206, while the count's chancery no longer used an

---

[7] Artem: Atelier de recherche sur les textes médiévaux, member of the Upresa 7002 'Moyen Age' of the Université de Nancy II and the C.N.R.S.

[8] *Thesaurus Diplomaticus*, ed. P. Tombeur et al. (Turnhout, 1997): one CD-ROM.

[9] In fact, some charters had an invocation, which disappeared when the charter was copied into a cartulary. For an example of a cartulary omitting the invocation, see *De oorkonden der graven van Vlaanderen (juli 1128 – september 1191), II-1: regering van Diederik van de Elzas (juli 1128 – 17 januari 1168)*, ed. Th. de Hemptinne and A. Verhulst (Brussel, 1988), pp. 182–83, no. 112 (cartulary of Saint-Vaast of Arras, MS B. M. Arras 1266, omitting invocation and witnesses). See also B.-M. Tock, *Une chancellerie épiscopale au XIIe siècle: le cas d'Arras* (Louvain-la-Neuve, 1991), p. 105, no. 2 and p. 161, no. 248.

[10] *Actes des comtes de Flandre (1071–1128)*, ed. F. Vercauteren (Bruxelles, 1938); *De oorkonden*, ed. De Hemptinne and Verhulst.

invocation (including it in only 6% of the charters), the monastic scriptoria still did so in 61% of the charters.[11]

Can we observe a cause and effect relationship here? Does the falling into disuse of the invocation show an insistence on the lay character of the comital power, as opposed to the monastic scriptoria and even the episcopal chanceries? This may be so, but the evidence needs to be viewed comparatively in distinct regional, rank, and chronological frameworks. Firstly, even during the eleventh century not all princes regularly used an invocation. In Ponthieu, only one third of the comital charters issued since the beginning of the twelfth century contain an invocation. In Normandy, the dukes used it most of the time: more than 90% of the ducal charters issued before 1066 (212 of 234 charters, that is) contain one.[12] All six original ducal charters issued between 1066 and 1121 preserved in French archives contain an invocation.[13] However, for the charters of Norman counts and viscounts, preserved as originals in France, and dated before 1121, of the twenty charters eleven do not contain invocations.

Secondly, the bishops also gave up the invocation, sometimes even sooner than the Flemish counts. In the bishopric of Thérouanne (which was in the county of Flanders), 27% of the charters issued under Bishop Didier (1169–91) have an invocation, but under Bishop Lambert (1191–1207) it was only 3%.[14] In Noyon, about 50% of the charters from 1148 to 1187 have an invocation, compared with 9% under Bishop Stephen (1187–1221).[15] In Reims, Archbishop William (1176–1202) did not use an invocation.[16] Archbishops Manasses II (1096–1106) and Raoul (1107–24)

---

[11] *De oorkonden der graven van Vlaanderen (1191 – aanvang 1206)*, ed. W. Prevenier, 3 vols. (Brussel, 1964–71), I, 361 and 568).

[12] *Recueil des actes des ducs de Normandie (911–1066)*, ed. M. Fauroux (Caen, 1961), p. 48.

[13] That is, if we agree that the formula 'Omnipotente Deo inspirante qui dat omnibus benefacientibus bene velle et posse pro bona voluntate', which is at the beginning of a charter of Duke Robert Curthose in 1092 for Le Bec-Hellouin abbey, can be considered an invocation, or a quasi-invocative preamble (Rouen, Archives départementales de la Seine-Maritime, 20 H carton 5).

[14] Data based on my edition (in progress) of the charters of the bishops of Thérouanne. Before 1169, 65% of the charters of Bishop John (1099–1130) have no invocation, compared with 55% under Bishop Milo I (1131–59), and 52% under Bishop Milo II (1159–69).

[15] *Les chartes des évêques de Noyon, 1148–1221. Etude diplomatique et édition*, ed. A. Rinckenbach, 3 vols. (unpublished dissertation Ecole des Chartes, Parisı, 1991), I, 68.

[16] See Archbishop William's charters in the *Thesaurus Diplomaticus*.

diminished the use of the invocation, but their successors Renaud II, Samson, and Henry of France generalized this use again.[17] It is also absent in eleventh-century episcopal charters from Normandy.[18] In Arras (also in Flanders), the charters lost their invocation sooner if they had been drafted by the recipient: before 1164, the chancery always used an invocation, while the monastic scriptoria omitted it sometimes (in six charters of 35). From 1164 to 1183, an invocation can be found in 55% of the chancery charters, but in only 20% of the recipient charters. From 1184 the invocation disappeared.[19] So neither comital nor episcopal charters offer unequivocal evidence about the use of invocations. The use and falling into disuse of the invocation cannot univocally be linked to monastic or clerical scriptoria, nor to the development of comital and ecclesiastical chanceries.

Thirdly, the purpose of the invocation was to ask for, or just to call to mind, God's protection and benediction: but for what or for whom? God's blessing could be asked for the issuer of the charter. The invocation should then be regarded a part of the *intitulatio* and be linked with the pious formula ('Dei gratia').[20] Should this be true, it would be very important for us. Although some charters support this idea, it does not seem the most important characteristic: the texts linking invocation and *intitulatio* are rare, and all are early medieval. In these cases the invocation is part of a person's title, not necessarily the issuer.[21] The invocation as a part of a title

---

[17] *Actes des archevêques de Reims, d'Arnoul à Renaud II (997–1139)*, ed. P. Demouy, 3 vols. (unpublished dissertation Université de Nancy, 1982), I, no. 163*.

[18] There is only one exception among the preserved originals dated before 1121: a charter of Archbishop Riculfus of Rouen, dated 872 (Rouen, Archives départementales de la Seine-Maritime, 14 H 156).

[19] Tock, *Une chancellerie*, pp. 105–07 and 161.

[20] K. Schmitz, *Ursprung und Geschichte der Devotionsformeln bis zu ihrer Aufnahme in die fränkische Königsurkunde* (Stuttgart, 1913), p. 97; H. Zielinski, 'Selbstaussage – Fremdaussage. Überlegungen zur Intitulatio des frühen Mittelalters', *Göttingische Gelehrten Anzeigen* 225 (1973), 91–118; H. Fichtenau, 'Forschungen über Urkundenformeln', *Mitteilungen des Instituts für Österreichische Geschichtsforschung* 94 (1986), 285–339 at p. 287.

[21] Many instances can be found in subscriptions of Merovingian councils: see the councils of Arles (524), Carpentras (527), etc., in *Concilia Galliae a. 511–695*, ed. C. de Clercq, Corpus Christianorum. Series Latina 148a (Turnhout, 1963). An example from the 'concilium Epaonense' of 517: 'Victorius, episcopus in Christi nomine civitatis Gratianopolitanae, relegi et subscripsi' (ibid., p. 35). Very few examples can be found later: e.g. an unpublished charter of Desiderius, bishop of Thérouanne, dated 1172: 'Desiderius, in Christi nomine Morinorum episcopus' (Bruges, Archief Bisdom, C 105 no. 2).

does not put the charter and the act under the protection of God, but just remembers the divine foundations of the issuer's power, and probably also its religious purpose. Sometimes it simply records that the issuer was inspired by God, as in the case of an eleventh-century benefactor of the abbey of Saint-Claude: 'Ego in Dei nomine Vuicardus dono Deo', 'I, Vuicardus, in God's name give to God'.[22] Most texts, however, support another idea, such as the charter of John, bishop of Thérouanne, dating from 1114: 'Quia apostolus dicit: quecumque facitis in verbo aut in opere, omnia in nomine Domini facite; in ejus igitur nomine Dei Patris omnipotentis et Filii et Spiritus Sancti, notum sit cunctis fidei catholice cultoribus quia ego Johannes, Dei gratia Morinorum episcopus', 'Because the apostle says: "Whatever you do in word and deed, do everything in the name of the Lord"; therefore in his name of God the almighty Father and the Son and the Holy Ghost, be it known to all believers in the Catholic faith that I, John, with God's grace bishop of Thérouanne [...]'.[23] *Notitiae* also usually open with an invocation.[24] Because these are diplomatic texts without issuer, the invocation can only concern the legal act.[25] Thus, by the invocation, the benediction of God is hoped to descend onto the act (gift, trial, et cetera) recorded in the charter, not onto the issuing power, whether a secular or an ecclesiastical one. Clearly linked with the protection of the act is the invocation within a charter's text, and not at the beginning of the charter. A very rare example can be found in a charter of Drogo, count of Vexin, around 1030: 'quapropter ego comes Drogo, dominicis preceptis

---

[22] Lons-le-Saunier, Archives départementales du Jura, paquet 31, liasse 6.

[23] *Cartulaire de l'Abbaye de Saint-Bertin*, ed. B. Guérard (Paris, 1841), pp. 225–26.

[24] A *notitia* was drafted by the beneficiary of the legal act, who also kept the record; it was not approved by, nor even seen by, the author. A charter may have been drafted by the beneficiary, but was to be approved by the issuer, who generally also was the author of the act, or was an independent third party (but could be the beneficiary). I here simplify the difference between charter and *notitia*, which raises many difficulties. See D. Barthélemy, 'Une crise de l'écrit? Observations sur des actes de Saint-Aubin d'Angers (XIe siècle)', *Bibliothèque de l'Ecole des Chartes* 155 (1997), 95–117 at pp. 99–100. Barthélemy's well-founded criticism cannot take away the need to distinguish what we could call unilateral and multilateral records, or (even if this is not exactly the same) between observers' and actors' records.

[25] Most *notitiae* do without invocation (see the *Cartulaire-chronique du prieuré Saint-Georges d'Hesdin*, ed. R. Fossier (Paris, 1988), dated 1097–1180), but see the *notitia* of an agreement between Arrouaise abbey and Mont-Saint-Quentin abbey of 1174 (in the cartulary of Arrouaise, MS B. M. Amiens 1077, fol. 62–63; the charters of Arrouaise abbey will be published by myself shortly).

salubriter admonitus, in nomine sancte et individue Trinitatis reddidi monachis [...]', 'therefore I, Count Drogo, for my salvation admonished by the Lord's precepts, in the name of the holy and undivided Trinity render the monks [...]'.[26] In conclusion, it is most likely that God's blessing, implored in the invocation, was invoked not for the issuer of the charter, but as a divine guarantee of the recorded legal act.

The intitulatio

The *intitulatio* may contain a pious formula ('Dei gratia') and a formula of humility ('licet indignus'). The case of Charlemagne shows that the pious formula was more politically inspired than pious. This is true for later times as well. John IV, count of Armagnac, used the formula 'par la grace de Dieu', but had to renounce this by order of King Charles VII.[27] During the entire eleventh and twelfth centuries bishops used a pious formula in Arras,[28] Thérouanne,[29] Reims,[30] and Noyon.[31] At Arras, even the archdeacons used a pious formula, but not the leaders of the cathedral chapter, such as the dean and the provost.[32] This may be explained by the fact that the latter only exercised the chapter's authority, and the archdeacon an episcopal authority. Unfortunately, because of the lack of studies about

---

[26] Rouen, Archives départementales de la Seine-Maritime, 14 H 805.

[27] D. Vondruss-Reissner, 'La formule "par la grâce de Dieu" dans les actes de Jean IV d'Armagnac', *Bibliothèque de l'Ecole des Chartes* 151 (1993), 171–83.

[28] This is so obvious that I forgot to mention it explicitly in my study of the chancery of Arras: Tock, *Une chancellerie*, pp. 107–09, 162.

[29] With few exceptions, most of them as a result of bad copies. But we indeed read 'ego Desiderius Morinensis episcopus' in a charter of Bishop Desiderius (1173, copy in the cartulary of the church of Thérouanne; *Cartulaire de l'église de Térouanne*, ed. Th. Duchet and A. Giry (Saint-Omer, 1881), pp. 41–42, no. 50; the text is complex and supposes the action of a superior, that is, divine, authority) and 'ego Desiderius Morinorum episcopus' in a charter of the same bishop (1185, original preserved in Paris, Bibliothèque Nationale de France, MS lat. 17.058, no. 3; D. Haigneré, 'Les chartes de l'abbaye de Notre-Dame de Licques, Ordre des Prémontrés (1078–1311)', *Mémoires de la société académique de l'arrondissement de Boulogne-sur-Mer* 15 (1890), pp. 33–175, at 62–63, no. 6).

[30] *Actes*, ed. Demouy, I, no. 166*.

[31] *Les chartes*, ed. Rinckenbach, I, 69–70.

[32] B.-M. Tock, 'Les chartes promulguées par le chapitre cathédral d'Arras au XIIe siècle', *Revue Mabillon*, 2nd ser., 2 (1991), 49–97 at pp. 58–60.

The Political Use of Piety 27

archdeacons' and cathedral chapters' charters, we do not know if this was the same in other dioceses as well.[33]

The use of a pious formula in comital charters is not as common. In Germany, the first examples date back to the mid-twelfth century.[34] In Flanders, this use was increasing until 1168. Of the charters of Count Robert I (1071–93), 71% contain a pious formula, compared with 50% of those of Robert II (1093–1111), 68% of those of Baldwin VII (1111–19), 74% of the charters of Charles the Good (1119–27), and 86% of Thierry of Alsace's charters (1128–67).[35] In Namur we also observe an increase, but this continued until 1196: of (only) 36 comital charters before 1196, 14% have a pious formula before 1166, 50% from 1171 to 1182, and 83% from 1182 to 1196.[36] In Hainault the use was decreasing,[37] and in Ponthieu it fluctuated.[38] In Normandy, the dukes used a pious formula in nearly all their charters.[39] In Picardy, as in Normandy, the lesser counts (of Arques, Aumale, Eu, Évreux, Meulan, Mortain, Ribemont, and Vermandois) did

---

[33] The *Thesaurus Diplomaticus* contains charters issued by archdeacons and cathedral chapters with and without pious formulas. Perhaps the case of Arras is special, because of the strict episcopal control over the chancery, even when it worked for the chapter.

[34] K. Brunner, 'Der fränkische Fürstentitel im neunten und zehnten Jahrhundert', in *Intitulatio II.: Lateinische Herrscher- und Fürstentitel im neunten und zehnten Jahrhundert*, ed. H. Wolfram (Wien, Köln and Graz, 1973), pp. 179–340 at pp. 203–07.

[35] Data based on *Actes des comtes de Flandre*, ed. Vercauteren, and *De oorkonden*, ed. De Hemptinne and Verhulst. Letters, treaties, and false charters are not included. Only five charters of William of Normandy (1127–28) survive: all have a pious formula. From 1191 to 1206, only 2% of the charters drafted by the chancery have an invocation, compared with 26% of those drafted by the recipients (*De oorkonden*, ed. Prevenier, I, 364 and 571).

[36] *Actes des comtes de Namur de la première race, 946–1196*, ed. F. Rousseau (Bruxelles, 1936), to be completed with the charters of the counts of Namur in the *Thesaurus Diplomaticus*.

[37] No systematic edition of the charters of the counts of Hainault exists. Many charters are printed in *Actes et documents anciens*, ed. Duvivier. The *Thesaurus Diplomaticus*, which gives the text of most of the counts of Hainault's charters, contains 117 charters, which can be divided into six periods: 1065–1117, 1133–50, 1151–60, 1161–70, 1171–80, 1181–90. The percentages of charters with a pious formula are 78, 58, 53, 52, 48, and 37% respectively. The pious formula is no longer used after 1190 (but from 1191 the count of Hainault is count of Flanders too).

[38] Percentages of charters with a pious formula: 63% until 1106, 18% under William I (1106–71), 28% under John (1171–91), and 23% under William II (until 1200). See *Recueil des actes des comtes de Pontieu, 1026–1279*, ed. C. Brunel (Paris, 1930).

[39] *Recueil des actes*, ed. Fauroux, p. 49.

not use a pious formula until 1120, if we may believe the evidence from the surviving original charters.[40] Besides, the title of count does not seem to have been very important here in the eleventh century: some counts do not mention it, such as Richard, count of Évreux, who in 1038 merely calls himself 'Ego Ricardus, Rotberti archiepiscopi filius', 'I, Richard, son of Archbishop Robert'.[41] The counts of Bar, in Lorraine, before 1190 hardly used a pious formula either.[42] The same is true for the counts of Rethel, in Champagne, before 1200.[43] This pious formula could express the religious purpose of a power,[44] or be a sign of gratitude towards God for being a count.[45] More likely it mainly concerns the religious foundations of power:

---

[40] There are some exceptions, such as two charters of the count of Talou of 1043 and 1046 (*Chartes de l'abbaye de Jumièges (vers 825 à 1204)*, ed. J.-J. Vernier, 2 vols. (Rouen and Paris, 1916), I, 63–64, no. 20; Fécamp, Musée de la Bénédictine, 5bis), and a charter of the count of Beaumont-sur-Oise issued before 1059 (Fécamp, Musée de la Bénédictine, 83).

[41] *Chartes de l'abbaye de Jumièges*, ed. Vernier, pp. 60–63, no. 19.

[42] *Actes des comtes de Bar, de Sophie à Henri Ier, 1033–1190*, ed. M. Parisse (Nancy, 1972): only three acts have a pious formula (no. 14 of 1145, no. 38 of 1178, and no. 58 of 1189).

[43] *Trésor des chartes des comtes de Rethel*, ed. G. Saige and H. Lacaille, 2 vols. (Monaco, 1902–16), I.

[44] K.F. Werner, 'Königtum und Fürstentum im französischen 12. Jahrhundert', in *Probleme des 12. Jahrhunderts. Reichenau-Vorträge 1965–1967*, Vorträge und Forschungen 12 (Stuttgart 1968), 177–225 at p. 199.

[45] O. Guillot, *Le comte d'Anjou et son entourage au XIe siècle*, 2 vols. (Paris, 1972), I, 354–56. Olivier Guillot notes that the few pious formulas of the eleventh century Angevin counts often date back to the beginning of their principate. But there are only ten pious formulas, and the eleventh-century charters were probably drafted by the beneficiaries. One charter seems to confirm Guillot's interpretation; 'Ego quidem Gaufredus, comitatus Andecavensis naturalis heres, sed preter eum per urbes plures et castra hujusmodi potestatis sub Dei ordinatione minister' (charter given in 1056 by Geoffrey Martel; *Cartulaire vendômois de Marmoutier*, ed. A. de Trémault (Vendôme, 1893), no. 117). As Guillot states, this charter clearly distinguishes the Angevin principate, inherited from the father, from the other power, given by God. However, this charter, drafted by Marmoutier abbey, is meant to legitimate the count of Anjou's authority in Vendôme, against the count of Vendôme, 'naturalis heres' of this land (D. Barthélemy, *La société dans le comté de Vendôme de l'an mil au XIVe siècle* (Paris, 1993), pp. 297–98). Nevertheless, a Flemish text supports Guillot's point of view: 'Ego Robertus, Dei gratia quicquid sum, comes Flandrensium fidelis [...] quia et paternae haereditatis, Deo annuente, obtineo principatum [...]' (*Actes des comtes*, ed. Vercauteren, pp. 16–19, no. 6). Robert I, second son of Count Baldwin V, had to conquer his county from his nephew Arnulf in the battle of Cassel, 1071 (*Lexikon des Mittelalters*, VII, col. 894).

The Political Use of Piety 29

it is only the most powerful princes who use it, those who regard themselves as being close to the king and to God.

The formula of humility is not as frequent as the pious formula. Laymen and laywomen never use it, with only four exceptions to my knowledge, three of which concern Richard II, duke of Normandy,[46] Baldwin IV, count of Hainault,[47] and Sophia, countess of Chiny,[48] These exceptions can probably be explained by the initiative of a monastic drafter. More important in this respect is Charles the Good, count of Flanders, because a formula of humility can be found in two of his charters.[49] This is not surprising, as this layman is considered a saint. Even if his saintliness largely stems from his martyrdom, he had perhaps already been considered to be holy before his death.[50] Bishops more frequently used the formula of humility, sometimes out of respect for a local tradition, and sometimes out of personal humility. In Arras we have the case of Bishop Godescalc, the first bishop whose chancery used a formula of humility. Godescalc behaved very humbly, too much so in the view of St Bernard, who was afraid that Godescalc would lose all his authority.[51] At Reims, only Archbishop Renaud (1083–96) frequently used a formula of humility. He restored the archbishop's power and authority, and placed religion and reform again at the centre of the archbishop's policy, after the disastrous pontificate of Manasses I.[52] Apparently not every count was allowed to state, by means of the pious

---

[46] Charter for the chapter of Saint-Quentin, 1015 (*Recueil des actes*, ed. Fauroux, pp. 100–02, no. 18): 'Northmannorum licet indignus dux et patritius'.

[47] Charter for Vicoigne abbey, 1138 (*Sacri et canonici ordinis Praemonstratensis annales*, ed. Ch. L. Hugo, 2 vols. (Nancy, 1734–36), I, col. 684: 'Ego Balduinus, iunioris Balduini comitis filius, comes Hainoniensis quamvis indignus'.

[48] Charter for Orval abbey, 1198 (*Cartulaire de l'abbaye d'Orval*, ed. H. Goffinet (Bruxelles, 1879), pp. 117–18, no. 79: 'ego Sophia, humilis comitissa de Chisneio'. Perhaps Sophia is said to be humble because she is a woman. This *intitulatio* continues: 'ego quoque filius ejus comes de Chisneio'.

[49] Charter for St. Walburgis's chapter in Veurne, 1123 (*Actes des comtes*, ed. Vercauteren, pp. 260–62, no. 114): 'ego Carolus, licet indignus, divina clementia Flandrensium comes'; charter for Auchy abbey (dated between 1119 and 1127) (ibid., pp. 286–90, no. 124): 'Karolus, Flandriarum comes inmeritus'.

[50] On Charles the Good, see Galbert of Bruges, *De multro, traditione et occisione gloriosi Karoli comitis Flandriarum*, ed. J. Rider (Turnhout, 1994), pp. XII-XII, and poems like the *Lamentatio de morte Karoli comitis Flandriae*, edited by Henri Pirenne in his edition of Galbert (Paris, 1891), pp. 177–84.

[51] Tock, *Une chancellerie*, pp. 30 and 209.

[52] *Actes*, ed. Demouy, I, 68*-72*.

formula in the *intitulatio*, that his power came from God: only the duke of Normandy and the count of Flanders did so, as well as the count of Namur just before becoming a margrave.[53] The count of Hainault did not think about using it. Other counts, whom we could call the lesser counts, were not allowed to use it. Only exceptionally did laymen and laywomen include in the *intitulatio* a formula of humility, which was, however, frequently used by bishops.

The sanctio

Although the purpose of a charter was to give perpetual memory and power to a legal act, it occurred that ill-intentioned persons tried to disregard the document. To avoid this, the natural protection given by the charter could be strengthened by a *sanctio*. This formula threatened the transgressors with either a secular penalty (generally a fine) or a religious penalty (excommunication). The attribution of a religious penalty normally was a clerical privilege, while the secular one was a regalian right, exercised by the princes. This distinction was not always respected, as we will see. Besides, it is important to notice that the mere inclusion of a *sanctio* is an implicit acknowledgment of the weakness of the charter.

Bishops' charters do not mention any secular penalties. Even in charters of imperial bishops, like those of Liège or Strasbourg, whose civil and territorial powers were greater than in northern France, the use of a secular penalty seems very rare.[54] On the other hand, bishops' charters frequently mention a religious penalty, even if this use is decreasing. This is the case in Noyon, where it fell from 40 to 10% of the charters between 1148 and

---

[53] On the creation of the margraviate of Namur in 1184, S. Hauser, *Staufische Lehnspolitik am Ende des 12. Jahrhunderts, 1180–1197* (Frankfurt, 1998), pp. 81–94.

[54] An exception is the charter of Baldric II, bishop of Liège, issued for the chapter of the Holy Cross in Liège in 1011: 'Si quis autem contra hanc nostre traditionis cartulam quod minime credimus uenerit, et eam infringere uoluerit, iram omnipotentis Dei incurrat et a liminibus sanctorum sequestratus appareat et partem cum dyabolo et sociis suis in inferni claustris habeat et insuper, cogente iudiciaria potestate, auri libras decem persolvat' (*La Belgique ancienne et moderne. Géographie et histoire des communes belges. Continuation. Arrondissement de Louvain, canton de Tirlemont, communes rurales*, ed. A. Wauters, 2 vols. (Bruxelles, 1875–76), I, 166–67). This charter is very early, dating from the beginning of the eleventh century, and, moreover, the fine had to be imposed by a judicial power, which can be the emperor's, and not the bishop's.

1221.⁵⁵ The threat with a secular penalty is rare in the count of Flanders's charters: before 1127, we only find five fines, one exile, and one loss of advocacy.⁵⁶ Surprisingly, we find more religious sanctions: 22, most of them being excommunications. This raises some problems. How can a count, being a secular prince, threaten with a religious penalty?⁵⁷ Some charters resolve the problem by stating that the count asked a churchman to pronounce the excommunication. A nice formula is found in some charters of Baldwin VII for the abbey of Saint-Amand.⁵⁸ We can ask whether these formulas express the count's or monastic feelings. The example of the charters of Saint-Amand, as well as other texts, seems to point to a monastic origin.⁵⁹ The count may have played a role, however. Why do 44% of the charters of Baldwin VII contain a religious penalty, compared with only about 10% of the other comital charters before 1128? Presumably Baldwin VII, or one of his *dictatores*, had a taste for religious penalties. The most important observation is that more than twenty charters needed the spiritual protection of the comital word.

After 1128, the number of penalties continues to decrease. In Count Thierry's charters we only find three threats with a fine.⁶⁰ Only one of the charters of his son, Count Philip (1168–91), contains such a threat.⁶¹ The explicit mention of the count's anger (*ira*) with the offenders probably was obvious and therefore superfluous.⁶² Spiritual penalties are found in fifteen

---

⁵⁵ *Les chartes*, ed. Rinckenbach, I, 75.

⁵⁶ *Actes des comtes*, ed. Vercauteren, nos. 9, 16, 32, 66, 87, 107, 111.

⁵⁷ Some *dictatores*, prudently, do not mention any penalty, but in the *corroboratio* use formulas which are usually part of spiritual penalties: 'et sigilli mei impressione confirmavi, ne qui sancte ecclesie inimicus inposterum audeat tale donum temere infringere aut minuere aut violare' (*Actes des comtes*, ed. Vercauteren, pp. 116–18, no. 42).

⁵⁸ 'Abbatem et fratres violatorem anathematis vinculo innodare rogavi' (*Actes des comtes*, ed. Vercauteren, pp. 185–86, no. 82). See also ibid., pp. 180–84, no. 81, and pp. 190–92, no. 85.

⁵⁹ A charter of Count Robert I for the abbey of Saint-Bertin has the same text as a charter of the abbot (*Actes des comtes*, ed. Vercauteren, pp. 52–53, no. 16).

⁶⁰ *De oorkonden*, ed. De Hemptinne and Verhulst, nos. 93 (£10), 94 (£30) and 142 (£50).

⁶¹ Charter for St. Donatian's chapter in Brugge (*Opera Diplomatica*, ed. A. Miraeus and J.F. Foppens, 4 vols. (Leuven and Brussels, 1723–48), II, 1188.

⁶² One mention in a charter of Thierry for Marchiennes abbey, 1150–55 (*De oorkonden*, ed. De Hemptinne and Verhulst, pp. 228–29, no. 142); and three mentions in charters of Philip: for Hasnon abbey, 1174 (R. Dubois, 'Prieuré de Lucheux et prévôté de Gros-Tison. Cartulaire factice', *Mémoires de la société des antiquaires de Picardie* 47 (1936),

(5%) of Thierry's charters, twelve of which date from the period 1128–45, and in and only three of Philip's.[63] In general, the count asked a churchman, a bishop or an abbot, to pronounce the excommunication. Some drafters seem to have been embarrassed by the relationship between the bishop and the count: 'Concedo et volo ut domnus Milo episcopus Morinensis, meo rogatu, excommunicationis sententia hanc mee devotionis traditionem confirmet', 'I concede and wish that lord Milo, bishop of Thérouanne, at my request, confirms this donation of my devotion through the sentence of excommunication'.[64]

In Hainault, before 1138, six of the sixteen charters contain a spiritual penalty. We only find one secular penalty: £100 for freemen, the loss of the eyes for the unfree.[65] After 1139 we read of only one religious penalty, in a charter of 1179.[66] Even before 1138, the expression of the religious penalty does not reveal a strong comital authority: the penalty can be in the bishop's subscription,[67] or can be left to God.[68] There is only one charter in

---

111–517 at pp. 397–99, no. 81), for Marchiennes abbey, 1180 (*Actes et documents*, ed. Duvivier, pp. 106–09, no. 54), and for Melrose abbey, 1185 (unpublished; text in *Thesaurus Diplomaticus*). Another text for Marchiennes abbey, of 1135, speaks about the 'severitas' of the count (*De oorkonden*, ed. De Hemptinne and Verhulst, pp. 57–59, no. 28). In Catalonia, around 1130, the 'ira comitis' replaced the 'ira Dei' (M. Zimmermann, 'Protocoles et préambules dans les documents catalans du Xe au XIIe siècle: évolution et signification spirituelle', *Mélanges de la Casa de Velazquez* 10 (1974), 41–76; 11 (1975), 51–79, in vol. 10, p. 53).

[63] Charters given by the count and a bishop, or with an episcopal seal are excluded here. The *Thesaurus Diplomaticus* enumerates more than 400 charters issued by Philip.

[64] *De oorkonden*, ed. De Hemptinne and Verhulst, pp. 71–72, no. 37 (Ten Duinen abbey, 1137). Another charter reads: 'Atque hoc ipsum auctoritate domini Milonis episcopi sub anathematis districtione confirmari volo et postulo' (Warneton abbey, 1138; ibid., pp. 79–80, no. 44).

[65] Baldwin II for Marchiennes abbey (*Actes et documents*, ed. Duvivier, p. 19). Another secular penalty is to be found in the king's subscription of a charter of Baldwin I for Hasnon abbey, 1065 (*Recueil des actes de Philippe Ier, roi de France (1059–1108)*, ed. M. Prou (Paris, 1908), pp. 59–63, no. 22).

[66] Baldwin V for Aulne abbey (L. Devillers, 'Mémoire sur un cartulaire et sur les archives de l'abbaye d'Aulne', *Annales du cercle archéologique de Mons*, 4 (1863), 237–80; 5 (1864) 193–422, in vol. 4, pp. 260–61). In a 1158 charter for Anchin abbey, Baldwin IV wishes a reward for those who will respect the charter: 'Pacem eidem loco servantibus pax eterna detur in celis' (*Actes et documents anciens intéressant la Belgique*, ed. Ch. Duvivier (Bruxelles, 1898), pp. 302–03).

[67] Baldwin II for Hasnon abbey, 1086 (J. Dewez, *Histoire de l'abbaye de Saint-Pierre d'Hasnon* (Lille, 1890), pp. 562–65). In a charter of Baldwin IV for the abbey of Saint-

The Political Use of Piety 33

which the count ordered an excommunication, but he left the execution to the abbot, not the bishop.[69]

The counts of Ponthieu seldom used the *sanctio* after the eleventh century: only seven times in 47 charters before 1169, date of the penultimate charter including a spiritual penalty.[70] With three exceptions, the Ponthieu charters do not ask a bishop to excommunicate violators of the legal

---

Feuillien in Le Roeulx (1138), the text reads: 'harum etiam traditionum testis est domnus Nicholaus, Dei gratia Cameracensis episcopus, et in presentia ejus eedem traditiones recognite sunt et ad utilitatem eiusdem ecclesie sigilli sui impressione sub excommunicatione confirmate' (L. Devillers, 'Description sommaire du cartulaire de l'abbaye de St-Feuillien au Roeulx', *Annales du cercle archéologique de Mons* 21 (1888), 285–316, at pp. 308–09, no. 1). The bishop's chancellor subscribed this charter, and the date specifies the year of the episcopate. Therefore, the charter was probably drafted by the biishop's chancery.

[68] Baldwin II for the abbey of Saint-Denis-en-Broqueroie, 1089: 'Quod si quis potentum ausus fuerit presumere, nisi desierit, potenter sustineat tormenta' (Ch. Duvivier, 'Quelles étaient l'importance et les limites du Pagus Hainoensis jusqu'au XIe siècle?', *Mémoires et publications de la société des sciences, des arts et des lettres du Hainaut*, 2nd ser., 9 (1863–64), 448–50, no. 68). Baldwin III for Saint-Denis-en-Broqueroie, 1117: 'quod qui presumpserit, si admonitus non emendaverit, sicut psalmus ait, destruat eum Deus in finem, evellat eum et radicem eius de terra viventium' (*Chartes du chapitre de Sainte-Waudru de Mons*, ed. L. Devillers, 4 vols. (Bruxelles, 1899–1913), I, 8–10, no. 6).

[69] Baldwin II for Crespin abbey, 1094 (Duvivier, 'Quelles étaient', p. 477, no. 22).

[70] All eleventh-century charters contain a spiritual penalty. In the twelfth century, this is the case in seven charters (*Recueil*, ed. Brunel, nos. 25, 27, 32 (ambiguous), 59, 61, 62, and 71). The last charter of a count of Ponthieu with a spiritual penalty was given to the abbey of Saint-Josse-au-Bois in 1185. This relates how the count had been excommunicated as a result of injustice he had done to the abbey. At the king's request, he gave up his claims, made peace with the abbey, and donated lands to it. The excommunication was lifted. The abbot—the charter does not mention the count asking for it—threatened transgressors of the agreement with excommunication: 'Abbas autem ejusdem ecclesie et sacerdotes qui aderant, assumptis stolis et candelis accensis, omnes ejus conventionis transgressores anathematis sententia dampnaverunt', 'The abbot of this abbey and the priests who were present, after having put on their stoles and having lighted the candles, condemned all transgressors of this agreement with the sentence of excommunication'. The count promised to pay a fine if he (or his heir) broke the agreement: 'Quod si, quod absit, ego, vel uxor mea, vel aliquis de heredibus nostris, istam conventionem aliquando violare temptaverit, et aliqua damna intulerit, non solum damna recenter illata sed etiam antiqua damna CLX modiorum annone et DC lib. Pontivensis monete tenebitur reddere [...]', 'In case—which should not be—I, my wife, or anyone of my heirs would ever try to violate this agreement and bring any damage [to the abbey], they not only will be held to return the recently caused damage but also the old damage of 160 measures of grain and £600 in money of Ponthieu'.

acts.⁷¹ They only express the wish that evildoers will be punished by an anathema, or directly by God.⁷² Only two *sanctiones* can be found in the charters of the counts of Namur, and none in the charters of the counts of Chiny.⁷³ In Normandy, the few charters given by lesser counts included in the Artem database show a similar, but more precocious evolution: before 1050 these charters contain a spiritual penalty; from 1070 onwards it is omitted.

We can probably explain the difference between the counts of Flanders and other counts by referring to the Gregorian reform, which reinforced the bishops' authority and independence from secular power. As a result of this reform, it was no longer permissible for a layman to order an excommunication by a bishop, except if the former was a powerful prince, such as the count of Flanders. Even this count did not frequently use these spiritual penalties, perhaps out of respect for the church, but certainly because his sword and his justice offered better guarantees.⁷⁴

Conclusion

The three parts of charters we have studied here do not show piety in the same way. The invocation protected the legal act, not the power issuing the

---

⁷¹ The exceptions are two early charters (*Recueil*, ed. Brunel, nos. 3 and 8), and a later charter for Saint-André-en-Gouffern (1143), the text of which is adapted from a papal bull, according to which the count asks the pope to excommunicate violators: 'Si quis igitur contra hanc nostre constitutionis paginam temere venire temptaverit, exoramus ecclesiasticos rectores qui in cathedra beati Petri, apostolorum principis, resident, ad quorum officium ecclesiasticus rigor pertinet, secundo terciove commonitus, si non satisfactione congrua emendaverit, quatinus potestatis honorisque sui dignitate privetur reumque se divino juditio existere de perpetrata iniquitate cognoscat, et a sacratissimo corpore et sanguine Dei Domini redemptoris nostri Jhesu Christi alienus fiat, atque in extremo examine districte ultioni subjaceat [...]' (*Recueil*, ed. Brunel, no. 27).

⁷² E.g. a charter for the priory of Abbeville, 1136: 'Quod si forte aliquis, quod quidem absit, diabolica operatione vel sinistro consilio deceptus, hanc meam et matris mee elemosinam quocumque modo demere vel auferre Deo omnipotenti et ejus apostolis Petro et Paulo, quibus eam pro remedio animarum nostrarum concessimus, temptaverit, in perpetuum anathema sit, Deoque omnipotenti rationem reddat, et nisi a temeritate sua resipuerit, eterne damnationis sententiam incurrat' (*Recueil*, ed. Brunel, no. 25).

⁷³ For the charters of the counts of Namur, note 36; for those of the counts of Chiny, *Thesaurus Diplomaticus*.

⁷⁴ In Germany, however, princes often used a religious penalty during the eleventh and twelfth centuries: J. Studtmann, 'Die Pönformel der mittelalterlichen Urkunden', *Archiv für Urkundenforschung* 12 (1932), 251–374 at p. 326.

charter: it can be found in any charter. The pious formula of the *intitulatio* confirmed that the power of the charter's issuer came from God. It can only be found in episcopal charters and in charters of particularly powerful princes, such as the count of Flanders, the duke of Normandy, and, though less so, in the charters of the counts of Hainault, Namur, and Ponthieu. The formula of humility is merely an ecclesiastical one, because humility is not on a par with authority. The use of the *sanctio* became rare during the twelfth century. Only a prince who was able to give orders to a bishop, such as the count of Flanders, was permitted to use this formula.

Piety, however frequent in eleventh-century charters, is restricted to only some princes during the twelfth century. It seems as if a prince had to be close to the king, or close to being a king, in order to be able to ask to be supported by God. Even the monastic drafters who wrote charters for a lesser count or a lord, thought it not appropriate to use a pious *intitulatio* or *sanctio*. These princes did not continue this use of piety during the twelfth century, probably because the gap between clerics and laymen, bishops and princes, was ever-increasing. At the end of the twelfth century, the Church in northern France was independent and moved away from the secular power. At the same time, the secular power was able to use secular tools, such as feudal law, justice, and arms.

The Crisis of Episcopal Authority in Guibert of Nogent's *Monodiae*

TRUDY LEMMERS

In the year 1112 the city of Laon was shaken by violent riots. No single horrible detail of the barbarities that took place at Laon seems to have been left unrecorded in Guibert of Nogent's autobiographical work, *Monodiae*.[1] In Guibert's work, *Songs for One Voice* (more commonly known as *De vita sua*) he dwells upon the maltreatment, plunder and manslaughter of his own age. Because the first book of the *Monodiae* is considered to be the first medieval autobiography since the *Confessiones* of St Augustine it has been widely studied by literary scholars.[2] In the first book Guibert follows the example of St Augustine, confessing his sins, and praising God, but in his second and third books he departs from the model of the *Confessiones*, providing a seemingly pessimistic account of his own times, the period of the twelfth-century

---

[1] Although the book is known as *De vita sua* since the first printed edition of the work in the seventeenth century, Guibert did not use this title. In his *De sanctis et eorum pigneribus* Guibert referred to the work as *libri monodiarum*. Guibert de Nogent, *De sanctis et eorum pigneribus*, ed. R.B.C. Huygens, CCCM 127 (Turnhout, 1993), pp. 79–175 at p. 99. See now my dissertation, *Guiberts van Nogents Monodiae. Een twaalfde-eeuwse visie op kerkelijk leiderschap* (Hilversum, 1998).

[2] On the relationship between the *Confessiones* and the *Monodiae* for example, S. Hallenstein, *Nachbildung und Umformung der Bekenntnisse Augustins in der Lebensgeschichte Guiberts von Nogent* (Hamburg, 1934); G. Misch, *Geschichte der Autobiographie: Das Hochmittelalter im Anfang* (Frankfurt am Main, 1959), iii, 1, pp. 108–167; P. Courcelle, *Les confessions de saint Augustin dans la tradition littéraire: antécédents et postérité* (Paris, 1963), pp. 272–76.

renaissance.[3] Modern historians have varied in their opinion of Guibert's character from a rational thinker to a moralizing biblical exegete, but his interest in the spiritual basis of ecclesiastical authority has not been widely studied.[4] The tragedy of Laon forms the centrepiece of his third book, and thus can be used to assess Guibert's attitudes towards the authority of contemporary rulers, as well as for economic history.[5] It will be argued here that in his depiction of chaos he sets out a fundamentally optimistic view of ecclesiastical authority with certain moral and spiritual conditions.

---

[3] In the second book Guibert's description of his life merges with the history of the convent of St Mary of Nogent, and in the third book with contemporary political history, namely the communal revolt of Laon.

[4] At the turn of the century Guibert was made a proto-modern historical critic, by, among others, G. Monod, *Le moine Guibert et son temps* (Paris, 1905), pp. 254–303. But in the last decades this reputation has been discredited, for instance J. Chaurand, 'La conception de l'histoire de Guibert de Nogent', *Cahiers de civilisation médiévale* 8 (1965), 354–95. A survey, with references, of Guibert's changing reputation as a historian is given by J.F. Benton in the introduction to his translation of the *Monodiae (Self and Society in Medieval France: The Memoirs of Abbot Guibert of Nogent (1064?–c. 1125)*, trans. J.F. Benton, Medieval Academy Reprints for Teaching 15 (Toronto, 1991; first edition New York, 1970), pp. 8–9); and R. Ray, 'Medieval Historiography', *Viator* 5 (1974), 33–59 at pp. 46–47. Guibert is often reproached for his so-called social conservatism and his didactic and moralistic remarks, for instance J. Kantor, 'A Psychohistorical Source: The Memoirs of Abbot Guibert of Nogent', *Journal of Medieval History* 2 (1976), 281–304. For a brief historiographical survey on this topic, R. Kaiser, 'Das Geld in der Autobiographie des Abtes Guibert von Nogent', *Archiv für Kulturgeschichte* 69 (1987), 289–314 at p. 292. In this survey, Kaiser states: 'Die Beurteilung Guiberts als erzkonservativer Mönch, der den wirtschaftlichen und sozialen Umwälzungen seiner Zeit völlig blind gegenüber gestanden haben soll, zieht sich fast bis heute wie ein roter Faden durch die stadtgeschichtliche Forschung'. Also, idem, 'Laon aux XIe et XIIe siècles', *Revue du Nord* 61 (1974), 421–26. Some historians have been tempted by Guibert's description of his own life to a psychological consideration of the man. In addition to Kantor and Benton as cited above, C.D. Ferguson, 'Autobiography as Therapy: Guibert de Nogent, Peter Abelard and the Making of Medieval Autobiography', *Journal of Medieval and Renaissance Studies* 12 (1983), 187–212.

[5] The development of the communal revolt is also narrated by Anselm of Gembloux, *Continuatio Anselmi Gemblacensis*, ed. L.C. Bethmann, *MGH SS* 6 (Hannover, 1840), p. 375; Suger of Saint-Denis, *Vita Ludovici Grossi regis*, ed. H. Waquet, *Vie de Louis VI le Gros* (Paris, 1964), pp. 176–78; Orderic, *Historia Ecclestiastica*, ed. Chibnall, VI, 90–91; Herman of Tournai, *Liber de miraculis s. Mariae Laudunensis*, ed. J.-P. Migne, PL 156 (Paris, 1853), cols. 961–1018 at cols. 964B-65B.

The Tragedy of Laon

According to Guibert, it had been the misfortune of the city of Laon that since ancient times neither God nor any lord was feared there.[6] The public authorities were involved in rapine and murder, depending upon each man's power and desire. The clergy was held in such contempt that neither their persons nor their goods were spared. When the king happened to visit the city he was shamefully fined on his own property. Peasants who came into Laon were thrown into prison and held for ransom, or when the opportunity occurred, were drawn into vexatious lawsuits. No man dared to approach the city unless he had the most securely guaranteed safe conduct. One day the clergy and the archdeacon offered the people of Laon the opportunity to create a commune.[7]

In fact a commune means an oath sworn between the lord of the city, sometimes a count, sometimes the bishop, and the burghers, in order to grant the burghers of the city certain privileges. A number of scholars describe the formation of communes as an initiative that came about as a response to violence and the illegal exercise of judicial authority. They consider the communal movement to be an effective means of settling disputes and of restoring unity and peace in the region.[8] This view is also mentioned by Guibert, for in the *Monodiae* he calls the commune a sworn association for mutual aid among the clergy, the nobles, and the people.[9] In another passage, however, Guibert defines a commune as a financial arrangement, which included the abolition of all financial exactions customarily imposed on serfs, and the payment of the customary levies

---

[6] It is clear that Guibert's description of the things that happened in the city of Laon essentially reflects a cleric's view. A successful attempt to focus on the images and self-images of town-dwellers has recently been made by R. Künzel, *Beelden en zelfbeelden van middeleeuwse mensen: Historisch-antropologische studies over groepsculturen in de Nederlanden, 7de-13de eeuw* (Nijmegen, 1997), pp. 149–224.

[7] Guibert de Nogent, *Autobiographie*, ed. and trans. E.R. Labande (Paris, 1981), pp. 317–320; trans. Benton, *Self and Society*, pp. 165–67; also trans. P.J. Archambault, *A Monk's Confession: The Memoirs of Guibert of Nogent* (University Park PA, 1996).

[8] A. Vermeesch, *Essai sur les origines et la signification de la commune dans le nord de la France (XIe et XIIe siècles)* (Heule, 1966), pp. 108–18, 175–83. On communes in medieval Europe, K. Schulz, *'Denn sie lieben die Freiheit so sehr...': Kommunale Aufstände und Entstehung des europäischen Bürgertums im Hochmittelalter* (Darmstadt, 1992).

[9] *Autobiographie*, ed. Labande, pp. 320–21: 'inter clerum, proceres et populum mutui adjutorii conjuratione'.

once a year.[10] According to Guibert, as will be demonstrated below, the commune of Laon certainly did not bring the desired peace to the city of Laon.

Gaudric, the bishop of Laon, who had played no part in the negotiations leading to the formation of the commune, was greatly angered and stayed away from the city for a long time. Guibert adds that because of Gaudric's insatiable greed he remained inactive as a pastor, forgetful of his sacred calling. Whenever one of the people, Guibert continues, was brought into a court of law, he was judged, not on his condition in the eyes of God, but on his bargaining power, and was deprived of even his last penny. This greed made it easy to induce the bishop to change his mind about the commune. When he was finally offered a huge amount of silver and gold, he swore to maintain the rights of the commune.[11] Just as readily as he had sworn, Gaudric went back on his oath. Determined to attack the commune to which he had sworn, he called together the nobles and the clergy. The bonds of the association were to be broken. On Maundy Thursday, Guibert writes, the very day when he should have performed the most solemn of all episcopal duties, that is the consecration of the oil and the absolution of the people from their sins, the bishop was not even seen to have entered the church.[12] He was intriguing with the king's courtiers to ensure that after the sworn association had been destroyed, the king would restore the laws of the city to their former state.[13]

When this became known to the burghers of Laon, they were seized by enormous amazement and enormous rage. Binding themselves by mutual oaths, a number of men conspired to murder the bishop and his accomplices. When this came to the bishop's attention, he ordered the people of his household and all the knights to protect him in public, and he summoned a great number of peasants from his episcopal manors to guard his palace.[14] These precautions, however, could not prevent Gaudric from being attacked in his palace by a raging crowd which forced him to flee and

---

[10] *Autobiographie*, ed. Labande, pp. 320–21: 'Communio autem—novum ac pessimum nomen—sic se habet: ut capite censi omnes solitum servitutis debitum dominis semel in anno solvant et, si quid contra jura deliquerint, pensione legali emendent, caeterae censuum exactiones quae servis infligi solent, omnimodis vacent.'

[11] *Autobiographie*, ed. Labande, pp. 320–23.

[12] The symbolic meaning of these events is explained by C. Carozzi, 'Le dernier des Carolingiens: de l'histoire au mythe', *Le Moyen Age* 82 (1976), 453–76.

[13] *Autobiographie*, ed. Labande, pp. 328–33.

[14] *Autobiographie*, ed. Labande, pp. 332–37.

drove him directly into the arms of his murderers. His corpse was brutally mutilated and after being stripped naked, was thrown into a corner in front of his chaplain's house. Hardly anyone passed by without casting at him some insult or curse, and no one thought of burying him.[15] The burghers of Laon, greatly fearing the king's judgement after this deed, called in the aid of Thomas, lord of Marle castle, to defend them against a royal attack. Thomas, however, knowing that his strength was not sufficient to hold the city against the king, advised them to follow him into his lands and to become his vassals. Immediately after the inhabitants of Laon had left their city, all the people of the district rushed upon the deserted city and robbed the possessions from the houses.[16]

While reading Guibert's eye-witness account of the communal revolt of Laon, one immediately senses his strong involvement with the events. Guibert did not like what he observed. He abhorred the course of events in the city, especially the role of money, which in his opinion had fundamentally disrupted the existing social order. It meant independence and power for the burghers of the city and corrupted the clergy and the nobility. There is, therefore, good reason for his description of the commune as a 'new and evil name', and this innovation is defined in terms of a financial arrangement.

'The root of all evil'

Despite Guibert's repugnance of money's disruptive effects, he does not treat it as the actual cause of the violent revolt. He opens the third book of his *Monodiae* with the words:

> As I promised to tell the story of the people of Laon, or rather to present their tragedy on stage, I must first explain that in my opinion the origin of all trouble came from the errors of the bishops of Laon.[17]

According to Guibert, the violent acts he is about to describe, namely maltreatment, plunder, and manslaughter, were caused by the conduct of

---

[15] *Autobiographie*, ed. Labande, pp. 336–45.

[16] *Autobiographie*, ed. Labande, pp. 362–77.

[17] *Autobiographie*, ed. Labande, pp. 268–69: 'De Laudunensibus, ut spopondimus, jam modo tractaturi, imo Laudunensium tragoedias acturi, primum est dicere, totius mali originem ex pontificium, ut nobis videtur, perversitatibus emersisse' (trans. Benton, *Self and Society*, p. 145).

the bishops of Laon. He therefore introduces the story of the communal revolt with a description of the lives of the earlier bishops, which function here as a negative hagiography. The root of all evil lay way back in the tenth century, when Adalbero held the episcopal office. According to Guibert, this bishop increased the prosperity of the clergy and the bishopric, but he defiled those benefits by his most extraordinary wickedness. One day he betrayed the last Carolingian pretender to the throne, Charles of Lotharingia, to whom he had taken an oath of fealty, in order to advance the interests of Hugh Capet. Guibert stresses the moral baseness of the deed by adding that the bishop resembled Judas by committing this crime on Maundy Thursday.[18]

Bishop Helinand, an eleventh-century bishop, seemingly did much for God's glory. His offence, however, was that those good works were intended only to increase his own popularity and adulation.[19] Bishop Enguerrand proved to be an unsatisfactory guardian of the church's rights, because at his accession he returned to the king everything which his predecessor had rightfully obtained for the benefit of the church of Laon. Furthermore, Guibert states that during the rule of three succeeding bishops this income had been lost to the church, and perhaps will be lost forever. He adds that Enguerrand had involved all succeeding bishops in this act of simony, because they would not dare to demand from the king restitution of the wealth which their predecessor had given up in return for being made bishop.[20] After a life filled with misdeeds, Enguerrand died without having received the last absolution.[21]

In 1106 Gaudric was consecrated bishop of Laon.[22] We have already learned that his violent death in 1112, as a result of his betrayal of the burghers of Laon, was the first act in the communal revolt. Some time before these events took place, however, Gaudric had committed another horrible crime. About three years before the tragedy of Laon took place, Gaudric had plotted with the leading nobles of the city to murder his enemy

---

[18] *Autobiographie*, ed. Labande, pp. 268–70. On these events, which happened in 991, Carozzi, 'Le dernier des Carolingiens'.

[19] *Autobiographie*, ed. Labande, pp. 270–72.

[20] *Autobiographie*, ed. Labande, pp. 274–75: 'Unde factum est, ut omnes qui secuturi sunt, episcopos hujus symoniae participes, sicut mihi videtur, fecerit, qui praesulatum tanta regii metus affectatione suscipiunt, ut repetere non audeant quae ille, ut episcopus fieret, damnabiliter indulsit.'

[21] *Autobiographie*, ed. Labande, pp. 272–80.

[22] *Autobiographie*, ed. Labande, pp. 280–94.

Guibert of Nogent's Monodiae 43

Gerald of Quierzy.[23] After the arrangements had been made, the bishop left the matter in the hands of his fellow conspirators and went on a journey to Rome. On Friday in the week of Epiphany, Gerald was murdered in the cathedral of Notre-Dame of Laon. Because of Gaudric's absence the purification of the cathedral was performed by the bishop of Senlis, and Guibert was asked to preach to the people on that occasion. As a good shepherd he admonished his flock and tried to make them aware of their sinful behaviour. Resembling an Old Testament prophet he warned them that the arising civil conflicts would eventually lead to their destruction. Guibert implied that bishop Gaudric had failed in his episcopal duties as Gaudric should have led the ceremony and should have preached to the people. In Guibert's opinion the people of Laon had no one to turn to, because their leaders had neither honour nor authority:

> Amid such things there is no sure standing, because the honour and power to whom you should have recourse in peril—that is your rulers and nobles—are fallen.[24]

Three years later, the bishop betrayed the burghers of Laon, which led to the revolt and the collapse of the commune.

According to Guibert these were the errors of the bishops of Laon: treason, simony, the seeking of personal glory, the bargaining away of church property, greed, murder, and failing in spiritual leadership. These errors were the origin of all trouble and had caused, according to Guibert, the total disintegration of society. Guibert does nothing to conceal the vile actions of the people of Laon, who were not entirely faultless themselves, but it was the bishops who bore responsibility and were blameworthy.

'A man of the house of his Father'

In the third book of the *Monodiae* Guibert paints an extremely bleak picture of his times. At first glance it seems as if he had lost all hope for the future when he wrote his work. Still, when we look more closely at the text, we can discern that in analyzing the origin of the communal revolt, Guibert also comes forward with the solution to the problem. We can find his ideal

---

[23] *Autobiographie*, ed. Labande, pp. 296–316.

[24] *Autobiographie*, ed. Labande, pp. 306–07: 'Inter haec itaque non est substantia quia eorum ad quos in periculis concurrendum vobis fuerat, rectorem vidilicet vestrorum ac procerum, honesta ruit atque potentia' (trans. Benton, *Self and Society*, p. 161).

of a perfectly ordered society hidden in his description of the chaotic events that took place in 1112. In Guibert's ideal, society consisted of two orders: freemen and serfs. This was considered to be a God-given order, which should not be interfered with. In his *Monodiae*, Guibert stresses this by quoting the words of the archbishop of Reims, who had preached on the day of the reconsecration of Laon cathedral after the communal revolt. According to Guibert the archbishop spoke these words:

> 'Serfs', said the [archbishop quoting the] Apostle, 'be subjected to your masters with all fear'. And lest serfs plead as an excuse that their masters are hard and greedy, they should hear how the Apostle continues, 'And not only to the good and gentle but also to the overmighty'. In the authoritative canons, those people are damned with anathema who teach serfs to disobey their masters for the sake of entering religion, or fly away elsewhere, much less to resist.[25]

The consequences of the disturbance of this God-given order are shown by Guibert in the aftermath of the formation of the commune: violence, death, and destruction. The actual cause of this disturbance was, however, to be found in the errors of the bishops of Laon. They who should have acted on behalf of the ones they ruled, had, from the tenth century onwards, acted only out of self-interest. Their power and honour had fallen. Guibert considered the people of Laon to be lost, a flock without a shepherd.

In Guibert's ideal world the bishops, as church leaders, were at the summit of the hierarchical pyramid. Not the king, as in Adalbero of Laon's ordering of society,[26] and not the pope, as in the ideals of the Gregorian reformers,[27] but the bishops. They were the ones responsible for the peace and unity in the Christian world. This position can be explained, on the one hand, by the Gregorian reform ideology, in which the position of the

---

[25] *Autobiographie*, ed. Labande, pp. 360–61: '"Servi" inquit Apostolus, "subditi estote in omni timore dominis". Et ne servi causentur duritiam vel avaritiam dominorum, adhuc audiant: "Et non tantum bonis et modestis, sed et discolis." Plane in autenticis canonibus damnantur anathemate, qui servos dominis religionis causa docuerint inobedire, aut quovis subterfugere, nedum resistere' (trans. Benton, *Self and Society*, pp. 183–84).

[26] Adalbero of Laon, *Poème au roi Robert*, ed. C. Carozzi (Paris, 1979); C. Carozzi, 'D'Albéron de Laon à Humbert de Moyenmoutier: la désacralisation de la royauté', in *La cristianità dei secoli XIe in occidente: conscienza e strutture di una società* (Milano, 1983), pp. 67–84.

[27] For instance, C. Morris, *The Papal Monarchy: The Western Church from 1050–1250* (Oxford, 1989), pp. 79–133; J. Laudage, *Gregorianische Reform und Investiturstreit* (Darmstadt, 1993), pp. 76–107.

emperor as head of lay society was being questioned, the clergy being supposed to lead the laity. On the other hand, it may also be due to the so-called *imbecilitas regis*, the king's weakness.[28] The effective power of the king of France in Guibert's times was restricted to the Ile-de-France. As a reaction to the king's waning peace, the bishops of the Frankish realm convened, from the late tenth century onwards, peace councils at which they forged alliances with nobles and monastic communities, namely the Peace of God. Guibert's ideal clearly bears traces of this movement.[29] Bishops as church leaders were burdened with the heavy responsibility of maintaining unity and peace, and should, according to Guibert, come up to high requirements. He formulates these explicitly in the sermon he pronounced on the day he was consecrated as abbot, and which appears in the second book of his *Monodiae*.[30] On the day of his installation, the Sunday before Christmas, Guibert opened this sermon with Isaiah 3.6–8:

> A man shall take hold of his brother, one of the house of his Father, saying: 'Thou hast a garment; be thou our ruler: and let his ruin be under thy hand'. And he shall answer saying: 'I am no healer and in my house there is no bread nor clothing: make me no ruler. For Jerusalem is ruined and Judah is fallen'.[31]

In Guibert's explanation of the verses' meaning to the assembled chapter, the man is effeminate in the face of the devil. He takes hold of his brother when he unites himself to a man born of God.[32] In other words, this fearful man, who seeks support, chooses the right person, namely one of the house of his Father. According to Guibert it is important that the man he takes hold of be:

> [a] man of the house of his Father because, he who is taken for the office of a pastor ought not to be found ignorant of the mysteries of the house of God. He who does not know the sacraments of the church is unworthy of its administration.[33]

---

[28] J. Dunbabin, *France in the Making 843–1180* (Oxford, 1985), p. 150.

[29] *The Peace of God: Social Violence and Religious Response in France around the Year 1000*, eds. T. Head and R. Landes (Ithaca and London, 1992).

[30] *Autobiographie*, ed. Labande, pp. 238–42.

[31] *Autobiographie*, ed. Labande, pp. 238–39; trans. Benton, *Self and Society*, p. 131.

[32] *Autobiographie*, ed. Labande, pp. 238–39: 'Vir est qui contra diabolum effoeminate se habet. Is fratrem apprehendit cum ad aliquam ex Deo natum se colligit.'

[33] *Autobiographie*, ed. Labande, pp. 238–39: 'Is quoque patris debet esse domesticus, quia qui ad officium corripitur pastoratus mysteriorum domus Dei reperiri non debet ignarus. Qui enim sacramentorum Ecclesiae nescius est, ipsius administratione dignus non est' (trans. Benton, *Self and Society*, p. 131).

In conclusion Guibert asks: 'How shall he preside over the church when he does not know the church? Therefore let him be one of the house.'[34]

Long before the Gregorian reform took place, from the early eleventh century onwards, a public debate took place on the true nature of priestly office.[35] This debate was triggered by a strong interest in the salvation of the Christian community. The line of thought was that a priest gained access to eternal life for the faithful by administering the sacraments. For this ritual function the priest was required to be pure, undefiled by the worldly stains of sex and money. The first requirement for the office was a pure inner life, as reflected in the outer life. Guibert also touches upon this in his sermon, for he continues:

> What is meant by a garment but a fine dress of outward works? Let the man who has a garment be called a ruler. It often happens that he who exceeds by his conduct, his word and his deed is sought for rule.[36]

According to Guibert the garment stands for the good deeds visible to all. This implies that a ruler by his excellent moral conduct should be able to set an example, he should be a moralist. This is important because in Guibert's opinion the ruler is responsible for the conduct, words, and deeds of his subjects.

The man who is sought to rule answers according to Isaiah: 'I am no healer', which in Guibert's opinion means:

> I have not the power to resist the growing ruin of disease for so many. You are looking at the outer clothing, which is not in my house, because the dress of the soul is not the same as that of the body.[37]

In other words, the inner and outer appearances are not in harmony. The

---

[34] *Autobiographie*, ed. Labande, pp. 240–41: 'Et quomodo praesit ecclesiae, qui nescit ecclesiam? Domesticus ergo sit' (trans. Benton, *Self and Society*, p. 131).

[35] Laudage considers this to be the basis of the actual Gregorian reform, as he explains in J. Laudage, *Priesterbild und Reformpapsttum im 11. Jahrhundert* (Köln and Wien, 1984).

[36] *Autobiographie*, ed. Labande, pp. 240–41: 'Quid in vestimento nisi pulchra intelligitur exteriorum operum habitudo? Princeps ergo rogatur ut sit vestimentum habet, qui crebro contingit, ut is expetatur ad regimen, qui in incessu, verbo et actu castigatiorem se exhibet' (trans. Benton, *Self and Society*, p. 131).

[37] *Autobiographie*, ed. Labande, pp. 240–41: 'Non sum, inquit, medicus, ut tot obviare valeam ruinis morborum crebrescentibus. Vestimentum exterius aspicitis, quod tamen in domo non est, quia non idem animi habitus qui corporis est' (trans. Benton, *Self and Society*, pp. 131–32).

body and soul are not wrapped up in the same garment. Because of the discrepancy between inner and outer, the outer deeds look good, but the intention is not. Therefore the man is not powerful enough to resist the growing ruin of disease for so many.

The man who is sought to rule continues by saying: 'In my house there is no bread', by which he means according to Guibert:

> 'The bread which is sought daily from God, the comfort of His divine refreshment which is poured in spiritually or the strengthening of that love in the inner man, without which there is never good rule.'[38]

That is, without the proper inner attitude, gained by divine nourishment, a man is not fit to rule. Because there is no bread in his house, he is not only unable to feed himself but he also cannot feed the ones he rules. Guibert explains: 'And so he to whom the spirit imbued with powers from on high supplies but little help, declines to be made ruler'.[39]

Guibert now discusses the state of this man's soul. Because of its bad condition he approves of his refusal to rule. He continues by saying: 'For Jerusalem [the soul] is ruined, that is the perishing of inner peace. And Judah [also an image for the soul] is fallen'. According to Guibert that is the loss of internal tranquillity, which is to be obtained after the confession of sins, in Guibert's opinion, the end of all evil. But this man, because of his blindness, is not able to perform confession.[40] Such a man has, therefore, a good reason to refuse the office of pastor. At the close of his sermon on why the soul has no strength to rule itself, Guibert comments, 'it is rightly prevented by others, and more rightly by itself from being the ruler of other men'.[41]

---

[38] *Autobiographie*, ed. Labande, pp. 240–41: 'Quia non est in domo illius panis qui a Deo hodie petitur quotidianus, confortatio vidilicet ejus, quae spiritualiter infunditur divinae refectionis, aut ipius, sine qua bene nusquam regitur, confirmatio in interiori homine charitatis' (trans. Benton, *Self and Society*, p. 132).

[39] *Autobiographie*, ed. Labande, pp. 240–41: 'Princeps itaque fieri jure recusat, cui id virium animus superne imbutus minime subministrat' (trans. Benton, *Self and Society*, p. 132).

[40] *Autobiographie*, ed. Labande, pp. 240–43: 'Hierusalem enim quia ruit, id est quia internae experientia pacis deperiit, et etiam Judas concidit, id est, ipsa peccatorum confessio, quod extremum malorum omnium est, post amissionem intimae tranquillitatis omnimodo desperatione defecit, juste occasio refutandi pastoratus se praebuit. Ubi enim mens emergentibus vitiis inquietatur, nimis turpiter incursatur, nec mens his male obcaecata per confessionem eadem detestatur' (trans. Benton, *Self and Society*, p. 132).

[41] *Autobiographie*, ed. Labande, pp. 242–43: 'Cum se regere non praevalet: juste per alios, justius per seipsam ab aliorum regimine arcetur' (trans. Benton, *Self and Society*, p. 132).

In short, on the day of his installation, Guibert preached a sermon on leadership. With reference to the book of Isaiah, he explains the making of a good church leader. According to Guibert he should be of the house of the Father, aware of the limits of human power and knowledge, and aware of God's omniscience and omnipotence. A man who knows himself and who knows God therefore has the strength to rule himself. Only such a pure man is fit to rule others, for he has the power to resist the growing ruin of disease for so many. According to Guibert, the bishops of Laon failed dismally in this respect, because, from the tenth century onwards, they were defiled by worldly stains, particularly money. They had broken the boundaries between the spiritual and the worldly spheres, and had defiled the sacred with the profane. Thus the God-given cosmic order, in which freemen were supposed to remain either in the spiritual or in the worldly domain, was disrupted. The bishops could no longer function as spiritual leaders, for as a result of their defilement, they had lost communication with the divine and had jeopardized the salvation of the people of Laon. In consequence, the disruption of the order that had commenced on a spiritual level now also continued on a lower level, as the boundaries between freemen and serfs were broken by the formation of the commune.

The nature of the priestly office was not, in Guibert's view, limited to the sacramental function. Even though he severely reproached Gaudric, in his *Liber quo ordine sermo fieri debeat*, he thought it of the utmost importance for a priest to lead a pure, virtuous life because of his pastoral functions, by which he refers to the task of preaching, by word or example.[42] Preaching was the most appropriate means for a pastor to lead his flock. Guibert illustrates this by the sermon he preached on the day of the purification of Laon cathedral, after the murder of Gerald of Quierzy.[43] By recording this sermon in the third book of his *Monodiae*, Guibert emphasizes the fact that, in his opinion, Gaudric should have performed that duty. As bishop he should have warned and admonished the people of Laon. It is no coincidence that a year after the communal revolt took place, Guibert offered his little book on preaching, a didactic work on how a preacher should behave and how his preaching could be most effective, to

---

[42] Guibert de Nogent, *Quo ordine sermo fieri debeat*, ed. R.B.C. Huygens, CCCM 127 (Turnhout, 1993), pp. 47–63 at pp. 50–51. In his views on leadership, Guibert leans heavily on Gregory the Great. We can trace Guibert's view on this subject back to the *Regula Pastoralis*.

[43] *Autobiographie*, ed. Labande, pp. 306–11.

Bartholomew of Jur, on his appointment as bishop of Laon.[44]

In addition to his sermon on the day of the purification of Laon cathedral, Guibert also considers good church leadership in the first book of his *Monodiae*. This may come as a surprise, because at first sight Guibert does not seem to present a very positive image of himself in his autobiographical first book, where he presents himself as a sinner, unworthy of the love of God and men. Also, Guibert says very little about his career as abbot, because the autobiography ends with his installation in office. Still, the facts Guibert tells about himself in the first book of his *Monodiae* fully correspond with the theoretical exposition on leadership in the sermon he preached on the day of his installation. In this first book Guibert describes himself as a man acting wilfully against God's commandments. However, he does not present this negative image for the sake of the image itself. This image is part of a larger scheme. If we study it more closely, it can be discerned that what Guibert actually describes is not the life of a doomed sinner, but the life of a sinful man who desperately tries to fight his evil human nature in pursuit of spiritual perfection. Such a process is never an easy matter. Many times Guibert stumbled and fell, but he was also able to rise, because no matter how deep he had fallen, God never turned his back on him. Finally he reached his goal. He describes this as a great moment of deeply religious experience:

> O God, I thank Thee that my childish desires entirely withered away and that it no longer pleased me to long for any earthly dignity. Thou didst then scourge me and throw me to the ground, O Father, O God, Chastener of my desires and vanities, and didst bring me back to reflection, binding me within so that my vagrant mind might have no escape, but should yearn from its innermost being for simple humility and sincerity of heart [...]. Then, by the sweet savour of Thy close friendship, I first learned the true meaning of singleness of will, of its purity, of an unbending resolve to be forever humble.[45]

---

[44] See the letter of dedication in *La tradition manuscrite de Guibert de Nogent*, ed. R.B.C. Huygens, Instrumenta patristica 21 (Den Haag, 1991), pp. 83–84.

[45] *Autobiographie*, ed. Labande, pp. 164–65: 'Deus tibi gratias, quia tunc intentio ad integrum puerilis, emarcuit, nec ad aliquam terrenam ulterius dignitatem suspirare collibuit. Flagellasti namque me in tempore illo, Pater, et corrector cupiditatum et levitatum mearum, Deus, afflixisti, et me ad cognitionem redegisti, ita ut me intra me constringeres, mensque hactenus vaga nusquam evolaret, sed ad solam humilitatem et cogitationis sinceritatem medullitus aspiraret [...]. Tum primum intimo illo tuo sapore addidici quid voluntatis unitas, quid ejusdem puritas, quid fuerit irreflexa perpetuae paupertatis intentio' (trans. Benton, *Self and Society*, pp. 99–100).

So after half a lifetime of strife, Guibert had finally succeeded. He could now be called 'one of the house of the Father', for he was familiar with the mysteries of the house of God. Guibert had united his will with the will of the Father. As he did not long any more for earthly dignity, he would be able to function as a good shepherd. Shortly after this experience, Guibert was elected abbot of St Mary of Nogent.

In Guibert's view, every man chosen to rule should experience this development. However, as follows from the description of the lives of the bishops of Laon, most rulers fell short in this respect, and therefore were not fit to rule. They knew neither themselves nor God. They were so sucked into the mud of their own sins that not only were they unable to understand the horror of their own actions, but they also brought ruin upon those they were responsible for. Only with the proper inner condition would a man be able to rule others. In his own opinion Guibert was such a man. Just as the Old Testament prophets had been able to see the invisible things of God through the things that were made, Guibert considered himself as one of the elect who could, for the benefit of his contemporaries, detect the spectacle of history through the violent confusion of events.

Conclusion

Probably it was the communal revolt of Laon which led to Guibert's writing. Some three years after these events had taken place, order had still to be restored to the towns of northern France. As a true medieval historian Guibert not only accounted for the things he heard or saw, but also gave meaning to these events. In his opinion the Laon uprising taught a lesson in leadership. In Guibert's ideal the world was a perfectly ordered place in which clergy and laity, freemen and serfs all had their own domains. It reflected a God-given order, in which the bishops, because of their intermediary position with the divine, were responsible for maintaining unity and peace. Through the prism of this order he perceived the world he lived in as being disintegrated, chaotic, and violent. Leadership had lost its honour and power, and therefore no one was safe. It was not, however, a world without hope. Guibert shows the way out of this chaos, to the final restoration of unity and peace, by expounding his ideal of church leadership through the negative examples of the bishops of Laon, and by illustrating it by the example of his own life. Guibert's model of leadership is to be considered as his solution to the crisis of ecclesiastical leadership in his own times, and therefore deserves our attention.

Relics as Tools of Power:
The Eleventh-Century *Inventio* of St Bertin's Relics and the Assertion of Abbot Bovo's Authority

KARINE UGÉ

The cult of relics, which thrived throughout the Central Middle Ages, entailed the writing of texts which had relics as their central theme: *translationes*, relating the transfer of relics from one shrine to another; *inventiones*, describing the discovery of relics whose location had been forgotten or ignored; *furta*, dealing with thefts of relics; *adventus*, detailing the arrival of newly found, acquired, or stolen relics at a new location; and *delationes*, the carrying around of relics in order to bolster a cult and raise money.[1] The different genres of relic narratives were particularly popular in northern France in the tenth and eleventh centuries because of the intensive traffic of relics caused by the disruptions, alleged or real, brought about by the Vikings, and by the subsequent wave of monastic foundations, refoundations, and reforms which spread throughout the region.[2] Among these relic

---

[1] On relic narratives, M. Heinzelmann, *Translationsberichte und andere Quellen des Reliquienkultes*, Typologie des sources du moyen âge occidental 33 (Turnhout, 1979); on relic thefts and the texts relating them, P.J. Geary, *Furta Sacra: Thefts of Relics in the Central Middle Ages* (Princeton, 1978); on *inventiones* as a literary genre, M. Otter, *Inventiones: Fiction and Referentiality in Twelfth-Century English Historical Writing* (London, 1996), pp. 21–57.

[2] F. Lifshitz, 'The Migration of Neustrian Relics in the Viking Age: The Myth of Voluntary Exodus, the Reality of Coercion and Theft', *Early Medieval Europe* 4 (1995), 175–92, shows how the fear of Vikings was used as a spurious explanation for thefts of relics camouflaged as transfers in tenth-century Normandy.

narratives, one group of texts is particularly remarkable through its association with a specific religious reform: the movement of Benedictine restoration associated with Gerald of Brogne in Flanders and Lotharingia. In this article, I will present an overview of this tradition and then focus on one text: the *Relatio de inventione et elevatione sancti Bertini* (henceforth: *Relatio*), written shortly after 1052 by Bovo, abbot of Saint-Bertin.[3] Because of its date and place of composition, Bovo's text fully belongs to this tradition of relic narratives. Nonetheless, his agenda went beyond the advertising of a cult and the bolstering of the corporate identity of the saint's community usually associated with *inventiones*. Indeed, Bovo used the models available to him, thanks to the continuous textual tradition which had flourished in Flanders since the mid-tenth century, to compose a seemingly standard *inventio*. A closer look at the *Relatio*, however, reveals how much its author perverted the conventions of the genre in order to create an extremely personal and self-serving text asserting his own authority within the monastic community.

To comprehend fully the specificity of this text, it is necessary to look first at the local tradition of relic narratives which inspired Bovo in writing his own account; that is the group of relic narratives which can be associated directly or indirectly with the Benedictine revival promoted by Gerald of Brogne in the central decades of the tenth century. Between 931 and 953, Gerald founded or re-established the Benedictine rule in at least nine monasteries; six of them—including Saint-Bertin—were located within the territory of his friend and patron Arnulf, count of Flanders, who forcefully used his authority over the abbeys in his territories to help Gerald in his mission.[4] Since no custumal from the abbeys that Gerald restored has survived, the specifics of his reforms remain elusive. However, one aspect of his religious beliefs, which he shared with Arnulf, is well known and documented, namely, his fondness for relics. The two men loved relics so much that they had few scruples when it came to obtaining them,

---

[3] *Bovonis Relatio de Inventione et Elevatione Sancti Bertini* (henceforth: *Bovonis Relatio*), ed. O. Holder-Egger, *MGH SS* 15 (Hannover, 1887–88), pp. 524–34.

[4] On Gerald of Brogne and his restoration movement, the memorial volume of the *Revue Bénédictine* 70 (1960); A. Dierkens, *Abbayes et Chapîtres entre Sambre et Meuse (VIIe— XIe siècles)* (Sigmaringen, 1985), pp. 197–248; D. Misonne, 'La restauration monastique de Gérard de Brogne', in *Naissance et Fonctionnement des Réseaux Monastiques et Canoniaux. Actes du Premier Colloque International du C.E.R.C.O.M., Saint-Etienne, 16–18 Septembre 1985* (Saint-Etienne, 1991), pp. 117–23.

and when they could not get them through friendly contacts, they did not hesitate to resort to military raids. Arnulf's and Gerald's acquisition of relics led to the production of an important corpus of texts relating to their thefts, or exploits (depending on the point of view of the author), and the later consequences.[5] It is not clear how much Gerald's abbacies stimulated contacts and exchanges of manuscripts among all his abbeys, but a common textual trend can be observed, and it can safely be asserted that the abbeys reformed by Gerald played a significant part in the spreading of relic narratives in that region.

Different types of relic narratives fulfil different purposes: *inventiones* were often composed to justify the foundation or refoundation of a monastic community at the site of the miraculous discovery. This is indeed the case with the *Inventio sancti Gisleni*, written around 940 by a monk of Saint-Ghislain (near Mons, Hainault).[6] According to the *Inventio* and the *Vita sancti Gisleni*, Ghislain had lived in the eighth century and, after his death, a religious community had formed around the church that he had built. However, save for references in the early tenth-century life of St Waudru, nothing was recorded about St Ghislain and his eponymous monastery before the mid-tenth century.[7] Things changed when Duke Gislebert of Lotharingia called upon Gerald of Brogne to restore the community, which had fallen—according to the *Inventio*—into a state of deep decay. Indeed, no fewer than three *vitae* and one *inventio* were devoted to Ghislain in the decades after Gerald's takeover in 931. The *Inventio* presents the miraculous finding of the relics as a prefiguration of and a prerequisite for Gerald's abbacy. St Ghislain had remained hidden in the ground because of the sins of his community ('peccatis enim nostris exigentibus, tantus patrocinator mortalibus profuturus palam aberat'),[8] and it was only after he revealed himself that Gislebert decided to invite Gerald to restore a proper monastic life under the Benedictine rule ('ergo

---

[5] On Gerald of Brogne and the cult of relics, D. Misonne, 'Gérard de Brogne et sa dévotion aux reliques', *Sacris Erudiri* 25 (1982), 1–26.

[6] *Inventio en miracula sancti Gisleni*, ed. O. Holder-Egger, *MGH SS* 15 (Hannover, 1887–1888), pp. 576–79.

[7] On the foundation of the monastery of Saint-Ghislain, A.-M. Helvétius, *Abbayes, évêques et laïques: Une politique du pouvoir en Hainaut au Moyen Âge (VIIe–XIe siècle)* (Bruxelles, 1994), pp. 213–34. On the hagiography of St Ghislain, also L. van der Essen, *Etude critique et littéraire sur les Vitae des saints mérovingiens de l'ancienne Belgique* (Louvain and Paris, 1907), pp. 249–59.

[8] *Inventio et miracula sancti Gisleni*, ed. Holder-Egger, p. 576 (ch. 1).

monachico ordine sub norma sancti habitus instituto, maioribus demum virtutibus monasterium attolitur').[9] Moreover, the *inventio* provided Gerald with the relics needed to gather his community around the cult of its patron saint and to bolster, if not to create, its sense of corporate identity. Furthermore, the author's insistence on the decay preceding the discovery of the relics and the arrival of Gerald—a literary device abundantly used by authors of *inventiones*—emphasized the role of the reformer and the rebirth of his abbey.[10]

Although Saint-Ghislain was the first documented monastic restoration Gerald performed, he had already prompted the translation of the relics of St Eugene, which had been brought from Saint-Denis in 919 to his own monastic foundation of Brogne (near Namur).[11] Because Brogne was a brand-new foundation on Gerald's own estates, its community had no hagiographic tradition and was in great need of relics and a specific liturgy. The text *Adventus sancti Eugenii martyris*, and the actual transfer of the relics, provided all of this. The text was read as a sermon on the feast day of St Eugene, on the anniversary of the arrival of his relics at Brogne.[12] It is not so much about the *adventus* of St Eugene's relics at Brogne as it is about their long tribulation before their removal by the abbot of Saint-Denis. The author begins with a brief account of St Eugene's life, which he knew from his old *passio*, then relates successively the transfer of his relics to Deuil, their translation to Saint-Denis to protect them from the Vikings, the arrival of Gerald at Saint-Denis and his departure with parts of St Eugene's body. This last episode is added at the end of the eighth lesson, which indicates, as Misonne has suggested, that the core of the text was that already in use at Saint-Denis, and that the monks from Brogne were content with recycling and making only superficial changes to the old Dionysian liturgy.[13] Nonetheless, rudimentary as it was in its composition, the *adventus*, as a first liturgical and historical text intended for Brogne,

---

[9] Ibid., p. 578 (ch. 6).

[10] See for example the story of the mid-seventh-century translation of St Benedict and St Scholastica from Monte Cassino, destroyed by the Lombards, to Fleury, written by Adrevald of Fleury in the late ninth century: *Historia translationis sancti Benedicti*, ed. E. de Certain, in *Les Miracles de Saint Benoit* (Paris, 1858; rept. New York, 1968), pp. 1–14.

[11] D. Misonne, 'La légende liturgique de la translation de St. Eugène de Saint-Denis à Brogne', *Revue Bénédictine* 74 (1964), 98–110.

[12] Ibid., p. 98.

[13] Ibid., pp. 109–10.

provided the new monastery with the necessary sacred connections with a patron saint, with the heroic times of the martyrs, and with the great abbey of Saint-Denis that it lacked because of the circumstances of its foundation.

The restoration of St Peter's abbey Gent by Gerald in 941 occasioned yet another quest for relics and the composition of new texts celebrating their arrival.[14] He was given that opportunity by the presence of the relics of saints Wandrille, Ansbert and Vulfran near Boulogne, in Arnulf's territory. The wandering of the Fontenelle monks throughout northern France with their relics has been abundantly studied.[15] It is enough to recall that monks of Saint-Wandrille seem to have settled at Gent at the end of the ninth or at the beginning of the tenth century. This situation entitled Gerald to present himself as abbot of Fontenelle, and so to claim a right to possess its patron saints' relics. In turn, he tried to use his possession of the relics to legitimize his failed attempt to re-establish Saint-Wandrille. With the military backing of Count Arnulf, he organized a raid on Boulogne in 944, seized the sacred bones and brought them home, along with many other relics, such as those of St Omer and St Bertin. The abbey of Saint-Bertin, not very far from Boulogne, was restored by Gerald in 944. A detailed account of the *adventus* was given by a monk of Gent who was probably a first-hand witness to the events.[16] At about the same time that Gerald brought the relics of saints Wandrille, Ansbert, and Vulfran from Boulogne to Gent, he effected a similar transfer of the relics of St Gudwald and St Bertulf, from Montreuil-sur-Mer (in today's Département de la Somme) and Renty (Département du Pas-de-Calais) respectively, to Boulogne and then to Gent. This episode also became the subject of a new

---

[14] *Annales Blandinienses*, ed. P. Grierson, in *Les Annales de Saint-Pierre de Gand et de Saint-Amand* (Bruxelles, 1937), pp. 1–73.

[15] F. Lot, 'La destruction de l'abbaye au IXe siècle et les pérégrinations des religieux de Saint-Wandrille', in *Études Critiques sur l'Abbaye de Saint-Wandrille*, Bibliothèque de l'École des Hautes Études 204 (Paris, 1913), pp. xxx-xli; H. van Werveke, 'Saint-Wandrille et Saint-Pierre de Gand (Ixe–Xe siècles)', in *Miscellanea Mediaevalia in Memoriam Jan Frederik Niermeyer* (Groningen, 1967), pp. 79–92; E. van Houts, 'Historiography and hagiography at Saint-Wandrille: The *Inventio et miracula sancti Vulfranni*', ANS 12 (1989), 233–51.

[16] *Une Translation de Reliques à Gand en 944: Le Sermo de Adventu Sanctorum Wandregisili, Ansberti and Vulframni in Blandinium*, ed. N. Huyghebaert (Bruxelles, 1978). The *Adventus* has survived today in its twelfth-century rehandled form; however, Huyghebaert was able to extract the original tenth-century account.

relic narrative, unfortunately no longer extant.[17]

All the texts mentioned are positive reactions to the coming or discovery of new relics, since they were written by members of the community which initiated the transfers and benefited from them. These texts, which were integrated in the liturgy of the relics' new place of residence, or were even, as in the cases of St Ghislain and St Eugene, the first liturgical texts of the community, celebrated the new covenant between the saints and their new hosts. They also praised the abbot able to assemble such strong patronage for his communities. However, Gerald's and Arnulf's intensive appropriation of relics also aroused hostility from some of the communities who considered themselves despoiled. For example, Hariulf of Saint-Riquier relates unsympathetically in his *Chronicon Centullense* (1088), how Arnulf took advantage of his capture of Montreuil-sur-Mer in 948 to seize St Richer's relics from the abbey of Saint-Riquier (Centula) and bring them to Saint-Bertin: those relics, according to Hariulf, were given back to the community of Saint-Riquier in 981 by Arnulf's grandson, his successor as count of Flanders.[18] Gerald's appropriation of the relics which had belonged to the monks of Fontenelle, and more specifically those of St Vulfran, also stirred contention later on. Once re-established in their house in the beginning of the eleventh century, the monks of Fontenelle disputed the presence of St Vulfran at Gent. Indeed, according to ninth-century sources from their abbey, they had carried only the bodies of St Ansbert and St Wandrille in their flight from the Vikings. In 1054, probably stung by reading the *Inventio sanctorum Wandregisili, Ansberti et Vulframni* during a trip to Gent, a monk from Fontenelle wrote as a counter-claim the *Inventio et miracula sancti Vulframni*, asserting that Vulfran's relics were discovered in 1033 in the main church of his monastery.[19]

---

[17] This lost text should not be confused with the *Sermo de adventu ss. Gudwaldi et Bertulfi*, ed. N. Huyghebaert, *Sacris Erudiri* 23 (1978–79), 87–113. The *Sermo* is a twelfth-century account of the *adventus* of Gudwald and Bertulf based on the relation given by the eleventh-century *Vita Bertulfi*. The *Vita Bertulfi* itself refers to a 'libellus qui de eorum adventu scriptus est', which was probably the original account of the *Adventus*.

[18] *Chronique de l'Abbaye de Saint-Riquier (Ve siècle–1104)*, ed. F. Lot (Paris, 1894), pp. 150–52. J. Laporte, 'Gérard de Brogne à Saint-Wandrille et à Saint-Riquier', *Revue Bénédictine* 70 (1960), 142–66.

[19] *Une Translation de Reliques à Gand*, ed. Huyghebaert, pp. c-ciii; Van Houts, 'Historiography and Hagiography', pp. 237–38.

The Inventio *of St. Bertin's Relics*

Although all the relic narratives mentioned here share the common point of stemming from Gerald of Brogne's monastic restorations and his acquisition of relics for his new houses, the textual relationships between them are extremely difficult, if not impossible, to untangle. The task of establishing filiation is made even more problematic because two major texts—the *Adventus sancti Wandregisili* and the *Adventus sancti Gudwaldi*—survive only in rehandlings or are only known through other sources. However, an axis of textual exchange between Saint-Wandrille, St Peter's Gent and Saint-Bertin is clearly discernible. Indeed, it is only likely that the monks of Saint-Wandrille would have been in contact with the abbey of Saint-Bertin during their wandering in northern France—Saint-Bertin is only 35 km. from Boulogne, and from 875 to 891, the monks settled at Blangy-en-Artois, some 40 km. from Saint-Bertin. Possibly, the acquisition by Saint-Bertin of a corpus of hagiographic texts from Fontenelle dates from that period of contacts.[20] Huyghebaert suggests that the author of the *Adventus sanctorum Wandregisili, Ansberti et Vulframni* came to know through Saint-Bertin all the Fontenelle sources that he quoted in his work: the *Vita Ansberti*, the *Vitae* and *Miracula Wandregisili*, and the *Gesta patrum Fontanellensium*.[21] However, since monks from Fontenelle had already settled at St Peter's Gent at the end of the ninth century, the exchange may have happened the other way around, Saint-Bertin receiving the Fontenelle manuscripts from Gent in 944 when Gerald came to Saint-Bertin to restore the Benedictine rule. In any case, it is clear that by the mid-tenth century, texts from Fontenelle were known at Saint-Bertin, since Folcuin, who wrote the *Gesta abbatum Sithiensium* in 962, modelled his own text on the *Gesta patrum Fontanellensium*.[22] Although he never quoted them directly, Folcuin closely followed the textual structure of the

---

[20] Saint-Omer, Bibliothèque Municipale, MS 764. About this manuscript, F. Wormald, 'Some Illustrated MSS of the Lives of the Saints', *Bulletin of the J. Rylands Library* (1952), 250–62; L. Deschamps, 'Notice sur un manuscrit de la Bibliothèque Municipale de Saint-Omer', *Mémoires de la Société des Antiquaires de la Morinie* 5 (1839–40), 173–208. An unreliable tradition also suggests that the relics of saints Wandrille and Ansbert were hidden at Saint-Omer around 846; Laporte, 'Gérard de Brogne à Saint-Wandrille', pp. 143–45, and A. D'Haenens, *Les invasions normandes en Belgique au IXe siècle. Le phénomène et se répercussion dans l'historiographie médiévale* (Louvain, 1967), pp. 258–59.

[21] *Une Translation de Reliques à Gand*, ed. Huyghebaert, p. lxvi.

[22] *Gesta sanctorum patrum Fontanellensis cenobii*, eds. F. Lohier and J. Laporte (Paris, 1936). On Fontenelle, also F. Lot, *Études Critiques sur l'Abbaye de Saint-Wandrille* (Paris, 1913).

Fontenelle *Gesta* and efficiently imitated their author's technique of mixing historiographic, hagiographic and diplomatic sources.[23]

Another textual link between Gent and Saint-Bertin might be one of the most widely consulted relic narratives of the Central Middle Ages, the *Historia translationis sancti Benedicti* by Adrevald of Fleury. This text relates the finding of the relics of St Benedict and St Scholastica at Monte Cassino by monks of Fleury and their subsequent translation to the Loire valley. Indeed, the full title of the *Adventus* of saints Wandrille, Ansbert, and Vulfran resembles of the *incipit* that Adrevald's text bears in many of its copies.[24] The same *incipit* is found in the manuscript of Adrevald's *Translatio* copied at Saint-Bertin around the millennium by Abbot Odbert.[25] Here again, Adrevald's text may have reached Saint-Bertin through exchanges with Gent. The *Historia translationis sancti Benedicti* also influenced the composition of relic narratives at Saint-Bertin since, as will be explained later, Bovo took inspiration from it when he wrote his *Relatio* shortly after 1052.[26] To finish with the textual interplay between Saint-Bertin, Saint-Wandrille and St Peter's Gent, it is interesting to recall that the *Inventio* of St Vulfran was written at Saint-Wandrille only one or two years after the composition of the *Relatio* of Saint-Bertin.[27] Although this might be fortuitous, it is striking that both authors used similar literary devices to make their point: discovery of the relics following the restoration

---

[23] On Folcuin's *Gesta*, K. Ugé, 'Creating a Useable Past in the Tenth Century: Folcuin's *Gesta* and the Crises at Saint-Bertin', *Studi Medievali* 37 (1996), 887–903.

[24] *Une Translation de Reliques à Gand*, ed. Huyghebaert, p. xxiv. The complete title of the *Sermo* is *Gloriosus a Deo dispositus adventus in Monte Blandinium rite vocato sanctorum Wandregisili, Ansberti et Vulframni* [...]. The *incipit* of the *Historia translationis sancti Benedicti* of Adrevald as found in the Saint-Bertin manuscript as well as in many other copies is: "Incipit gloriosus et a Deo dispositus aventus in cenobio Floriacensis rite vocato electi (...)". Of course, Adrevald's work bears that title in many manuscripts (*Historia translationis sancti Benedicti*, ed. De Certain). On this text and its manuscript tradition, A. Vidier, *L'Historiographie à Saint-Benoît sur Loire et les Miracles de St. Benoît* (Paris, 1965); J. Hourlier, 'Le témoignage de Paul Diacre', in *Le Culte et les Reliques de Saint Benoît et de Sainte Scholastique*, ed. A. Beau et al., *Studia Monastica* 21 (1979), 205–11; idem, 'La translation d'après les sources narratives', ibid., 214–39; and T. Head, *Hagiography and the Cult of Saints. The Diocese of Orleans, 800–1200* (Cambridge, 1990).

[25] Saint-Omer, Bibliothèque Municipale, MS 350.

[26] *Bovonis relatio*, ed. Holder-Egger.

[27] Van Houts, 'Historiography and Hagiography', pp. 237–38 gives 1054 for the date of the redaction.

of an abbey, exaggeration of the physical and spiritual decay of the monastery in the period before the discovery and references to documents used as sources. But of course, by the eleventh century, these characteristics were already well-established *topoi* of relic narratives, especially *inventiones*, and are also found, for example, in the *Inventio sancti Gisleni* that I have already mentioned.[28]

Although direct borrowings—shared phrases, idiosyncratic language, and the like—between the texts previously mentioned and Bovo's *Relatio* cannot be found, it is manifest that Bovo drew on a textual tradition flourishing in the region, and especially in the communities which had been touched by Gerald of Brogne's enterprise. However, the circumstances of St Bertin's *inventio* and Bovo's goals in writing its *Relatio* were significantly different from the circumstances and purpose of the aforementioned texts: the abbey already possessed relics supposed to be St Bertin's, his cult had been continuous throughout the period, nobody was contesting the community's possession of the relics, and, finally, the monastery had never been abandoned or so severely damaged that it needed to be refounded.[29] In these circumstances, why did Bovo feel compelled to write his text? Before approaching his specific motivation, it is important to look at the tradition of historical writing at Saint-Bertin upon which Bovo built his own narrative. Throughout the Middle Ages, the abbey of Saint-Bertin maintained a continuous tradition of producing many of the traditional medieval genres: annals,[30] chronicles,[31] *Gesta abbatum*,[32] and hagiographic texts.[33]

---

[28] See the examples in Otter, *Inventiones*.

[29] On the history of Saint-Bertin from its foundation to the eleventh century, Ugé, 'Creating a Useable Past'.

[30] *Annales Sithienses*, ed. G. Waitz, *MGH SS* 13 (Hannover, 1881), pp. 34–38, running from 532 to 856, and the now lost annals of Saint-Bertin, written at the end of the ninth century (O. Holder-Egger, 'Zu Folcwin von St. Bertin', *Neues Archiv* 6 (1881), 417–38, and *Les Annales de Saint-Pierre de Gand et de Saint-Amand*, ed. Grierson, pp. xv-xvii).

[31] *Iohannis Longi chronica sancti Bertini*, ed. O. Holder-Egger, *MGH SS* 25 (Hannover, 1880), pp. 736–866, written by John of Ypres, abbot of Saint-Bertin from 1331 to 1334, and running from the foundation of the abbey around 645 to his time.

[32] *Folcuini Gesta abbatum Sithiensium*, ed. O. Holder-Egger, *MGH SS* 13 (Hannover, 1881), pp. 600–35, written by the monk Folcuin and running from the foundation of the abbey to 961. Folcuin's *Gesta* was given a continuation by Simon, monk of Saint-Bertin and abbot of St Peter's Gent, covering the period from 1021 to 1145 (*Simonis Gesta abbatum sancti Bertini Sithiensium*, ed. O. Holder-Egger, *MGH SS* 13 (Hannover, 1881), pp. 635–63).

[33] *Vitae Audomari, Bertini, Winnoci*, eds. B. Krusch and W. Levison, *MGH SS Rer. Mer.* 5 (Hannover and Leipzig, 1910), pp. 729–86, written in the early ninth century. St

The historiographic tradition at Saint-Bertin started as a reaction against the division of the monastery by Abbot Fridugis (820–34) in a community of monks centred around the shrine of St Bertin, and a community of canons, centred around the shrine of St Omer. The monks, imbued with their spiritual superiority and deprived of their control over the shrine of St Omer, never accepted the situation, and all their further writings, historical, liturgical, and hagiographic, were infused with that frustration. From that point on, Saint-Bertin's authors became experts in producing texts that asserted their own power and authority not only inside the restricted field of the conflict with the canons.[34] In that process, they demonstrated a remarkable ability to use any models they could put their hands on in a very personal way.[35] Bovo was not only inspired, in a general way, by the polemical nature of previous texts, but he also directly used some of them as sources, especially Folcuin's *Gesta abbatum Sithiensium* and his life of St Folcuin, bishop of Thérouanne.[36] Because of this strong tradition of historiography at Saint-Bertin, it is not only interesting to consider Bovo's *Relatio* in the context of earlier relic narratives, but it is also important to keep in mind the background offered to him by his own house. Bovo was all the more able to make good use of these texts considering that, according to Simon, who wrote the continuation to Folcuin's *Gesta*, he was a very educated man, well learned in the liberal arts. He also commissioned a third life of St Bertin from the monk Folcard, who later made a career for himself in England.[37]

Bovo's *Relatio* reports the discovery of the relics of St Bertin in 1050 and their subsequent translation in 1052. It is useful to begin with a brief account of the events as they are told by Bovo. In 1033, during the abbacy of his

---

Bertin's and St Omer's other *vitae* are published in *AA.SS. Septembris t. II*, ed. J.B. Sollerius (Paris and Rome, 1868), pp. 590–613 and *AA.SS. Septembris t. III*, ed. J.B. Sollerius (Paris and Rome, 1868), pp. 402–17 respectively.

[34] Fridugis's division of the community is described in the *Gesta abbatum Sithiensium*, ed. Holder-Egger, p. 614 (ch. 47).

[35] For example, Folcuin's *Gesta* was most likely modelled on the ninth-century *Gesta abbatum Fontanellensium* (Van Werveke, 'Saint-Wandrille et Saint-Pierre de Gand'). Folcuin never directly quoted the *Gesta* from Fontenelle, but the structure of the two texts is strikingly similar.

[36] *Vita Folcuini episcopi Morinensis*, ed. O. Holder-Egger, *MGH SS* 15 (Hannover, 1887–88), pp. 423–30. It was written by the same Folcuin who wrote the *Gesta abbatum Sithiensium*, when he was already abbot of Lobbes (after 962).

[37] *Simonis gesta abbatum*, ed. Holder-Egger, pp. 638–39 (chs. 10–15).

The Inventio *of St. Bertin's Relics* 61

predecessor, so Bovo tells us, the abbey of Saint-Bertin was struck successively by two calamities: a fire seriously damaged its main church and, shortly afterwards, an epidemic killed eleven of the forty monks who made up the community.[38] Since the buildings had been hastily restored after the blaze, they started to crumble after a few years; so Bovo, four years into his abbacy, decided to undertake the major work of rebuilding and enlarging the church.[39] As workers were attempting to displace the main altar, their tools hit a layer of hard stones and old cement which suggested that something was buried underneath. After the bishop of Thérouanne, the monks, the canons of Saint-Omer, and lay witnesses had gathered around the altar, Bovo presided over the excavation. They found, buried far beneath under the altar, a leaden casket containing bones, which were identified by a silver cross as *Sanctus Bertinus Abbas*. Bovo specifies that it took three searches to find the cross, and that he himself found it.[40] The *inventio*, however, was subjected to a long investigation, and it was not until two years later that the archbishop of Reims performed the translation of the relics.[41]

Bovo's text presents interesting features: it is significantly longer than many texts of its kind—ten pages of the MGH edition—and it is a first person account of a very recent event. Most *inventiones* on the other hand are shorter, anonymous, and told by a third party who was not contemporary with the discovery.[42] Bovo's introduction is particularly important for understanding his intentions in writing the account, as well as in terms of his technique of writing. He starts with an exchange of letters between himself and Wido, archbishop of Reims, who had performed the translation of the relics.[43] In the first epistle, Bovo explained how he, urged by his

---

[38] *Bovonis Relatio*, ed. Holder-Egger, pp. 526–27 (ch. 1). In the twelfth-century chronicle of Lambert of Saint-Omer, the entry for 1033 reads: 'Templum sancti Audomari crematur' (*Lamberti Audomaris Chronica*, ed. G.H. Pertz, *MGH SS* 5 (Hannover, 1844), pp. 65–66 at p. 65).

[39] *Bovonis Relatio*, ed. Holder-Egger, pp. 527–28 (ch. 3).

[40] Ibid., p. 528.

[41] The translation was done on 1 May, 1052, *Bovonis Relatio*, ed. Holder-Egger, pp. 531–33 (chs. 8–12).

[42] However, the fifth-century *Revelatio sancti Stephani*, which may have been a model for Bovo (see below), is a first-person account of the finding of St Stephen's relics by Lucian (*Revelatio sancti Stephani*, ed. S. Vanderlinden, *Revue des Études Byzantines* 4 (1946), 178–217).

[43] In the course of the eleventh century bishops relied more and more heavily on the authority of their metropolitan for the identification and elevation of relics; this evolution

fellow monks, wished to give a written account of the events for posterity. Neither accepting nor refusing the task allegedly pushed upon him, but obviously dying to do it, the abbot begged the prelate to commission him as the author of the work. Of course, the archbishop approved of his project and enjoined the abbot to send him a copy of his work, 'in order that you be recognised for your writings [...] since what you described really happened and since they went into my hands, nothing will have to be added or removed.'[44] These first two letters fulfil three closely related purposes: they legitimize the abbot's initiative, since the *Relatio* becomes a commission from the archbishop; they guarantee that the integrity of the text will be protected, since nothing will be added to or removed from it, and it will represent the only accepted version of the facts; and finally, they guarantee that Bovo will be recognized as the author of his text. The third missive inserted by Bovo confirms the previous two letters and goes even further by emphasizing the active involvement of the archbishop in his guarantee of the text: 'if ever the troubles brought about by the scourge of rivalry tried to introduce changes, I would turn myself toward your [...] benevolent protection. Indeed, it is fair that, trusting your noble protection, I would shield myself behind the walls of your defense.'[45]

The relationship between fiction and reality in this correspondence is not easy to unravel: it could reflect more or less faithfully a true exchange or it could be a purely literary device. Whatever the case, Bovo's request for legitimization and protection is clear and understandable in view of the circumstances. Indeed, another set of relics was already honoured as St Bertin's, and the discovery of the new ones during Bovo's building campaign raised serious questions. Interestingly, Bovo's *Relatio* did not address the problem of the two sets of St Bertin's relics with his own authorial voice, but again, he used the epistolary genre to confer more authority to the story. In this case, they were letters exchanged between Drogo, bishop of Thérouanne, and the same Wido of Reims.[46] The letters, according to Bovo, were read aloud in a ceremony assembling abbots,

---

was ratified in 1025 by Gerald of Cambrai at the synod of Arras (N. Herrmann-Mascard, *Les reliques des Saints. Formation coutumière d'un droit* (Paris, 1975), p. 90).

[44] *Bovonis Relatio*, ed. Holder-Egger, p. 525. Such a transfer of authorial responsibility from the author to the patron is a *topos* of medieval narratives (M. Sot, 'Rhétorique et technique dans les préfaces des *gesta episcoporum* (IXe–XIIe s.)', *Cahiers de Civilisation Médiévale* 28 (1985), 181–200).

[45] *Bovonis Relatio*, ed. Holder-Egger, p. 525.

[46] Ibid., pp. 530–31 (ch. 5).

archdeacons, and monks in front of the new relics. The bishop explained the situation to his superior because ordinary people, *vulgus minus intelligens*, were very upset by the two St Bertins and were probably requesting explanations from the ecclesiastical authorities.[47] Clearly, however, the ordinary people were not the only ones to find the situation puzzling, since it took two years of investigation before the elevation could be performed. Eventually, in his answer to the bishop of Thérouanne, Wido carefully advised Drogo and Bovo to place the old and the new Bertin in the same shrine, and to translate them together.[48] One of Bovo's models for inserting this correspondence was Adrevald of Fleury's *Translatio sancti Benedicti*. It is clear that the exchange of letters between Drogo of Thérouanne and Wido of Reims about the *inventio* and the identity of the relics is reminiscent of the letter addressed around 750 to the monks of Fleury by Pope Zachary, which Adrevald of Fleury inserted in his *Miracula*.[49] The authenticity of the papal letter is much disputed, but by inserting it, Adrevald was making his point very clearly.[50] The monks of Monte Cassino never recognized Fleury's possession of Benedict's and Scholastica's relics; but, the pope's injunction to the community of Fleury to give Benedict's relics back to Monte Cassino was an explicit admission that the relics were indeed at Fleury. In addition, Bovo's technique of introducing his account with an epistolary exchange may have been inspired by the fifth-century *Inventio sancti Stephani*, which was among the most widespread *inventio* accounts of the Middle Ages, especially in northern France.[51] Indeed, Stephen's *Inventio* is known in western medieval sources as a set of two epistles: the second epistle is the Latin translation of the account given in Greek by Lucian, the priest who found Stephen's relics near Jerusalem, and it is introduced by a first epistle sent by the priest Avitus, who translated the text, to the bishop of Braga. Avitus had received a few of Stephen's relics from Lucian and he asked his compatriot Paul Orosius, on his way to Spain, to bring them to Braga. Avitus added the letters to the relics in order to authenticate them.

---

[47] Ibid., p. 531.

[48] Ibid., p. 531.

[49] Adrevald, *Miraculorum sancti Benedicti. Liber primus*, ed. E. de Certain, in *Les Miracles de Saint Benoît* (Paris, 1858; rept. New York, 1968), pp. 38–39.

[50] Vidier, *L'Historiographie à Saint-Benoît sur Loire*, pp. 160–61; J. Hourlier, 'La lettre de Zacharie', in *Le Culte et les Reliques de Saint Benoît et de Sainte Scholastique*, eds. A. Beau et al., *Studia Monastica* 21 (1979), 241–52.

[51] *Revelatio sancti Stephani*, ed. Vanderlinden.

Let us now look more closely at Bovo's interpretation of the events regarding the discovery of St Bertin's relics. The story starts with the fire of 1033, which Bovo did not consider pure bad luck, but rather as the consequence of God's wrath in the face of the laxity of spiritual life in a monastery turned into a 'den of thieves'. The situation was so bad that even St Omer and St Bertin could no longer play their natural role as intercessors.[52] This fire, however, was not enough to induce a long-lasting change in the community and, after a brief period of contrition, the monks fell back again into their old sins. It was only after a severe epidemic, which killed a good part of the community, that the surviving monks undertook a true *conversio*.[53] In 1046, as the church was threatening to collapse, Bovo started his project of rebuilding a larger sanctuary for the community, in the course of which work he found the hidden relics of St Bertin.[54] Soon after, the monks had a new shrine of gold and topaz built for their rediscovered patron saint, who immediately performed miracles. These included the first rains for a very long period, allowing the withered crops to blossom and fructify.[55] In his account of the discovery of the relics and its circumstances, Bovo put himself at centre stage: he decided to rebuild the church, he found the leaden urn, he discovered the cross with the name of St Bertin. He also sharply contrasted his own abbacy with the period of spiritual and physical disintegration of the abbey during the time of his predecessor—whom he does not blame directly. The episode of the reconstruction and *inventio* confers on Bovo's abbacy a character of renewal for Saint-Bertin. Not only did he rebuild the church of St Bertin, but by finding his true relics he also re-established his true cult. The attribution to God's wrath of the fire which destroyed the church contrasts with Bovo's own period of a new covenant between God, St Bertin and the saint's community. This is inherent in the stories of *inventiones*: as in *furta sacra*, the saints remain active in the process: they are not merely found; rather, they let themselves be found. Thus, the *inventio* is also a *revelatio*.[56] Bovo's presentation of his role as the refounder of his abbey is, however, in contradiction to the facts since his predecessor, Roderic, was actually the spiritual reformer of Saint-Bertin. Indeed, in 1021, Roderic was called by

---

[52] *Bovonis Relatio*, ed. Holder-Egger, p. 526 (ch. 1).

[53] Ibid., p. 527 (ch. 2).

[54] Ibid., pp. 527–28 (ch. 3).

[55] Ibid., p. 528 (ch. 4).

[56] Otter, *Inventiones*; Geary, *Furta Sacra*.

Count Baldwin from his monastery of Saint-Vaast at Arras, which had recently been restored according to the reform of Richard of Saint-Vanne, to re-establish the regular life at Saint-Bertin.[57] It is as a reformer, a *studiosus imitator* and *ferventissimus amator* of the Benedictine rule, that Roderic was remembered later in the historiography of Saint-Bertin.[58] It is conceivable that Bovo, facing the tough task of succeeding him, had to make the claim of being a pious leader and refounder in his own right.

Thus, the episode of the *inventio* would be enough to suggest that Bovo saw and presented himself as chosen and rewarded by St Bertin for being a good abbot. Indeed, Bovo's text is as much about himself as about St Bertin and his relics, and the abbot was not shy about stating this clearly in three passages. The first one is a comment made after the description of the fire: 'God with the help of His rod, compelled the reform and punished the sins which had to be atoned for by piety, and He administered lesser punishments on those who were good, as was demonstrated later at the right time.'[59] The second passage is a more symbolic prefiguration of the *inventio*, as it relates a monk's vision of a magnificent man, dressed in white, who came to inspect the monastery and blessed the place with his right hand.[60] The third expression of Bovo's election is found after a long historiographical passage referring to a very traumatic event for the monks of Saint-Bertin: the division of the monastery into separate communities of canons and Benedictine monks, imposed shortly after 820 by Abbot Fridugis. Bovo followed most of Saint-Bertin's authors, regarding the separation as sinful, but he concluded by saying: 'it was enough that I gathered our children under my protection for the sins of the monastery to go away and for the blessed relics, which had been hidden in emergency, to make themselves visible.'[61] The justification of this statement is not clear, because since 950 the canons had their own provost, distinct from the abbot of Saint-Bertin, although the two communities had close relations, which were not always cordial. No other source corroborates that the situation changed during Bovo's abbacy.[62] In any case, what is significant

---

[57] *Simonis gesta abbatum*, ed. Holder-Egger, pp. 636–38 (chs. 1–9).

[58] Ibid., p. 637 (ch. 5).

[59] *Bovonis Relatio*, ed. Holder-Egger, p. 527 (ch. 1).

[60] Ibid., p. 527 (ch. 2).

[61] Ibid., p. 529 (ch. 6).

[62] From the division into two communities until the reform by Gerald of Brogne, the canons and the monks shared one abbot, who could be a monk or a canon.

is the fact that he wanted his readers to believe that he had in one way or another re-established some sort of unity between the monks and the canons, and that he was therefore rewarded by St Bertin.[63]

Because Bovo's finding of St Bertin's relics was questionable, he had to provide some explanation and justification for the circumstances which had made the community ignorant of the location of the true relics for such a long time. To do this, he resorted to the archives of Saint-Bertin and more specifically to the tenth-century life of Folcuin, bishop of Thérouanne.[64] Bovo asserts that, because the abbey was threatened by the Vikings, Folcuin translated the relics of St Bertin and re-buried them in 846—Bovo and the *Vita Folcuini* both use the word *recondere*, which means 'to hide', 'to bury very deep'. Bovo's explanation is actually supported by the *Vita Folcuini*, although its author associates the hiding of Bertin with the theft of St Omer's relics by Abbot Hugh, who had tried to translate them to his other abbey of Saint-Quentin. According to the *Vita*, Folcuin brought the relics of St Omer back to his church and re-buried them; three years later, he exhumed and re-buried St Bertin.[65] St Omer's relics remained in their secret place until they too were discovered in 941, but unfortunately, no narrative of this *inventio* has survived.[66]

---

[63] The manuscript tradition of Bovo's *Relatio* could have told us more about the use he wanted to make of his text. Unfortunately, the two medieval manuscripts (from Saint-Bertin and Clairmarais) on which J. Mabillon based his edition in the *Acta Sanctorum ordinis S. Benedicti*, 6 vols. (Paris, 1668–1701; rept. Macon, 1935–50) III, part 1, pp. 153–68) seem to have disappeared. For his *MGH* edition, Holder-Egger copied the text from Mabillon but he was able to find a sixteenth-century copy of the first three letters in Saint-Omer, Bibliothèque Municipale, MS 746, t. II. Simon, the author of the continuation of Folcuin's *Gesta*, inserted the passage describing the fire and the epidemics in his chapter on Abbot Roderic (*Simonis gesta abbatum*, ed. Holder-Egger, pp. 636–37 (chs. 2–5)). At some point, excerpts of the *Relatio* were also inserted in the mass of Saint-Bertin.

[64] *Bovonis Relatio*, ed. Holder-Egger, p. 529 (ch. 5): 'meminisse coepi Vita sancti Folcuini [...]'.

[65] *Vita Folcuini episcopi Morinensis*, ed. Holder-Egger, p. 428 (ch. 7).

[66] According to Lambert of Saint-Omer's *Chronica* (ed. Pertz, p. 65): '941. Inventio Sancti Audomari et Bertini'. In his *Vita Folcuini*, Folcuin alluded to the *inventio* of St Omer (*Vita Folcuini episcopi Morinensis*, ed. Holder-Egger, p. 428 (ch. 7)): 'Et praecavens in futurum, ne parili modo aut alio quovis ingenio corpus auferretur sanctum, terra illud abscondit, ubi per plurimos annos homines quidem latuit; at revelatum est ubi Dominus voluit'. However, neither in his *Gesta* nor in his *Vita Folcuini* did he mention the discovery of St Bertin.

The question of the authenticity of Bovo's find remains, and will always remain, unanswerable. The hiding of the relics in the ninth century and their rediscovery in the eleventh are not implausible, although we should not forget that the *Vita* of Folcuin was written more than a century after his death. Bovo's setting of his *Relatio* in a very historical context (the destruction and rebuilding of the church, which are most likely actual events), the introduction of letters and historical sources into the narrative, as well as the participation of the author in the events reinforce that impression of historicity. Both historicity and credibility were sensible goals for an author so anxious about the legitimization and the integrity of his text. Nevertheless, one detail of the narrative seems inconsistent: Bovo asserts that he found the little silver cross under St Bertin's right shoulder, suggesting that the skeleton was still intact.[67] However, the words he used to describe the saint's container is *scrinium*, a little box or reliquary, and *urna*, which suggests that it could not contain an intact body. Indeed, Drogo of Thérouanne wrote in his letter to Wido of Reims that the bones were cremated (*ossa cinerati*).[68] Besides this inconsistency in the text, the textual tradition in which Bovo's *inventio* arises also sheds light on the degree of historicity one should expect from such a text. In her study of eleventh- and twelfth-century *inventiones* from post-Conquest England, Otter has stressed that the truth which these texts embodied was essentially symbolic and that, despite the efforts of their authors to ground their account in a familiar and historical context, *inventiones* usually happened in very unlikely circumstances.[69] These observations prove to be correct regarding the earlier continental *inventiones* as well. This is not surprising, since Otter also argues that the genre was probably brought to England by Goscelin of Canterbury, a monk of Saint-Bertin who lived in England from the 1050s until his death in the beginning of the twelfth century. Regarding Goscelin, it is interesting to note that, as a monk of St Augustine's Canterbury from about 1090 until his death, he was involved in the antagonism between his community and the monks of Christ Church. He wrote in that context a good amount of polemical writing strikingly reminiscent of the way the authors from Saint-Bertin dealt with their own

---

[67] *Bovonis Relatio*, ed. Holder-Egger, p. 528 (chs. 3–4).

[68] Ibid., p. 531 (ch. 5). The circumstances of their cremation are unclear, but they could have undergone an ordeal by fire for authentication at the time of the first translation; on the ordeal of relics by fire, Herrmann-Mascard, *Les reliques des Saints*, p. 134.

[69] Otter, *Inventiones*, p. 41.

conflicts.[70] This suggests that the earlier Bertinian historiographical culture made its way through the eleventh and twelfth centuries, and that Bovo's work should also be seen in light of its local tradition. To go back to the *inventiones* and their ambiguous relationship with 'historical truth', a few examples can be usefully presented. I have already mentioned the *Revelatio sancti Stephani*, which, as shown by its manuscript tradition, was very well-known and influential in Flanders and Lotharingia.[71] This story may have been a source for the *Inventio sancti Gisleni*: the two texts present narrative parallels and both the abbeys of Brogne and Saint-Ghislain possessed an eleventh-century manuscript of the *Revelatio*. The *Revelatio sancti Stephani* was also known to Goscelin of Saint-Bertin, whose *Inventio* of St Ivo resembles the older text.[72] As for St Ghislain, Helvétius has convincingly demonstrated that he never existed: he was an invention of Duke Gislebert, who needed a pretext for founding a monastic community there, in order to bolster his domination over the region of Hainault.[73] Despite the old pretension of Fleury to have the relics of St Benedict, their presence in France was always fiercely fought by the monks of Monte Cassino. Other *inventiones* are even more clearly the product of the unbridled medieval imagination regarding saint cults and relics. The discovery of the skull of John the Baptist in eleventh-century Aquitaine is only one among the multitude of highly unlikely discoveries of relics produced by monastic communities in order to answer their need for power, supremacy, or money.[74]

---

[70] Ibid., pp. 21–22. On Goscelin of Saint-Bertin, *The Life of King Edward Who Rests at Westminster, Attributed to a Monk of Saint-Bertin*, ed. and trans. F. Barlow (London, 2nd ed. 1992), pp. 132–49; T.J. Hamilton, *Goscelin of Canterbury: a Critical Study of his Life Works and Accomplishments*, 2 vols. (unpublished Ph.D. thesis University of Virginia, 1973). On Goscelin and the rivalry between St Augustine's and Christ Church, R. Sharpe, 'Goscelin's St. Augustine and St. Mildreth: hagiography and liturgy in context', *Journal of Theological Studies* 41 (1990), 502–16.

[71] Vanderlinden's edition of the *Revelatio sancti Stephani* is exclusively based on manuscripts from Belgian libraries and the Bibliothèque Nationale in Paris; despite that geographical limitation, he was able to gather a corpus of more than thirty medieval manuscripts.

[72] *Goscelini Cantuariensis monachi Vita sancti Yvonis episcopi Persae in Anglia depositi et ejus sociorum*, ed. J.-P. Migne, PL 155 (Paris, 1854), cols. 79–90.

[73] Helvétius, *Abbayes, évêques et laïques*, pp. 229–31.

[74] *Inventio capitis sancti Johannis*, ed. D. Papebrochius, *AA.SS. Iunii t. V* (Paris and Rome, 1867), pp. 650–52. On relics and forgeries in Aquitaine, R. Landes, *Relics, Apocalypse and the Deceits of History: Ademar of Chabannes, 989–1034* (Cambridge, MA, 1995).

More than other hagiographic texts, relic narratives and especially *inventiones* lend themselves to a narrative structure which makes them look much like historical texts, sometimes even miniature chronicles. It is remarkable that in many cases the authors of such translations and inventions went back, in much detail, to the origins of the monastery in which the relics were allegedly brought or found, and to the events which made the finding possible. However, since the historicity of these narratives is often questionable, what really matters both to us and to their medieval readers, is their symbolic meaning: the finding or coming of new relics meant the beginning of a new covenant between the saint and the community. It is only normal that these texts should have created interest in the context of intensive monastic reform and social change—in the tenth and eleventh centuries on the Continent and after the Conquest in England. In the case of the *inventio* of St Bertin, however, Bovo subverted the conventions and symbolism of the genre in order to produce a very individual and self-serving version of the new covenant. This is not only characteristic of the well-rooted trend to use narratives as tools of power at Saint-Bertin, but also reveals the personality of an author who, in quite original ways for his time, insisted so much that his authorship be recognized for posterity. In this regard, the legacy left by Bovo in the memory of Saint-Bertin may not have met his expectations. At the time of his death, a gap already existed between the community's perception of the events and the meaning Bovo tried so hard to impose on them. What was recalled in his epitaph was not his discovery of Saint-Bertin's relics, but his reconstruction of the church.[75] The little we know about him from sources other than his own writing, is told in the *Gesta abbatum Sithiensium*, written by the monk Simon, as a continuation of Folcuin's tenth-century *Gesta*. It is ironic that the only passage from the *Relatio* that Simon quoted—the story of the fire and the epidemic—was inserted in the chapter on Bovo's predecessor, the reformer Roderic.[76] Although Simon devoted the following chapter to Bovo's discovery of the relics and his writing of a *commentariolus* attesting the regularity of the *inventio* and translation, neither did he put much emphasis upon an event which was supposed to refound St Bertin's true cult. Equally, he did not emphasize Bovo's role in

---

[75] *Simonis gesta abbatum*, ed. Holder-Egger, p. 639 (ch. 15): 'Hanc fabricam primo templi fundavit ab imo; Quam divinarum portans virtute rotarum. Rexit et erexit contraque pericula texit.'

[76] *Simonis gesta abbatum*, ed. Holder-Egger, pp. 636–37 (chs. 2–5).

the discovery, or attribute it to his qualities as a religious leader.[77] Furthermore, his tone when writing about Roderic was clearly warmer and more enthusiastic than were the conventional words of praise he gave to Bovo. The tepid attitude of the monastic community of Saint-Bertin both toward Bovo and his unearthing of Saint-Bertin's new relics confirms the self-serving character of the facts and the text of the *Relatio*. It looks as if the community did not need these new relics. Bovo's interpretation of the discovery as a sign of his own election was not very appealing to the community either, all the more so since his role as an abbot did not measure up to his own self-image. Furthermore, the lay community, local potentates and common people alike, remained equally cold toward the *inventio*. Nevertheless, they were an important presence in Bovo's story: before the opening of the coffin, Bovo had invited the *castellani* of the town as witnesses and, since it was Saturday, day of the judicial court, the populace had gathered in town 'to make fun of the honourable people' and did not wait long to rush to the church.[78] The lay community was of course as much concerned with St Bertin's relics as was the monastic community, since the good working of society as a whole, from good weather, as shown in the 'first rains' miracle, and public health, to peace and justice, depended on his intercession.[79] Lay people, pilgrims as well as Saint-Bertin's neighbours, were not passive actors of the cult, and its success or failure depended on their adhesion or refusal. I have already mentioned that the *vulgus* had been very sceptical toward the new relics and had pressed the ecclesiastical authorities to provide explanations and clarify which ones were the proper relics. The aristocracy, who were of course the most likely to honour the 'true' relics with donations, were not very enthusiastic either. On 1 May 1052, the day of the elevation of the new relics, Countess Adela, daughter of Robert the Pious and wife of Baldwin V of Flanders, was present at the ceremony with her brother Odo and an important escort, but not the count himself.[80] According to the series of miracles that Bovo added at the end of his story, Adela offered a shroud made of precious fabric to wrap the relics in and gave a saltworks ('terra salinaris') to the monas-

---

[77] Ibid., p. 638 (ch. 12).

[78] *Bovonis Relatio*, ed. Holder-Egger, p. 528 (ch. 3).

[79] On the public utility of relics, E. Bozoky, 'Voyage de reliques et démonstration du pouvoir aux temps féodaux', in *Voyages et Voyageurs au Moyen Age. XXVIe Congrès de la S.H.M.E.S. (Limoges-Aubazine, mai 1995)* (Paris, 1996), pp. 267–80.

[80] *Bovonis Relatio*, ed. Holder-Egger, p. 531 (ch. 8).

The Inventio *of St. Bertin's Relics*

tery.[81] Bovo states that the land donation was authenticated by a charter, but if it ever existed, it is no longer among the seven surviving charters issued during Bovo's abbacy.[82] Furthermore, among these charters—agreements with local lords and privileges from Count Baldwin, Emperor Henry IV and Pope Victor II, dating from 1051 to 1063—none is a donation to the abbey or refers to the discovery of the relics, apart from the 1052 charter recording the *inventio* and the elevation.[83] Neither the charters nor Simon's *Gesta abbatum* suggest that donations to Saint-Bertin increased and that the cult was boosted in the years after the *inventio*. Indeed, Bovo was not even able to finish the rebuilding of the church that he had undertaken and, at his death in 1065, the work was left unfinished, probably from lack of financial means.[84] The legacy of Bovo's *Relatio de inventione et elevatione sancti Bertini* suggests that, however much the authors of relic narratives tried to historicize their story, plausibility was not the secret of their success. In order to attract support from the religious community as well as from the secular world, the finding of new relics and the writing of the corresponding narrative had to be meaningful and useful for the community itself.

---

[81] Ibid., p. 532 (ch. 11).

[82] The charters from Saint-Bertin present a very delicate problem: the originals disappeared during the French Revolution, and they survive only in eighteenth-century copies and in the twelfth-century manuscript of Folcuin and Simon's *Gesta abbatum* (Boulogne-sur-Mer, Bibliothèque Municipale, MS 721). For Simon's *Gesta*: *Cartulaire de l'Abbaye de Saint-Bertin*, ed. B. Guérard (Paris, 1841), and for the other charters, *Les chartes de Saint-Bertin d'après le Grand Cartulaire de Dom Dewitte*, ed. D. Haigneré, 4 vols. (Saint-Omer, 1886), I (648–1240). Simon included only two charters dated from Bovo's abbacy: the papal privilege (13 May 1057) and a privilege given by Count Baldwin (6 May 1056) (*Cartulaire*, ed. Guérard, pp. 180–83 and 184–87). Dewitte copied these privileges in his *Grand Cartulaire* but he also added a 1051 charter between Saint-Bertin and the Count of Saint-Pol, Henry IV's privilege (6 December 1056) and two undated charters, one of them a land donation, which he attributes to Bovo's abbacy without giving any evidence. Since Dewitte is a very unreliable source and the monks from Saint-Bertin were experimented forgers, the charters copied by Dewitte are to be considered with caution.

[83] *Les chartes*, ed. Haigneré, nos. 73, 76, 77, 78, 79, 80. Charter no. 74, dated 2 May 1052, records the elevation and gives a summary of the discovery.

[84] *Simonis Gesta abbatum*, ed. Holder-Egger, p. 638 (ch. 10).

Monastic Freedom vs. Episcopal and Aristocratic Power in the Twelfth Century: Context and Analysis of the *De libertate Beccensis*

JULIE POTTER

Medieval monastic writers of north-west Europe often put pen to parchment in order to preserve and protect the privileges of their houses. Records of gifts and rights bestowed by an abbey's benefactors were created and collected and later could be produced to support the monks' claims in the event of any dispute. Records produced by monastic scriptoria which contained details of the house's property included not only charters, which in the eleventh and early twelfth century were often drafted and written by the monastic beneficiaries, but also various types of narrative writing such as chronicles and the lives of saints or abbots of the house.[1] These documents recording an abbey's historical privileges were tools which gave both material and spiritual weight to monastic claims over lands and privileges contested by rival secular and ecclesiastical powers. Historians in the past have shown that monastic narrative accounts containing details of privileges and properties, as well as forged charters, were commonly produced in eleventh- and twelfth-century scriptoria in response to specific threats. These narrative records and

---

[1] For a discussion of the interrelated nature of charters and chronicles in the eleventh and twelfth centuries, M. Chibnall, 'Charter and Chronicle: the Use of Archive Sources by Norman Historians', in *Church and Government in the Middle Ages: Essays presented to C.R. Cheney*, eds. C.N.L. Brooke et al. (Cambridge, 1976), pp. 1–17.

forged charters often provide our clearest indication of both what was at stake in a particular dispute and how a monastery went about using historical writing as a tool for protecting its privileges and possessions. Through the exploration of monastic narrative history and chronicles we can increase our understanding of particular clashes between secular and ecclesiastic powers as well as how such clashes were mediated.

The text known as the *De libertate Beccensis*, written in the first half of the twelfth century, is a prime example of a monastic narrative history created in response to threats to the abbey's privileges by neighbouring secular and ecclesiastic powers.[2] It appears as a deliberate reshaping of a set of abbots' lives in polemic form to meet three specific challenges to the liberties of the Norman abbey of Le Bec-Hellouin: firstly the demand by Henry I in 1124 for an oath of homage from the abbot of Bec; secondly the demand by Archbishop Hugh of Rouen in 1136 for a written profession of obedience from the abbot: and lastly the demand by Robert, count of Meulan, newly created lord of Brionne in the 1090s, for the rights of patronage over the abbey.

To understand the interest and importance of the *De libertate* one must first have an understanding of the abbey's origins and circumstances. The abbey of Bec was founded in 1034 by a simple knight named Herluin in the service of Count Gilbert of Brionne, cousin of Robert I of Normandy, who was assassinated in 1040 while acting as guardian of the young William the Bastard.[3] The abbey's initial patrimony consisted only of Herluin's limited inheritance and was not very generously backed by his lord, the count of Brionne.[4] The community followed the Rule of St Benedict under Herluin's direction, but the foundation was not a dependency of, or directed by, any greater monastic house or order. This virtually unique lack of reliance at the time of foundation on any considerable secular or ecclesiastical power

---

[2] BN MS lat. 2342, ff. 185v–190; *De libertate Beccensis monasterii*, ed. J. Mabillon, in *Annales Ordinis Sancti Benedicti* (Paris, 1738), V, 601–05; trans. P. Fisher, *On the Liberty of the Abbey of Bec*, appendix in S. Vaughn, *The Abbey of Bec and the Anglo-Norman State 1034–1136* (Woodbridge, 1981), pp. 134–43.

[3] For the earliest account of the foundation of Bec by Herluin, Gilbert Crispin, *Vita Herluini*, ed. J.A. Robinson, in *Gilbert Crispin: Abbot of Westminster* (Cambridge, 1911), pp. 87–110; also ed. G.R. Evans, in *The Works of Gilbert Crispin Abbot of Westminster*, eds. A.S. Abulafia and G.R. Evans (Oxford, 1986), pp. 185–212.

[4] For analyses of the early patrimony of Bec, V. Gazeau-Goddet, 'L'Aristocratie autour du Bec au tournant de l'année 1077', *ANS* 7 (1985), 89–103.

was to prove the basis of many of the abbey's later claims to independence. In 1042 what had been a relatively insignificant house was transformed by the arrival of Lanfranc, a well-known Italian scholar and teacher. Initially dismayed by the ignorance and transgressions of his fellow monks, he considered life as a hermit, but was persuaded by Herluin to remain as prior and take on the reform of the house. His reputation soon attracted interest in the small community. Soon after his elevation as prior in 1045 Lanfranc began to accept both claustral and extra-claustral students at Bec.[5] His success as a teacher helped the abbey to attract both plentiful recruits and benefactors. By the early twelfth century the abbey of Bec had become one of the most respected houses in Normandy. Lanfranc had become abbot of Caen in 1063 and then archbishop of Canterbury in 1070. Among the students he had attracted to Bec while prior was Anselm, who became prior of Bec in 1063 before succeeding Herluin as abbot in 1078. In 1093 Anselm himself became archbishop of Canterbury, an office he fulfilled until his death in 1109.[6] By the time of Anselm's death, Bec had supplied a number of abbots and prelates to houses in England and Normandy and had established bonds of friendship with many of the most powerful families in England, Normandy and France.[7] Bec had transformed from a simple knightly foundation into an extremely wealthy and influential abbey.

In the very years when Bec was transformed from an insignificant and impoverished community to a great and wealthy abbey with many dependencies, the forms of both ducal and ecclesiastical government were gaining new precision and a longer reach. William the Conqueror had established his authority over the powerful secular families of Normandy and united them behind him in the Conquest of England. With the acquisition of a kingdom came adoption and development of a more structured administration in Normandy and a gradual increase in the use of written documents.[8] With William's support and to a certain extent under

---

[5] Gilbert Crispin, *Vita Herluini*, ed. Robinson, pp. 96–97; *Vita Lanfranci*, ed. M. Gibson, in *Lanfranco di Pavia e l'Europa de Secolo XI*, ed. G. d'Onofrio (Rome, 1993), pp. 661–715. For the career of Lanfranc, M. Gibson, *Lanfranc of Bec* (Oxford, 1978).

[6] For the career of Anselm, R.W. Southern, *Saint Anselm: A Portrait in a Landscape* (Cambridge, 1990).

[7] Among the most notable of the families which patronized Bec in the eleventh century were the Crispins, the Beaumonts, the lords of Gournay, and the Clares (descendants of Count Gilbert of Brionne).

[8] C.H. Haskins, *Norman Institutions* (Cambridge, MA, 1918); also M.T. Clanchy, *From*

his direction the church in Normandy, and then in England, was reformed and revitalized. At the same time, during his reign and those of his sons, the overall balance of power between the church and secular rulers in western Europe was being contested and redefined. In this climate of increasing regularization the Norman monasteries often found themselves having to defend the freedom of action and liberties which they had enjoyed in the earliest stages of the monastic revival against the challenges of those now increasingly claiming authority over them. At the abbey of Bec, one of the responses to the threat of encroaching secular and ecclesiastical powers survives in the form of a text, known as the *De libertate Beccensis*, composed by a prolific but anonymous twelfth-century monk of the abbey.

The text appears in a Paris manuscript which contains a number of the works of an anonymous monk of Bec.[9] The initial folios of the manuscript contain a list of the works of the monk including several tracts which do not appear in the book, some of which survive elsewhere, and some of which have been lost. In addition to a number of the works of the anonymous monk referred to in the list at the front, there is a copy of a widely circulated *Letter of Prester John to the Emperor Manuel Comnenus* tacked on to the end of the manuscript.[10] The internal dating of the *De libertate* and other works by the same anonymous monk of Bec implies that he was writing in the early to mid-twelfth century.[11] The main text is written in an early- to mid-twelfth century hand. It is possible, yet far from

---

Memory to Written Record: England 1066–1307 (Oxford and Cambridge, MA, 1993; first edition London, 1979), for the increasing use of written records in the Anglo-Norman world.

[9] BN, MS lat. 2342. P. Glorieux suggests, with reservations, that this anonymous monk could also have been the author of the letters by a monk of Bec contained in BN MS lat. 13575 and might possibly be identified as the young Alan of Lille. P. Glorieux, 'Alain de Lille, le moine et l'abbaye du Bec', *Recherches de Théologie Ancienne et Médievale* 39 (1972), 51–62.

[10] BN MS lat. 2342, ff. 191–193.

[11] The *De libertate Beccensis* gives an account of the abbey ending with the death of Abbot Boso in 1136; *De libertate*, ed. Mabillon, pp. 601–05. The *Miracula sancti Nicholai*, by the same author, though not surviving in BN MS lat. 2342, contains an account of a miracle at Bari in 1129; other miracles in this collection suggest that the author was at Bec from c. 1103; *Miracula sancti Nicholai*, in *Catalogus Codicum Hagiographicorum Latinorum: Bibliotheca Nationali Parisiensi*, eds. Hagiographi Bollandiana (Brussels, 1890), II, 405–32. For discussion, J. Potter, *The Earliest Narratives of the Foundation of the Abbey at Bec* (unpublished M.Phil. thesis Cambridge University, 1992), pp. 12–18.

certain, that the main body of the manuscript was compiled by the author himself, though there is clearly more than one copyist at work.[12] The list of the author's works on folios one and two is in a different hand from the main text and is probably late-twelfth-century, and the *Letter of Prester John* at the end must post-date 1170.[13] In addition, the same scribe who copied the *Letter of Prester John* was also responsible for a folio inserted into the *De libertate*.[14]

The text is arranged as an account of the lives of the first four abbots of Bec: Herluin, Anselm, William and Boso, who died in 1136. Nothing much is said concerning the activities of each abbot when in office, but rather emphasis is laid on each election and installation of a new abbot. The primary aim of the text appears to be to demonstrate that none of these abbots had ever had either to do homage to the duke or king, or to give a written or sworn profession of obedience to the archbishop of Rouen. The text explains that when Herluin was appointed abbot over the tiny community in 1034, he was ordained by the bishop of Lisieux because the see of Rouen was vacant at that time. According to the author, Herluin never did homage to anyone for the possession of the church, nor did he ever make a profession to a bishop, because it was not the custom for any abbot to do so to a bishop outside the area. After Herluin's death the monks elected Anselm, 'without any declaration or permission from an ecclesiastical dignitary'.[15] King William 'handed over the abbatiate to him by the gift of the pastoral staff [...] but he did not require any homage from him'.[16] As the church of Rouen was again vacant, the king ordered Gilbert, bishop of Évreux, to bless the new abbot, which he did, 'without any mention of a profession'.[17] When William of Beaumont succeeded Anselm as abbot in 1093, the duke of Normandy, Robert Curthose, ordered that the new abbot should be blessed without mention of a profession.

---

[12] Gibson describes BN MS lat. 2342 as an autograph manuscript, though it is unclear what evidence she bases this statement upon; M. Gibson, 'History at Bec in the twelfth century', in *The Writing of History in the Middle Ages: Essays Presented to R.W. Southern*, eds. R.H.C. Davis et al. (Oxford, 1981), p. 171.

[13] Manuel Comnenus ruled from 1143 to 1180, and other evidence places the *Letter* in the 1170s.

[14] BN MS lat. 2342, ff. 186–186v.

[15] *De libertate*, ed. Mabillon, p. 635; *Liberty of Bec*, trans. Fisher, p. 134.

[16] *De libertate*, ed. Mabillon, p. 635; *Liberty of Bec*, trans. Fisher, p. 135.

[17] *De libertate*, ed. Mabillon, pp. 635–36; *Liberty of Bec*, trans. Fisher, p. 135.

In 1124 the issue of homage came to a head with the election of Abbot Boso. When King Henry I heard of the election he refused to approve it. The *De libertate* explains that, 'Boso was at odds with Henry for certain reasons which went back to the former relationship between Henry and Anselm, and was thereby still involved in a great deal of dispute'.[18] The nature of the dispute gradually becomes clear in the text. Boso had been a close associate of Anselm and had represented the archbishop at the Council of Clermont in 1095 at which Pope Urban II had forbidden lay investiture. It was for this reason that Boso in 1124 tried to refuse office rather than put the abbey at risk by incurring the king's wrath. According to the *De libertate*, however, the monks of Bec, helped by the king's affection for their house and the good offices of Geoffrey, archbishop of Rouen, were eventually able to gain Henry I's approval and Boso was presented with the abbatiate by the king with no mention of homage. In addition the king ordered the archbishop of Rouen to bless the new abbot without making any mention of a profession. The account then closes with Abbot Boso's death in 1136.

Although the abbot's traditional exemption from swearing homage to the king or duke represents one of the main points of the text, it was almost certainly the demands of the archbishop of Rouen in 1136 for an oath of obedience from Boso's successor Theobald which provided the primary incentive for the composition of the *De libertate*. Bishop Hugh of Amiens became archbishop of Rouen in 1130 and immediately took up the struggle which had recurred on and off since the eleventh century to re-assert the rights of the church of Rouen over the great Norman abbeys, many of which refused to give a profession of obedience to the archbishop. When Hugh became archbishop, the abbots of Jumièges, Saint-Wandrille and Saint-Ouen had not yet been blessed. In 1131 Archbishop Hugh appealed to Pope Innocent II for support in his demands for the professions of these abbots, taking the abbots-elect of Jumièges and Saint-Ouen with him to the papal court at Reims. The abbots for their part claimed to possess ancient papal privileges of exemption from episcopal control, but when Innocent was to examine these privileges, proceedings were interrupted by the bishop of Châlons-sur-Marne, who said that he knew that a monk of Saint-Médard had forged papal privileges for both the church of Saint-Ouen and St Augustine's Canterbury. At this stage both the abbots of Saint-Ouen and of Jumièges were compelled to make professions and in return receive the

---

[18] *De libertate*, ed. Mabillon, p. 638; *Liberty of Bec*, trans. Fisher, p. 139.

archbishop's blessing. After this episode Innocent II wrote to the remaining abbot-elect, Alan of Saint-Wandrille, demanding that he make a profession of obedience to the archbishop. But by now King Henry I had heard of the events at Reims and immediately wrote to the pope complaining that the professions of the abbots of Jumièges and Saint-Ouen had been extorted outside the duchy and that Hugh had acted in a novel way against the king's rights. Unwilling to offend Henry, Innocent wrote to Archbishop Hugh commanding his compliance with the king's will.[19]

The opportunity for Hugh to renew his demands came with the death of Abbot Boso of Bec in 1136 and the election of his successor Theobald. Henry I had died in 1135 and royal control in Normandy was weak. Archbishop Hugh at first refused to ratify Theobald's election, objecting that he had not been consulted, but the bishop of Évreux intervened to win the archbishop's approval. The blessing was another matter. Hugh demanded a written profession of obedience, which Theobald steadfastly refused to give on the grounds that no previous abbot of Bec had made a profession, the argument outlined by the *De libertate Beccensis*.[20] Another of the works of the anonymous monk of Bec which appears in the same manuscript, also deals with the issue of professions. In the tract *De professionibus abbatum*, the author argues against episcopal demands for abbatial professions in general on the grounds that the profession of obedience required of a monk should be sufficient.[21] The period of fourteen months in 1136 and 1137 during which Theobald and the monks of Bec resisted what they regarded as the novel demands of the archbishop was almost certainly the period when the tracts *De professionibus* and *De libertate Beccensis* were composed. While the *De professionibus* was a direct argument against the demand for a profession, in the *De libertate* the aims of the author were slightly wider. As he states in the preface:

> I think it is worth the effort to put in writing, for those who are here now and for those who will come after us, the status and privilege with which the church of Bec has stood from its beginning. For it seems reprehensible if, through our neglecting to transcribe those events of former times, any

---

[19] For discussion, T.G. Waldman, *Hugh of Amiens, Archbishop of Canterbury* (unpublished Ph.D. thesis Oxford University, 1971), ch. 3.

[20] A. Saltman, *Theobald, Archbishop of Canterbury* (London, 1956); also J.-F. Lemarignier, *Études sur les privilèges et exemptions et la juridiction ecclésiastique des abbayes normandes depuis les origines jusqu'à 1140* (Paris, 1937), pp. 205–19.

[21] BN MS lat. 2342, ff. 159–162v.

sort of disturbance should at some time befall this church. Knowledge of the past can often be very valuable.[22]

With this task in mind, the *De libertate* not only stresses Bec's case against the archbishop's demands, but recounts the background of the abbey's exemption from homage which had come to a head with the election of Abbot Boso in 1124. At another point he recounts the ritual with which Abbot William was received as abbot at Bec in 1093, 'so that, whenever it is necessary, those who succeed us may know the correct method of performance'.[23] The text therefore stands as a kind of guide to the dos and don'ts surrounding the election and installation of a new abbot, with emphasis on the big don'ts of swearing homage to the lay ruler or swearing a profession of obedience to the archbishop of Rouen.

There is one further issue concerning the liberty of the abbey which is addressed by the *De libertate*. The text includes the tale of how Abbot Anselm in the early 1090s resisted the efforts of Robert I, count of Meulan, to establish lordship over the abbey of Bec. In doing so, the author defends Bec's tradition of independence from any one lay patron and most specifically from the lord of Brionne. In the early 1090s, Robert Curthose, duke of Normandy, granted the castle of Brionne, which had been held as a ducal castle ever since it had been taken from the rebel Guy of Burgundy in 1050, to Count Robert of Meulan, the son and heir of Roger of Beaumont. According to the *De libertate*, after taking possession of this castle, the count wished the abbey of Bec to pass into his lordship because it had been built in the fief of the castle of Brionne.[24] With this aim Count Robert approached Anselm through messengers, promising gifts to the abbey from his possessions if the abbot would consent to his proposition. Anselm replied that the abbey was not his to give but belonged rather to the duke. After the messengers left, the monks of Bec were in terror, 'as if they had heard that their whole church was to be demolished', and immediately went to the duke to obtain his support against the count's claim.[25] The duke was enraged, as were a number of the abbey's powerful benefactors at the ducal court, who swore that they would remove all of the gifts their families had made to Bec if the count of Meulan held the abbey under his lordship in

---

[22] *De libertate*, ed. Mabillon, p. 635; *Liberty of Bec*, trans. Fisher, p. 134.

[23] *De libertate*, ed. Mabillon, p. 638; *Liberty of Bec*, trans. Fisher, p. 139.

[24] *De libertate*, ed. Mabillon, p. 636; *Liberty of Bec*, trans. Fisher, p. 135.

[25] *De libertate*, ed. Mabillon, p. 636; *Liberty of Bec*, trans. Fisher, p. 135.

Context and Analysis of the De Libertate Beccensis

any way.[26] A few days later the count, unaware of the monks' action, came to Bec himself to test the abbot's feelings on the matter. The text reads:

> The monks, perceiving his arrival, confronted him at once in a high frenzy, as if he had come to pull down the place; these were, to be precise, Farman the cellarer, Eustace, Albert and Robert. Nevertheless, they asked Count Robert in a restrained tone why he had come. The latter, on his side, began to use affectionate language, in his customary manner. This had an effect of intense provocation on the monks, who, despising the sly cunning of the role he was adopting, started to give him forceful replies. While both sides strove vigorously over this matter, Father Anselm came up and, planting himself mid-way between the two parties, checked their quarrelling. Then, seated, he said among other things to the count: 'My lord count, you do not have the least power to obtain this object you are toiling for, because our lord does not desire it, nor the nobles on whose favours we live, nor, apart from this, have the authorities here and our sons the monks any kind of wish to grant it. This castle is not part of your inheritance, but the gift of your lord prince, who, at any time he wants, may take back his own property. But what need is there to fight between ourselves over this business? Find out the will of our lord and yours, and from this his judgement and orders will follow automatically.' At this Eustace stood upright and raising his right hand towards the abbey said: 'By that church, whose monks we are, if you, Father Anselm, and our lord prince, Robert, should grant your assent to this, as I hope you would not, we should all quit the place before we would allow it.' He turned to the count and with extreme firmness said to him: 'Lord Robert, by that church I swear to you, as long as I and the rest of the monks who now belong to this institution are alive, that by no method or artifice of yours shall the liberty of Bec be subservient to you.' After Eustace and the other monks had spoken at length against the count in the presence of the abbot,[27] Robert went off in a towering rage. The monks paid absolutely no heed to his anger, their hearts being completely set on keeping the liberty of their church unmolested.[28]

Soon after, the count travelled to the ducal court, but found the monks again there before him, and the duke set against his wish to bring Bec into his lordship. Not long after that the duke removed the castle of Brionne from Robert of Meulan, probably because of the powerful count's suspect

---

[26] William Crispin, William of Bréteuil, and Roger of Bienfaite are specifically named in the text.

[27] Fisher's translation is 'Father', but 'abbot' seems clearer in this context.

[28] *De libertate*, ed. Mabillon, p. 636; *Liberty of Bec*, trans. Fisher, p. 136.

loyalty, as suggested by Orderic Vitalis, rather than purely from ducal anger over his designs on Bec, and Roger of Bienfaite was installed as castellan.[29]

This episode is fascinating in many respects, but most intriguing is the question of whether it originally belonged in the *De libertate Beccensis* at all. This story is contained on a separate page written in a different hand, and the rest of the text does not require it in order to make sense. Indeed the episode stands apart in its subject from the issues surrounding the election and installation of abbots which form the basis of the main text. It is also notable that the hand of the *De libertate* insert seems to be the same hand as the copy of the *Letter of Prester John to the Emperor Manuel Comnenus* at the end of the manuscript, which suggests that the insert, unlike the main body of the text, was copied in the late twelfth century. There are several possibilities to consider when trying to determine the origins of the insert. It could have been either a new composition, or a part of some other text now lost, which was inserted into the *De libertate* by the late twelfth-century copyist. It could be that the insert was composed by the anonymous author of the *De libertate* earlier in the twelfth century as part of the original text, was deliberately left out by the first copyist of the manuscript, and later inserted as a correction. Or possibly the insert could represent the written version of a story which had survived through oral transmission at Bec, added to the text by the late twelfth-century copyist. It is conceivable that the text of the insert was borrowed from a lost text, though no evidence of such a text survives. The idea of a lost segment of the original, later added as a correction, offers interesting possibilities. The insert does deal with an incident concerning the liberty of Bec and therefore fits with the title of the work. Also, when the author in an earlier stage of the main text notes that Herluin 'never did homage to anyone for the possessions of his church, since he owned almost everything from his own father's estate', he could be foreshadowing the issue highlighted by the insert.[30]

---

[29] Orderic, *Historia Ecclesiastica*, ed. Chibnall, IV, pp. 204–11. Roger of Bienfaite, who was the grandson of Count Gilbert of Brionne, might well have posed a similar problem for the abbey, but his castellanship only lasted briefly. Shortly after the imprisonment of Robert of Meulan, Roger of Beaumont was able to successfully reconcile the duke and his son the count, and the castle of Brionne was restored to the count, though Roger of Bienfaite refused to yield it and had to be forcefully ejected in a joint expedition by Duke Robert and Robert of Meulan.

[30] *De libertate*, ed. Mabillon, p. 635; *Liberty of Bec*, trans. Fisher, p. 134.

However, in order to fit this theory with the evidence of the manuscript one would need to explain why its first copyist deliberately omitted the episode. This problem is not insurmountable. Relations between the monks of Bec and their powerful Beaumont neighbours fluctuated throughout the twelfth century. The Beaumont lords and their vassals were generous and influential patrons of Bec in the twelfth century, but their influence in the Risle valley and the Vexin, where many of Bec's possessions lay, was such as could also seem somewhat threatening. If the abbey came to be perceived as having fallen under the control of the Beaumonts, it could damage the abbey's relationships with other families of benefactors, as was made evident by the sharp reaction of the benefactors of Bec at Duke Robert's court when the count of Meulan's intentions were made known to them.[31] Yet at times during the twelfth century, when Beaumont power was at its height, it might not have seemed wise to celebrate Anselm's opposition to Robert of Meulan. The years between 1136 and 1138, when the *De libertate* was probably completed, were such a time. What might have seemed a good story to include in the early 1130s would have seemed less good after the death of Henry I in 1135, when Waleran II of Meulan, Count Robert's son, effectively became the supreme secular power in the Risle valley and throughout Upper Normandy.[32] It could be, therefore, that what initially appears to be a later insert could in fact represent the work of a later scribe making a correction to the manuscript on the basis on an earlier draft by the author, now lost. This theory, however, rests on rather too many complicated and uncertain elements.

Perhaps the most likely solution is that the story offered in the insert descended in an oral tradition at Bec as part of the community's store of anecdotes from the life of Anselm, widely regarded as Bec's greatest teacher. His conversation and stories from his life were remembered, treasured, and sometimes written down by his students.[33] One can well

---

[31] 'When they (William Crispin, William of Bréteuil, and Roger of Bienfaite) learned the facts of the case, roused to vigorous displeasure they swore loud and terrible oaths that they would remove whatever their parents had bestowed upon the church of Bec, if the count of Meulan held the monastery under his lordship in any conceivable way' (*Liberty of Bec*, trans. Fisher, pp. 135–36).

[32] D. Crouch, *The Beaumont Twins: The Roots and Branches of Power in the Twelfth Century* (Cambridge, 1986), pp. 29–38.

[33] *The Life of St Anselm Archbishop of Canterbury by Eadmer*, ed. and trans. R.W. Southern (Oxford, 1962); R.W. Southern and F.S. Schmitt, *Memorials of St Anselm* (Oxford, 1969).

imagine that this tale of how Anselm resisted the claims of the new lord of Brionne and thus saved the abbey's independence might have been passed down through several generations of monks at Bec. The insert episode itself bears indications of a background of oral transmission: dramatic conversation is heavily used, and the names of certain benefactors and monks are preserved in a rhetorical way. This would seem the most likely interpretation of the differences in style and subject between the main text and that of the insert, in view of the structure of the manuscript.

Looking at the text of the *De libertate* as a whole, we get a sense of how in the twelfth century many 'legal' cases were still being constructed on the basis of memorable events. In the eleventh century the memory of witnesses had operated as the primary safeguard for claims over lands and rights. By the thirteenth century such arguments were beginning to be resolved primarily on the basis of written authorities.[34] The efforts of the monks of Bec to commit important events in the memory of the community to writing reflects their struggle, which was shared by numerous other religious houses, to safeguard their liberties in a world where the rules of the game were changing. A comparison of the several narrative texts which survive from Bec from the early twelfth century also offers a most instructive example of how individual members of the monastic community, while sharing at least the core of a clear narrative tradition over several generations, could reshape the material towards achieving different ends.[35] If we look at the *De libertate* in conjunction with the lives of abbots William and Boso which cover many of the same events, we find no direct borrowing between the two texts and even quite different perspectives at points, yet there is clear coherency of narrative tradition with a common use of certain Bec sources, such as Anselm's correspondence.

The *De libertate* offers enormous interest as a text which illustrates some specific episodes at the abbey of Bec which formed part of the wider struggles between church and ruler over lay investitures and between abbey and archbishop, and between pope and king over monastic privileges of exemption. In addition, the insert concerning Robert of Meulan, whether

---

[34] Clanchy, *From Memory to Written Record*.

[35] Cf. A.G. Remensnyder, *Remembering Kings Past: Monastic Foundation Legends in Medieval Southern France* (Ithaca and London, 1995); D. Foote, 'Taming Monastic Advocates and Redeeming Bishops: The *Triumphale* and Episcopal *Vitae* of Reiner of St. Lawrence', *Revue d'Histoire Ecclésiastique* 91 (1996), 5–40; K. Ugé, 'Creating a Useable Past in the Tenth Century: Folcuin's *Gesta* and the Crises at Saint-Bertin', *Studi Medievali* 37 (1996), 887–903.

written in the first or second half of the twelfth century, illustrates that the monks of Bec were very aware both of the benefits which accrued from acquiring influential benefactors, and of the potential danger from powerful benefactors and neighbours who wished to infringe the abbey's liberty. Overall, the *De libertate* demonstrates how 'historical' writing was increasingly and successfully used as a tool by monastic communities faced by challenges to their liberties and privileges from neighbouring secular and ecclesiastic powers.

Part Two
Land and Kinship

Bishops as Contenders for Power in Late Anglo-Saxon England: The Bishopric of East Anglia and the Regional Aristocracy[1]

CHRISTINE SENECAL

Conceptions of the late Anglo-Saxon church, and its bishops in particular, have undergone profound changes in the last generation of scholarship. Historians used to focus on the connections between the episcopate and the king, passing over the relationship between bishops and local aristocrats as an unimportant issue.[2] This perspective, however, ignores the complex and often symbiotic relationship between secular lords and bishops, a relationship not always coloured by royal influence, and not always marked by opposition. Recent work on the bishopric of Worcester, as well as other studies, have done a great deal to change the old view, showing the often dependent and mutually beneficial connections between the regional aristocracy and bishops.[3] Bishops relied not only on the king,

---

[1] I would like to thank Robin Fleming for her generous guidance in the research and writing of this article, as well as Richard Ables, Mary Frances Smith, and Ann Williams for their valuable remarks. Any errors remaining, are, of course, the fault of the author alone.

[2] F. Barlow, *The English Church: 1000–1066* (London, 1979), p. 99. Also, E. John, 'The King and the Monks in the Tenth-Century Reformation', in idem, *Orbis Brittaniae and Other Studies* (Leicester, 1966), pp. 154–80.

[3] A.F. Wareham, 'St. Oswald's Family and Kin', in *St. Oswald of Worcester: Life and Influence*, eds. N.P. Brooks and C.R.E. Cubitt (London, 1996), pp. 46–63 for a discussion

but on the established elite for grants of land, gifts of wealth, and the enhancement of their reputations.[4] At the same time wealthy families stood to gain from their association with a bishop, using his see as a focus for their guilds, as a source of leased estates, and as a focus for patronage, giving the aristocracy an opportunity to flaunt publicly their wealth and status. On the other hand, the bishops—particularly secular bishops—did have competitors, because there was a limit to the amount lords could patronise different ecclesiastical centres. Therefore, bishops' competitors were often their monastic neighbours, who had benefited from royal support since the tenth-century reform and had threatened to overrun the secular bishops' spheres of influence. This paper demonstrates how the bishops nevertheless succeeded in establishing their power through social relationships with the aristocracy and free peasantry of the region, and compares the landholdings of the bishopric to the lordships of the great secular and ecclesiastical magnates.

The sort of give-and-take between an episcopal community and the aristocracy over generations was not unique to England in the tenth and eleventh centuries, but because of the limitations of the sources much less is known about the relationship between local landholders and bishops than between bishops and kings.[5] The sources mislead in three ways: first, the evidence preserved in the cartularies of the reform abbeys presents an overtly royal and monastic image of the exercise of power at the expense of the secular bishops; second, there was a decline in the late Anglo-Saxon period in the use of charters, often the best sources of information about local society; and third, the charters that do survive (Worcester's being the

---

of the extensive connections between the bishop of Worcester and his well-heeled family; E. Craster, 'The Patrimony of St. Cuthbert', *EHR* 69 (1954), pp. 177–99 for the interaction between a bishopric and its local secular community; A. Williams, '*Princeps Merciorum gentis*: The Family, Career and Connections of Ælfhere, Ealdorman of Mercia, 956–83', *ASE* 10 (1982), 143–72; eadem, 'The spoliation of Worcester', *ANS* 19 (1997), pp. 383–408; T. Reuter, 'Property Transactions and Social Relations between Rulers, Bishops, and Nobles in Early Eleventh-Century Saxony: The Evidence of the *Vita Meinwerci*', in *Property and Power in the Early Middle Ages*, eds. W. Davies and P. Fouracre (Cambridge, 1995), pp. 165–99.

[4] M.F. Smith, *Episcopal Landholding, Lordship and Culture in Late Anglo-Saxon England* (unpublished Ph.D. thesis Boston College, 1997).

[5] B.H. Rosenwein, *To Be the Neighbor of St. Peter: The Social Meaning of Cluny's Property, 909–1049* (Ithaca and London, 1989), for a continental perspective.

great exception) were more often royal diplomas rather than private aristocratic charters.[6] Historians must therefore turn to other sources in order to see how bishops interacted with their local neighbours. Fortunately, such a source does exist in Little Domesday Book, which preserves a wealth of information about these relationships in Norfolk and Suffolk. Little Domesday's unique depiction of lordship enables us to interpret the balance of power in East Anglia, and accordingly, how the bishop of Elmham rated in his own diocese. The relationship between the authority of the bishop and that of his aristocratic and ecclesiastical peers can be studied through the choices made by the free peasantry in giving their commendation. The loyalties of such people give some insight into the competition for men between the bishop, the earls, the lords, and the monasteries of East Anglia.

The position of the East Anglian bishopric during the tenth and mid-eleventh centuries was precarious. The Danish wars had destroyed the ancient see in North Elmham, and episcopal organization was slow to return. In the mid-tenth century Bishop Theodred of London had exercised authority in Suffolk through his control of the minster church at Hoxne, which was served by a community of canons. By the late tenth century the East Anglian see had been re-established at North Elmham, where it would stay until the 1070s, but with a relatively meagre endowment.[7] The see ranked a distant third in ecclesiastical wealth in the region after Bury St Edmund's abbey and Ely abbey.[8] Additionally, Stigand, archbishop of Canterbury, who had been the bishop of East Anglia before his brother Æthelmær received the position, had a personal patrimony far more valuable than that of his former sees.[9]

Thus, this recently refounded episcopal see, whose most important landholdings were divided between two centres (North Elmham and Hoxne) in two different shires (Norfolk and Suffolk) found itself competing with other ecclesiastical establishments for the patronage of wealthy donors, as well as establishing itself as a religious community distinct from its former bishop Stigand.[10] An additional challenge for the newly refounded see was

---

[6] N.P. Brooks, 'Anglo-Saxon Charters: The Work of the Last Twenty Years', *ASE* 3 (1974), 211–31, for difficulties working with Anglo-Saxon charters.

[7] Map 1; for the early history of the see, *VCH Suffolk*, II, 1–37; *VCH Norfolk*, II, 217–19, 315–28; and Barlow, *The English Church*, pp. 216–17.

[8] Table 1.

[9] M.F. Smith, 'Archbishop Stigand and the Eye of the Needle', *ANS* 16 (1994), 199–219.

[10] Map 2.

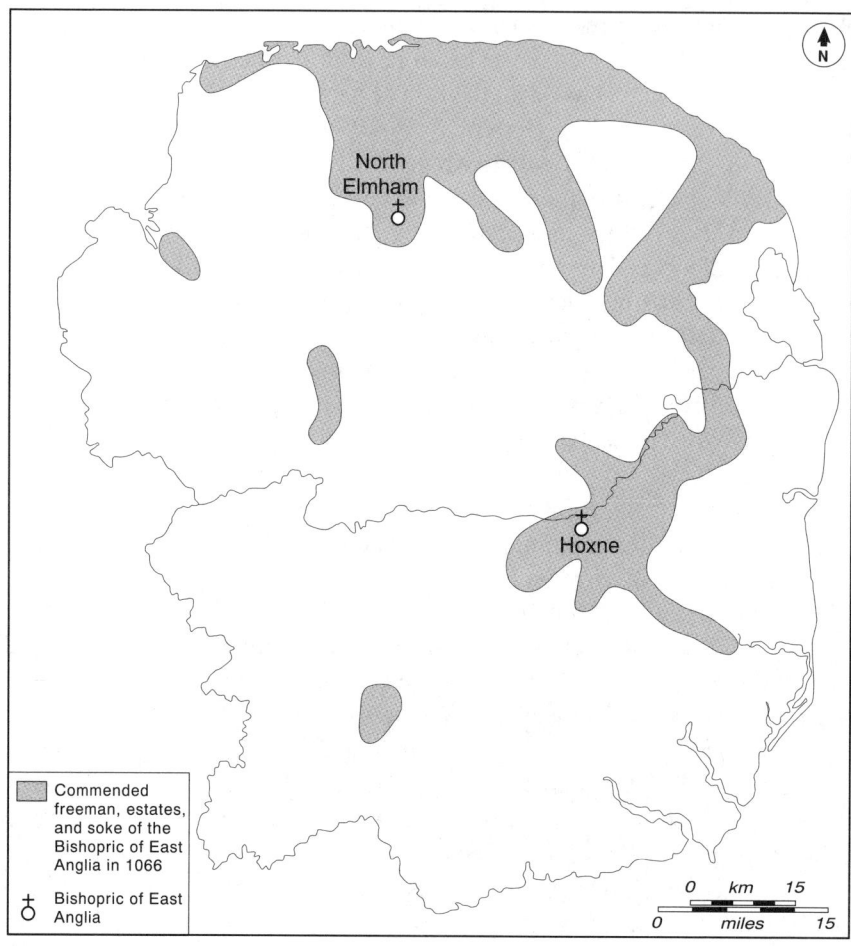

Map 1: The Commended Freeman, Estates and Soke of the Bishopric of East Anglia in 1066

The Bishopric of East Anglia and the Regional Aristocracy

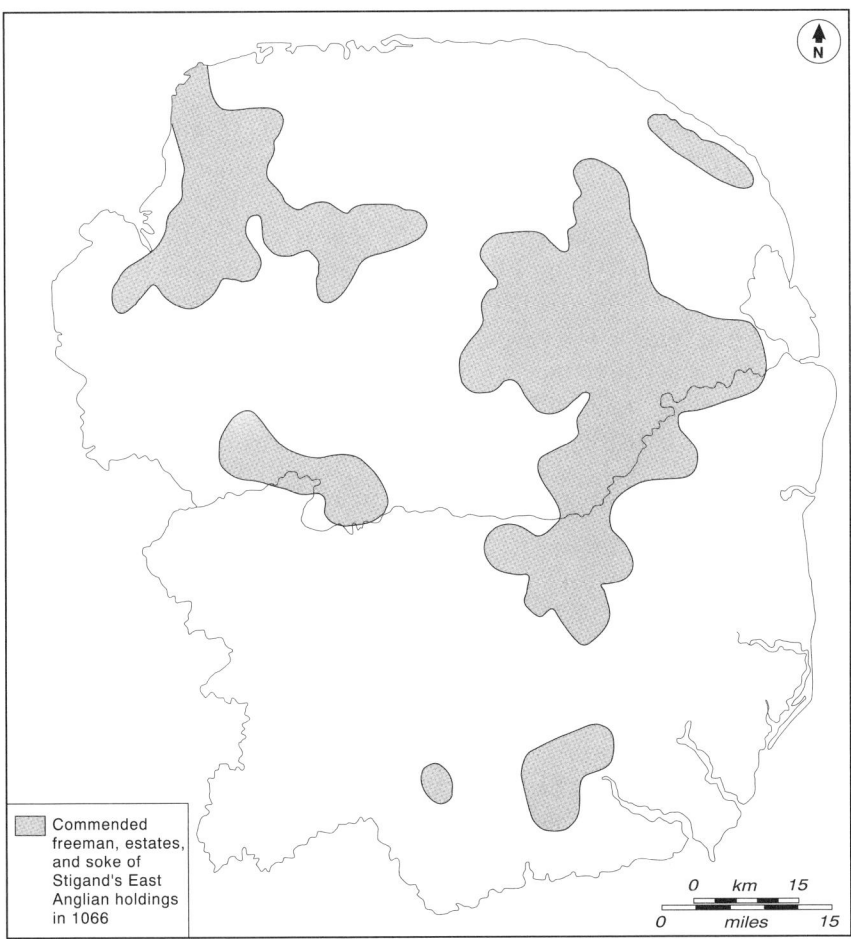

Map 2: The Commended Freeman, Estates and Soke of the Archbishop Stigand's Anglian Holdings in 1066

that it could not offer its clients the prestige provided by the reformed Benedictine monasteries. The reformed communities were known to have royal favour, and therefore to patronize a monastic centre was to be in accordance with royal taste. In the early 1040s the thegn Ælfric Modercope appointed Bishop Ælfric of East Anglia as the executor of his will, and divided his religious donations between the bishopric and local monasteries.[11] Gifts of land passed to the abbeys of Ramsey (Huntingdonshire), St Benet's (Norfolk), Ely (Cambridgeshire) and Bury St Edmund's (Suffolk), while Modercope left his tent and his best bedclothes to Bishop Ælfric. Tents were left to favoured heirs in Anglo-Saxon wills, and were used for housing saints' bones after exhumation.[12] Ælfric's heriot places him in the middle rank of the aristocracy, and his gift demonstrates the strong bonds with Bishop Ælfric.[13] Similar connections may have contributed to the slow increase in the patrimonial wealth of the bishopric, and indeed the see seems to have emerged from the Norman Conquest better than some of its local monastic competitors.[14] The ability of the bishops to prosper during a turbulent political age and to weather the storm of the Conquest was connected to their attention to local power, and stemmed from cultivating connections with both the aristocracy and the free peasantry, known as freemen.

Freemen stood in the middle rank of English society, and can be compared to *cnihts* in the West Midlands who carried out administrative and escort duties for the bishop of Worcester. The line between the more prosperous freemen and the lesser thegns, however, is more difficult to draw, and the services of freemen, *cnihts*, and middling thegns are often indistinguishable.[15] The obligations placed upon a freeman arose from a

---

[11] *Anglo-Saxon Wills*, ed. Whitelock, no. 28. In late Anglo-Saxon England high-status landholders, from earls' sons to relatively modest local landholders, were referred to as thegns.

[12] *Anglo-Saxon Wills*, ed. Whitelock, no. 3, for Wynflæd leaving Ælfwold a red tent.

[13] *Anglo-Saxon Wills*, ed. Whitelock, no. 28; N.P. Brooks, 'Arms, Status and Warfare in Late-Saxon England', in *Ethelred the Unready: Papers from the Millenary Conference*, ed. D. Hill, BAR, British ser. 59 (1978), pp. 81–103. Brooks discusses how heriots were paid to rulers after the deaths of landholders.

[14] Acquisition of estates by the bishop of East Anglia c. 1066–86, *DB*, II, ff. 194a-b, 195a, 199a, 201b; losses of St Benet's, ibid., ff. 146b, 150a, 194b, 244a, 248a-b, 251a, 259b, 264b; but the abbey also gained land, ibid., f. 217a-b.

[15] F.W. Maitland, *Domesday Book and Beyond. Three Essays in the Early History of England* (Cambridge, 1987; first edition 1897), pp. 23–25, 36–37, 66–79; J.B. Gillingham, 'Thegns and Knights in Eleventh-Century England: Who Was Then the

series of personal and tenurial relationships that he had with several lords.[16] The most onerous bond was the tenurial relationship involving the payment of rent, and the restriction that freemen could not sell their land to whomever they wished. A second obligation was when freemen were in the soke of one lord, but the ownership of the land was under the control of another lord.[17] Third, the most 'slender personal bond' was that of personal obligation, referred to in Domesday as 'simple commendation' ('tantum commendatio').[18] A freeman lived under one or more of these obligations, but the most powerful freemen were bound only by the personal ties of simple commendation, which allowed them to select lords for themselves.[19] Unlike continental homage, commendation did not necessarily imply land in exchange for services, nor did it connote that one was obligated to submit to a single lord. An example of the 'polygamous' nature of these relationships can be seen at Bastwick (Norfolk), where one freeman was commended only to Bishop Æthelmær, and another was half commended to the freeman and half to the bishop.[20]

Commendation did little to restrict freemen's freedom and actually served to give them status and protection, advantages which Maitland called 'extra-legal': 'What the man has sought by his submission is *defensio, tuitio*; the lord is his *defensor, tutor, protector, advocatus*, in a word, his warrantor.'[21] This protection could manifest itself when the lord vouched for his freeman in the local courts, leased him lands, or provided necessities.[22] The lord, of course, demanded a price in exchange, often requiring the freeman to give him land

---

Gentleman?', *TRHS*, 6th ser. 5 (1995), 129–53 at pp. 138–39. *DB*, II, f. 421a, Alti and Ketil were 'freemen [and] thegns'; below, n. 36.

[16] For ease of reading this article uses the term freemen also to describe sokemen.

[17] Soke here refers to legal jurisdiction.

[18] For a debate on commendation, Maitland, *Domesday Book and Beyond*, pp. 66–79; C. Stephenson, 'Commendation and Related Problems in Domesday', *EHR* 59 (1944), 289–310; and B. Dodwell, 'East Anglian Commendation', *EHR* 63 (1948), 289–306. The present author agrees with Dodwell and Maitland, who argue that commendation was a personal bond based on lordship rather than tenure.

[19] Dodwell, 'East Anglian Commendation', p. 306: 'we may thus conclude that commendation alone was but a slender personal bond [...]. Where it was still entirely personal it was not essentially permanent, for it could be broken at will.'

[20] *DB*, II, f. 201a.

[21] Maitland, *Domesday Book and Beyond*, pp. 70–71.

[22] For a discussion of these issues, R. Fleming, *Domesday Book and the Law: Society and Legal Custom in Early Medieval England* (Cambridge, 1998), F [Domesday legal text cited by Fleming [F] and text number] 3038, F 102, F 665, F 2946, F 2937, F 72.

upon the man's death, but the lord could also collect customs or rents, and collected fines if his man was killed.[23] An example of how this system of mutual back-scratching operated can be seen by turning once again to Ælfric Modercope. He was given permission by the king to bow down to two lords, the abbot of Bury St Edmund's and the abbot of Ely.[24] The fact that Ælfric also endowed these two monasteries in his will further demonstrates that his commendation was not forced, but was something from which he benefited: perhaps donating land was the price of protection. Another example can be seen in the case of the freeman Brungar. When some people in Suffolk accused this freeman of stealing horses, his lord went to the local assembly and discussed the case with the abbot of Bury St Edmund's, who had soke over the accused man. The two lords together settled the case and they left the assembly 'in a friendly manner'. Brungar, however, paid a high price for this defense: Little Domesday records that before the Conquest, his lord was holding the horse-thief's land.[25]

Freemen who were able to choose their lords made sure that their commendation was spread among patrons who gave them the most protection, and therefore avoided doubling up with similar patrons. For instance, if a man wanted the protection of a local wealthy family, he apparently only needed to submit himself to one member of the family—or so the evidence of Domesday suggests. For instance, the family of Ketil had freemen scattered throughout their estates. Nonetheless, among the relatives none shared the commendation of the same freemen.[26] In a more significant example, even though Archbishop Stigand and his brother Bishop Æthelmær of East Anglia were each lords of hundreds of men, they did not split the commendation of a single freeman.[27] This pattern does then

---

[23] Fleming, *Domesday Book and the Law*, F 3038, F 2545, F 686, F 2163, F 2659.

[24] *Anglo-Saxon Writs*, ed. Harmer, no. 21; *Anglo-Saxon Wills*, ed. Whitelock, no. 28.

[25] *DB*, II, ff. 401b, 402a; R. Ables, 'Sheriffs, Lord-Seeking and the Norman Settlement', *ANS* 19 (1996), 19–49.

[26] R. Fleming, *Kings and Lords in Conquest England* (Cambridge, 1991), pp. 141–43.

[27] In several instances, however (*DB*, II, ff. 191b, 197b, 310b, 438a) Stigand had the men commended to him, and the soke was the bishop's, or vice versa; or Stigand and his brother held their own freemen, but in the same place (*DB*, II, ff. 380a, 380b, 438a); and upon occasion a freeman was held under Stigand or was commended to him but lived on the holding of Bishop Æthelmær (*DB*, II, ff. 175b, 379b). In none of these instances, however, are the brothers sharing the commendation of the same man. The key distinction was that a freeman did not have to commend himself to the lord to whom he owed soke. R. Ables, 'An Introduction to the Bedfordshire Domesday', in *The Bedfordshire Domesday*, eds. A. Williams and G. Martin (London, 1991), p. 29.

suggest that one reason a man might wish to commend himself was for the very specific protection by a family, and that to accomplish this, one only needed to commend oneself to a single member of that kindred. Interestingly, the freemen of East Anglia did not consider commending themselves to two ecclesiastical lords as 'doubling up' their protection, and those who commended themselves to the bishop were as likely to split their commendation with a secular as with an ecclesiastical lord.[28]

In fact, raw numbers alone do not convey the struggle for local authority in East Anglia. To see this dynamic, an examination of the geographical position of commended freemen is needed. When the estates of the ecclesiastical centres in East Anglia and their commended freemen are viewed, it is obvious that the freemen of the bishop were centred in areas where they were far from monastic communities.[29] Thus in Suffolk, the bishop's freemen and landholdings were in the east, away from Bury St Edmund's, the wealthiest ecclesiastical centre in East Anglia, and a great lord of freemen.[30] The inability of the bishop to make inroads into the monks' spheres of control is striking, and shows how effectively the monastic communities had monopolized lordship in the areas under their influence. The freemen themselves determined this arrangement in part, realizing that the abbots' authority in these 'monastic zones' made their choice of lords obvious, for the monks were the most powerful voice of authority there. This can be seen across East Anglia. In the Norfolk hundred of Clackclose, for example, where the abbeys of Bury St Edmund's, St Benet's and Ely had little land but many freemen, the East Anglian see had no freemen, soke, or land at all.[31] The bishop had been unable to make inroads into those localities.

On the other hand, freemen did not hesitate to commend themselves to the bishop in areas where the wealthiest secular landholders, not the monks, held land. Thus, freemen only selected the bishop as their lord when their lands lay outside the areas which the monastic establishments controlled.

---

[28] Table 2.

[29] This study does not take into account the holdings of Ramsey abbey, which was located in Huntingdonshire. The abbey had estates in Norfolk and Suffolk, only valued at about £40.

[30] Map 3.

[31] The term hundred refers to the primary subdivision of the late Anglo-Saxon shire. The only non-ecclesiastical landholders of significance in the hundred were Thorketil and Toli, freemen who held over £10. *DB*, II, ff. 135a, 136a, 148a, 149a, 159b, 160a, 190a-b, 205b, 206a-b, 209a, 212b, 213a, 215a-b, 230a-b, 231a-b, 250b, 251a-b, 273b, 274a-b, 275a-b, 276a.

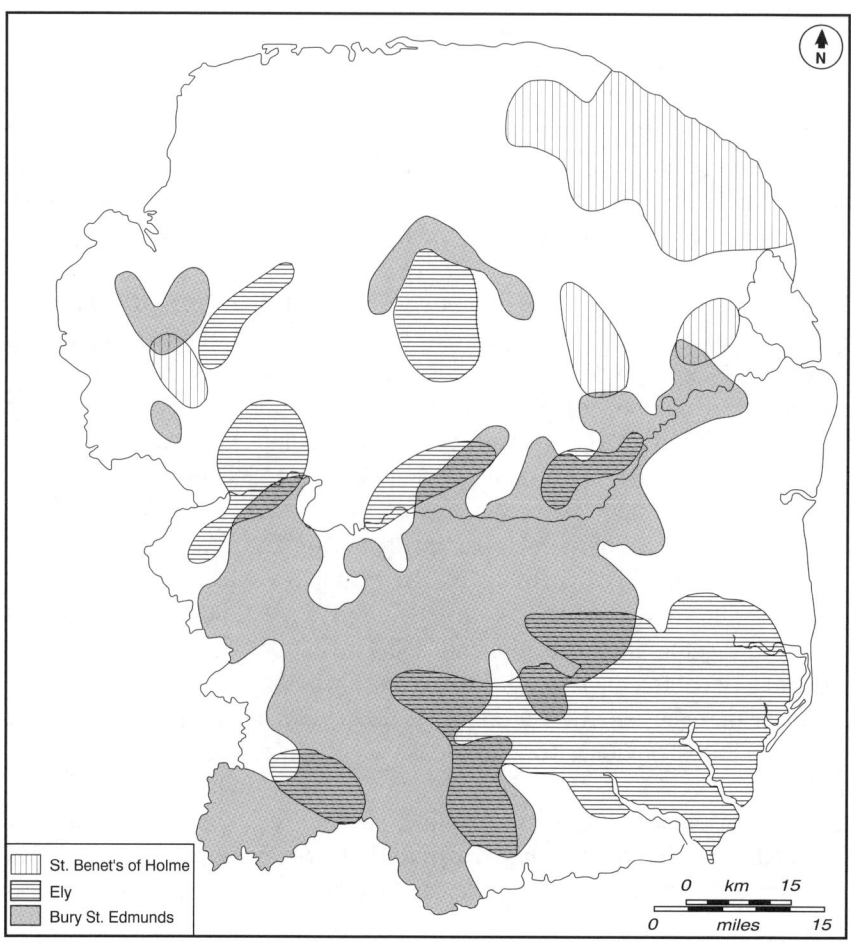

Map 3: The Commended Freeman, Estates, and Soke of East Anglia's Monastic Communities in 1066

The Bishopric of East Anglia and the Regional Aristocracy 99

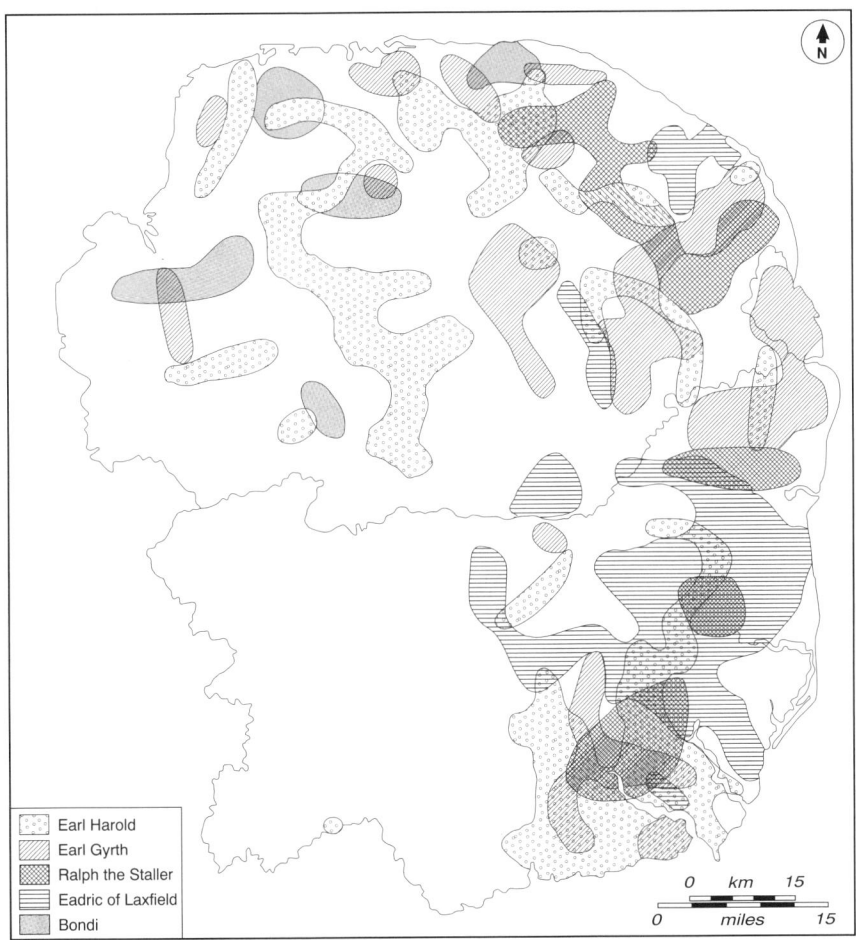

Map 4: The Commended Freeman, Estates, and Soke of the Wealthiest Aristocrats in East Anglia in 1066

For example, in the Norfolk hundred of Launditch, which included the site of the episcopal church, Stigand's freemen and Earl Harold Godwineson were the only other important landholders.[32] Given the tight grip that monastic centres had upon so much of Norfolk and Suffolk, it is not very surprising that the bishop looked for allies wherever he could find them, and therefore often formed relationships with the most important secular landholders in East Anglia. These lords—the earls Harold and Gyrth, Ralph the staller, Eadric of Laxfield—held in areas close to the bishop's land, and the bishop split soke, freemen, and/or commendation with all of these aristocrats.[33]

Indeed, when the commendation, soke, and freemen of these secular lords are compared with the bishops', a large overlapping of spheres of influence can be seen.[34] These lords and the bishop were able to compete for lordship and develop friendships only in these areas, because both had to contend with the areas tightly under control by the monastic communities. The bishop's friendships with his thegnly neighbours can be seen in the instances in which the bishop divided his lesser freemen—not his freemen in commendation, but the ones who had no say in their choice of lords. He only did so among secular neighbours, such as Earl Harold, and never among his monastic competitors.[35] The bishop's connections with the local aristocracy worked to his advantage, sometimes resulting in the acquisition of lands. Before 1066, the thegn Anand held an estate at Langley (Norfolk) with Bishop Æthelmær.[36] They were *socii* or fellows, a term which here denotes a partnership based on friendship rather than blood.[37] After Anand died, Æthelmær inherited his land. More important than the individual instances of the ways the bishop exploited his thegnly friendships, however, is the fact that the bishop and the established elite

---

[32] No one besides Stigand, Harold and Bishop Æthelmær held over £15 in the entire hundred. *DB*, II, ff. 120b, 138a, 140b, 144b, 165a-b, 166a, 178b, 179a, 197b, 121a, 136a-b, 137a, 191b, 207b, 209b, 214a, 226b, 227a, 232b, 235b, 236a, 239a, 252b, 256b, 257a, 264a, 274b, 275a.

[33] Table 2.

[34] Map 4.

[35] Table 2.

[36] *DB*, II, ff. 195b, 196a; Anand was described as a freeman, but as he held his land directly from King Edward, and had estates valued at £7, he can be regarded as a thegn. *DB*, II, ff. 152a, 195b, 196a.

[37] R.E. Latham, *Revised Medieval Latin Word-List from British and Irish Sources with Supplement* (Oxford, 1965), s.v.

formed a buffer against the monastic centres where they could build their lordships.

Not all interactions between the bishop and the thegns ran smoothly, of course. Æthelmær's competition with Eadric of Laxfield, one of the wealthiest landholders in East Anglia, demonstrates this point. Eadric only held freemen in common with the bishopric in Bishop's Hundred in Suffolk, which was, as the name indicates, one of the most important areas for the see. The fact that neither Eadric nor the bishop shared men, soke, or estates outside of this small area is interesting, and perhaps suggests that Eadric was making inroads into the bishop's authority there. Furthermore, in the estate of Chippenhall in Bishop's Hundred, the bishop split the soke of nine men with Eadric, which is unusual, considering that the whole hundred was dominated by the see.[38]

There were also exceptions to the general exclusivity of the monastic areas of control. Monastic centres differed in their ability to attract freemen. Bury St Edmund's had the most impermeable territory, and in fact, the only secular lord of kingdom-wide importance holding a significant amount in the abbey's areas of influence was King Edward himself.[39] On the other hand, St Benet's of Holme did have occasional intruders into its spheres of control. Eadric of Laxfield once again played the aggressor, having land and freemen commended to him on several locations where St Benet's territories lay. On the other hand, Ralph the staller cultivated genial relations with the abbey. In fact, evidence suggests that St Benet's was the most important recipient of Ralph's pious benefactions, with the staller granting soke, land, and freemen to the abbey.[40]

The overall status of the see of Elmham on the eve of the Conquest was relatively good. Even though the bishop was only able to cultivate lordship in areas away from those monopolized by the monastic centres, considering his see's relatively recent refoundation, he was able to attract many men into his sphere of influence. This is shown by comparing the number of

---

[38] *DB*, II, f. 329. Further evidence for Eadric's encroachment on the bishop's lordship can be found in *DB*, II, ff. 319b, 320a, where, on the estate of Eye (Suffolk), Eadric is recorded as having soke over the men of the bishopric on that estate, 'that is, [the soke which] the bishop should have had'. Eadric's encroachment is all the more apparent when it is realized that Eye was among the thegn's largest estates (valued at £15).

[39] Map 3; royal demesne in Norfolk and Suffolk was valued at £160 (Fleming, *Kings and Lords*, pp. 68–69). Within the ten hundreds most dominated by Bury, the king held only about £35 and only Wihtgar Algarson and Siward of Maldon held over £40.

[40] *DB*, II, ff. 134 a-b, 217b-218a, 158a, 229b, 158b, 217b, 229b.

freemen commended to lords in East Anglia with the value of these same lords' East Anglian holdings. All things being equal, the ratio of commended freemen to estate values should be the same from lord to lord if no lord was particularly sought after.[41] But, since not all lords could offer their freemen equal protection in the neighbourhood and local courts, the ratios are not equal. Of the major landholders, the monastic centres had the highest ratio of commended men to land. Even though the bishop did relatively well, with a ratio of 1.3 commended freemen to each £1 of demesne, he could not compete with the monastic centres or the earls. Stigand's ratio of commended freemen to estate value is especially low— 0.7 men to each £1 of land—probably because the archbishop spent most of his time in Canterbury, Winchester and at the royal court. The freemen knew they wanted allies who could consistently back them up in the local court. Thus, the fact that Bishop Æthelmær did relatively well in attracting freemen's commendation in areas outside the spheres of influence of the monastic communities shows that freemen did consider him to be a good local lord—one who could more easily give favours than his more powerful brother.[42]

In assessing the dynamics for control over the hearts and minds of the men of Norfolk and Suffolk, it perhaps makes most sense to view the bishop as a part of the local aristocratic network: he held in the same places as important secular lords and was allied with the most powerful thegns in East Anglia; yet, like the secular aristocrats, he was unable to attract freemen in territories dominated by the monastic centres. The most important example of how the bishop's interests were inextricably connected to the local aristocracy is the fact that the last Anglo-Saxon bishop of the see, Æthelmær, was the brother of Stigand, whose family dominated the region.[43] The fact that Archbishop Stigand invested his own personal wealth in the see, both before and after his time as bishop there, made the bishopric successful. For example, with dubious legality, Stigand took the valuable estate of Hemsby in Norfolk (valued at £26) away from a thegn and gave it to his brother Æthelmær for the see.[44]

---

[41] Table 1.

[42] For correlation between status of freemen and lords, Ables, 'Sheriffs, Lord-Seeking and the Norman Settlement', pp. 30–31.

[43] Smith, 'Archbishop Stigand', p. 206: '[documents] suggest a very uneasy relationship of long duration between the abbey and the diocesan bishopric, a situation apparently exacerbated by Stigand and his family.'

[44] *DB*, II, f. 195a.

Little Domesday's unusual recordings of commendation and freemen depict the balance of power in East Anglia in a way unlike any other sources from this period. Nowhere else are the complex patterns of lordship on a local scale so plentiful, and therefore nowhere else can we see how much the bishop's ability to be sought out as a lord governed so much of his authority in the region. Unfortunately, Little Domesday is the only source that describes these kinds of relationships to such a great extent, but surely had we comparable information regarding other shires it is likely that we would see similar patterns.

Table 1: *Ratio of Instances of Commendation to Value of Important Landholders' East Anglian Estates*[45]

Landholder	Value of land in East Anglia[46]	Instances of commendation	Ratio of men to land
Bury St Edmund's	£360	1,100	3.1
Stigand	290	190	0.7
Ely	220	610	2.8
Eadric of Laxfield	200	400+[47]	2.0+
Bishop Æthelmær	180	240	1.3
Earl Gyrth	100	110	1.1
Earl Harold	90	170	1.9
St Benet's of Holme	90	100	1.1
Ralph the staller	50	40	0.8

---

[45] Figures for Domesday estate values and instances of commendation are approximate.

[46] This author's totals for the estate values of Bury St Edmund's and Ely differ considerably from those of D. Knowles, *The Monastic Order in England: A History of Its Development from the Times of St. Dunstan to the Fourth Lateran Council 943–1216* (Cambridge, 1940), p. 102.

[47] It is impossible to assess the correct number of instances of commendation for Eadric of Laxfield, due to the fact that several individuals called Eadric lived in East Anglia in 1066. The figure here is given by K. Mack, 'The Stallers: Administrative Innovation in the Reign of Edward the Confessor', *Journal of Medieval History* 12 (1986), p. 132.

Table 2: Assets Shared by the bishop of East Anglia and Other Landholders[48]

Where	What was shared	How it was divided	Who shared
Bradfield	1 freeman	cmd bishop, soke B.S.E.	Æthelmær and B.S.E.
Welnetham	1 freeman	cmd bishop, soke B.S.E.	Æthelmær and B.S.E.
Stanningfield	1 freeman	cmd bishop, soke B.S.E.	Æthelmær and B.S.E.
Chippenhall	soke	½ bishop, ½ Eadric of Laxfield	Æthelmær and Eadric of Laxfield
Syleham	1 freeman	Stigand's freeman, held by bishop	Æthelmær and Stigand
Barsham	1 freeman-*commendation*	½ bishop, ½ Earl Gyrth and Ælfric	Æthelmær and Gyrth/Ælfric
Thurleston	1 freeman-*commendation*	½ bishop, ½ Ælfric father of Wihtgar	Æthelmær and Ælfric father of Wihtgar
Whitlingham	1 freewoman	bishop's property, held under Stigand	Æthelmær and Stigand
Wickmere	2 freemen	held by bishop and Harold	Æthelmær and Harold
North Elmham	24 freemen	bishop's men, Stigand's soke	Æthelmær and Stigand
Langley	estate	held together as *socii*	Æthelmær and Anand
Scratby	1 freeman	bishop held, cmd Abbot of Holme	Æthelmær and St Benet's of Holme
Hemblington	1 freeman	bishop had cmd, soke and held by Ralph the staller	Æthelmær and Ralph the staller
Brundall	1 freeman	cmd bishop, soke Ralph the staller	Æthelmær and Ralph the staller
Rollesby	1 freeman-*commendation*	cmd split	Æthelmær and St Benet's of Holme
Billockby	1 freeman-*commendation*	split cmd, on St Benet's of Holme's estate	Æthelmær and St Benet's of Holme

[48] cmd = commendation; B.S.E. = Bury St Edmund's.

Mintlyn	15 freemen	bishop had cmd, Stigand had soke	Æthelmær and Stigand
Chickering	1 freewoman	soke bishop's, cmd Eadric of Laxfield	Æthelmær and Eadric of Laxfield
Horham	2 freemen	soke is bishop's, but 1 is Stigand's, 1 is Eadric of Laxfield's	Æthelmær, Stigand and Eadric of Laxfield

Two Models of Marriage: Kinship and the Social Order in England and Normandy[1]

ANDREW WAREHAM

In early eleventh-century Normandy aristocratic rebellion was punishable by exile and forfeiture, and in England by execution and mutilation, but following the unification of the Norman duchy and the English kingdom there was a more tolerant attitude towards the punishment of traitors on both sides of the Channel.[2] Nevertheless, the *Leges Willelmi* set out blinding and castration as punishment for rebellion, and King William I 'was not misled by carnal affection to spare the crimes of his blood-relatives'.[3] Kings William II and Henry I punished their cousins to the letter of the *Leges Willelmi*, and under Henry I 'the guilty could not gain release through kinship'.[4] The

---

[1] Publication of this paper has been made possible by a grant from the Scoulouldi Foundation in association with the Institute of Historical Research. The Early Medieval Seminar at the IHR provided helpful comments, and I am grateful to the convenors. On terminology, endogamy is marriage to a relative within the prohibited degrees of kinship determined by ecclesiastical law, and exogamy is the marriage to a man or woman with whom no kinship bonds are shared or recognized.

[2] W. Stubbs, *The Constitutional History of England in its Origin and Development* (Oxford, 1874), pp. 292–95 raises the issue of the comparatively harsh punishment of royal kinsmen in the Anglo-Norman period; for a more recent view of such issues, J.B. Gillingham, '1066 and the Introduction of Chivalry into England', in *Law and Government in Medieval England and Normandy: Essays in Honour of Sir James Holt*, eds. G. Garnett and J. Hudson (Cambridge, 1994), pp. 31–55.

[3] *Gesetze der Angelsachsen*, ed. F. Liebermann (Halle, 1903), I, 488; William of Poitiers, *Histoire de Guillaume le Conquérant*, ed. and trans. R. de Foreville (Paris, 1952), p. 128.

[4] Below n. 95; Orderic, *Ecclesiastical History*, ed. Chibnall, VI, 18.

circumstances under which harsh or lenient punishments were inflicted for noble rebellion had a close bond with marriage and kinship, but the exact nature of that relationship remains unclear. Historians, however, have been interested in medieval marriage and kinship principally because of a perceived conflict between secular and ecclesiastical models of marriage. When nobles married their kinswomen they were held to have defied the church's teachings, and challenged its control of land and wealth.[5] This article explores the interaction between kinship, power, and punishment from the perspective of three noble families, and considers ecclesiastical responses to contrasting marriage strategies. The kindred of Ealdorman Uhtred, and the families of William FitzOsbern and Ralph of Tosny arranged a series of marriage alliances with aristocratic and ruling families in the eleventh century, but in 1075 the heirs of Uhtred and FitzOsbern were punished in contrasting manners for their rebellion against their royal kinsman.

Exogamy in Northumbria c. 996–1066

De obsessione, a text written by a Durham cleric c. 1075–1125, describes Ealdorman Uhtred of Northumbria's struggle against Viking and Scottish attacks from his power base at Bamburgh, and records the recovery of six of the bishopric of Durham's villages, which were used by his kinswomen as dowry gifts.[6] The text permits an analysis of the role of marriage, kinship, and feud in sustaining his family's power. Ealdorman Uhtred's first marriage was to Ecgfrida, daughter of Bishop Ealdhun of Durham, c. 996–1006. Her father gave the six villages in the Tees valley as dowry to Uhtred, but the marriage agreement stipulated that the land was to revert to the bishopric in the event of the couple's separation. Uhtred's second marriage to Sige, daughter of Styr of York, was connected with his appointment to rule over Yorkshire from c. 1006, and his third marriage to

---

[5] G. Duby, *Medieval Marriage: Two Models from Twelfth-Century France*, trans. F. Forster (London, 1991); J. Goody, *The Development of the Family and Marriage in Europe* (Cambridge, 1983).

[6] Symeon of Durham, *De obsessione Dunelmi, et de probitate Uchtedi comitis, et de comitibus qui ei successerunt*, in *Symeonis Monachi Opera Omnia*, ed. T. Arnold, 2 vols. (London, 1882), I, 215–20; *The Early Charters of Northern England and the North Midlands*, ed. C.R. Hart (Leicester, 1975), pp. 146–50; C.J. Morris, *Marriage and Murder in Eleventh-Century Northumbria: A Study of De Obsessione*, University of York, Borthwick Institute Paper no. 82 (York, 1992), pp. 1–5. *De obsessione* is the source unless otherwise stated for the history of Ealdorman Uhtred's family c. 996–1072.

King Æthelred II's daughter Ælfgifu almost certainly coincided with his presence at the royal court c. 1009–15.[7] Each marriage brought Uhtred practical benefits, marking a steady expansion of his power southwards.

De obsessione, however, suggests that the second and third unions were to lead to Uhtred's death: it records that when he married Sige he promised to kill Thurbrand Hold, her father's principal enemy, and that in 1014 Uhtred refused Cnut's request to betray King Æthelred because he owed his lands and office to his father-in-law. *De obsessione* claims that in 1016, when Uhtred was at Cnut's court under safe conduct, he was killed at the instigation of Thurbrand Hold. The *Anglo-Saxon Chronicle*, however, records a different series of events: Ealdorman Uhtred had defected to Sweyn of Denmark as early as 1013, and joined Cnut before the death of King Æthelred in 1016.[8] The various versions of the *Anglo-Saxon Chronicle* dealing with the early eleventh century were compiled in southern England and the Midlands, providing an unsympathetic account of Ealdorman Uhtred's actions.[9] He may not have been actually bound by obligations of loyalty arising from exogamous marriages, but that was how his death was portrayed in the Durham tradition.

Ecgfrida, daughter of Bishop Ealdhun, took as her second husband the Yorkshire noble, Kilvert son of Ligulf. Serial exogamy provided Uhtred's eldest son Ealdred with a network of political influence. Through the second marriages of both his father and mother, Ealdred had links with two important Yorkshire families. His daughter Æthelthryth married the powerful Yorkshire lord of Kirkdale, Orm son of Gamel.[10] As a result of these connections Ealdred, who ruled over the Bamburgh region, was able to resist the authority of Cnut's military commander, Earl Erik, who had been granted authority over all of northern England in 1016.[11] From 1024 Erik ceases to appear in charter witness lists, and after 1030, when

---

[7] *Anglo-Saxon Charters: An Annotated List and Bibliography*, ed. P.H. Sawyer (London, 1968), nos. 921–22, 926, 931, 933–34.

[8] *The Anglo-Saxon Chronicle*, eds. Whitelock et al., pp. 92, 95.

[9] *The Anglo-Saxon Chronicle: A Collaborative Edition: MS D*, ed. G.P. Cubbin (Cambridge, 1996), p. lxviii, for Worcester replacing York as the dominant influence upon the D manuscript in the eleventh century.

[10] Orm built Kirkdale church c. 1055–65, E. Okasha, *Handbook of Anglo-Saxon Non-Runic Inscriptions* (Cambridge, 1971), no. 64.

[11] *The Anglo-Saxon Chronicle*, eds. Whitelock et al., p. 95; *Encomium Emmae reginae*, ed. A. Campbell (London, 1949), p. 22; Symeon of Durham, *Historia regum*, in *Symeonis Monachi Opera Omnia*, ed. T. Arnold, 2 vols. (London, 1885), II, 197.

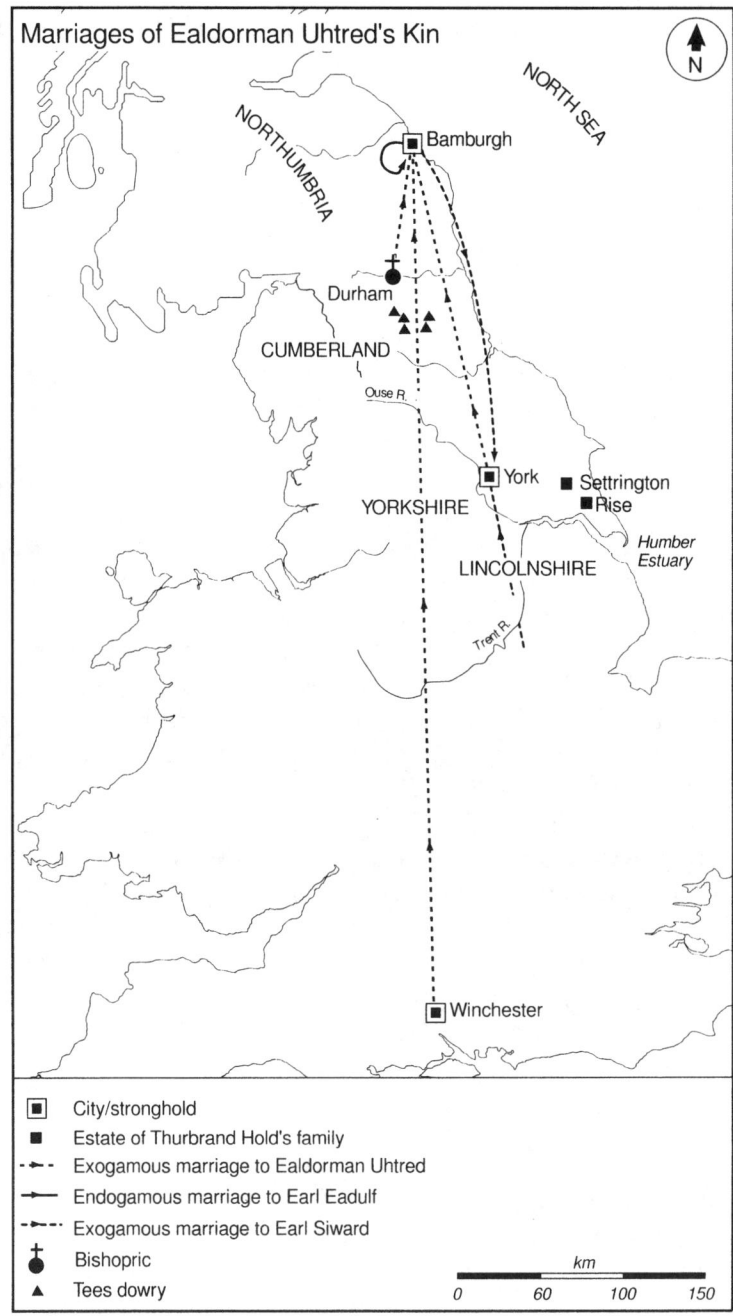

Map 1: Marriages of Ealdorman Uhtred's Kin

Table 1: Ealdorman Uhtred's Family and Kin

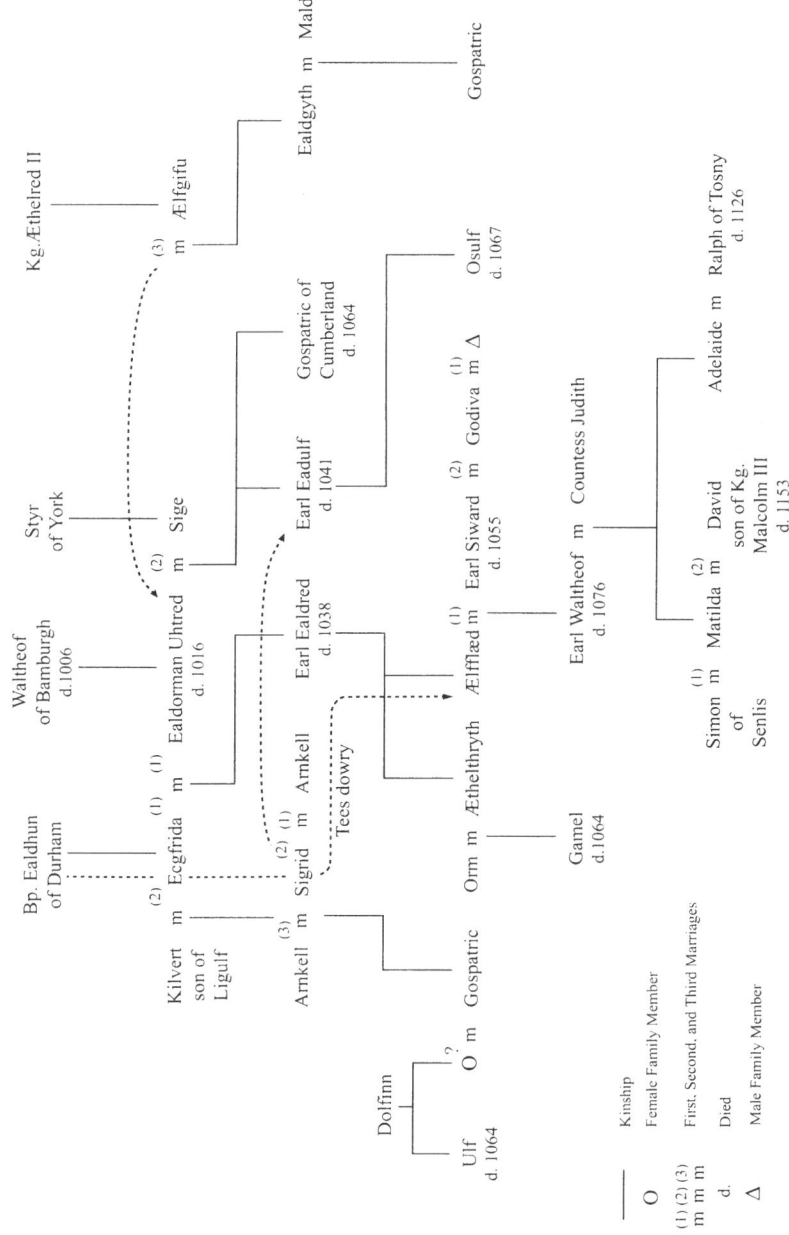

his son Hákon drowned, Earl Ealdred was safe from the threat posed by that family.[12] The influence that Ealdred wielded as a result of three sets of marriage ties, via his father, mother, and daughter, with prominent Yorkshire families perhaps enabled him to revenge his father's death by killing Thurbrand Hold, whose family was based in Holderness in south-east Yorkshire.

Ealdred's half-sister Sigrid married on three occasions; her first and third marriages were unions with other northern families not identified as kin, but her second marriage was to her other half-brother, Eadulf. This endogamous union was probably arranged after Eadulf succeeded Earl Ealdred (d. 1038). Earl Eadulf, however, was murdered on the orders of King Cnut in 1041, and his successor Earl Siward of Yorkshire married Ealdred's daughter, Ælfflæd.[13] Her dowry comprised the six Tees villages claimed from the bishopric of Durham by hereditary right through her grandmother Ecgfrida. In the 990s the six Tees villages passed successively to Ecgfrida's husbands, but then reverted to the bishopric of Durham, before being used in the mid-eleventh century as the marriage portions of Ecgfrida's daughter, Sigrid, and her granddaughter, Ælfflæd.[14] Serial exogamy provided lords with temporary control over extensive estates in the border region between Northumbria and Yorkshire, but those estates were not integrated into their patrimonies.

Earl Siward also served as earl of Northampton, and was married to Godiva, a wealthy Northamptonshire landowner.[15] He received a life grant over five of the thirty-five hides in the East Midlands which Godiva had granted to Peterborough abbey before their marriage.[16] Shortly after Siward's death in 1055 the monks of Peterborough abbey regained those five hides. Marriage provided Siward with temporary control over estates to the north and south of his own power base at York, but the rights of

---

[12] *Anglo-Saxon Charters*, ed. Sawyer, nos. 951, 953–56, 958–60; *The Chronicle of John of Worcester*, eds. and trans. P. McGurk et al. (Oxford, 1995), p. 511; *The Anglo-Saxon Chronicle*, eds. Whitelock et al., p. 101.

[13] *The Anglo-Saxon Chronicle*, eds. Whitelock et al., p. 106; Symeon of Durham, *Historia regum*, ed. Arnold, II, 198.

[14] Those estates eventually passed to the third husband of Sigrid, widow of Earl Eadulf, rather than to the son of Siward and Ælfflæd.

[15] *The Early Charters of Eastern England*, ed. C.R. Hart (Leicester, 1966), pp. 107–08, 246; *Anglo-Saxon Writs*, ed. Harmer, no. 59. Godiva had been married before her union with Siward, and he may also have been married to a woman with Scottish connections.

[16] *The Early Charters of Eastern England*, ed. Hart, pp. 108, 246.

Uhtred's kindred (and of the bishopric of Durham), as well as those of Peterborough abbey (and Godiva's kindred) were successfully maintained. Male exogamy was clearly important, but female serial exogamy should not be underestimated. Ecgfrida, her daughter Sigrid and Godiva were married at least seven times in all, with two separations, and only one remarriage following the death of a husband.[17]

Royal and ecclesiastical legislation on marriage was influenced by such practices.[18] King Edgar's Coronation Oath of 973, and the law codes *Quadripartitus* and *Textus Roffensis* included brief pronouncements against endogamy, but the 'staleness' of the Oath has been commented upon, and in Liebermann's edition those statements only take up a tenth of the lines devoted to remarriage and marriage contracts.[19] *Quadripartitus* and *Textus Roffensis* provide a detailed consideration of what was to happen if a woman married again, guaranteed the rights of friends and kin of a woman to help her if she was legally summoned in her husband's neighbourhood, and specified a minimum half-share of a husband's property as dower.[20] Secular and ecclesiastical authorities disapproved of endogamy, but serial exogamy over long distances created far more problems for legislators. Old English stems 'wed' and 'sib' denoted compact and peace, as well as marriage and kinship, while there are forty-

---

[17] Ecgfrida retired to Durham as a holy woman, and only Sigrid's third marriage arose from her second husband predeceasing her. For contrasting male and female mortality rates, S.F. Wemple, *Women in Frankish Society: Marriage and the Cloister 500 to 900* (Philadelphia, 1981), p. 102; cf. K.J. Leyser, *Rule and Conflict in Early Medieval Society: Ottonian Saxony* (London, 1979), p. 54.

[18] Similar patterns were present in south-east England and the far south-west. Ealdorman Byrhtnoth of Essex and Ealdorman Æthelweard of Cornwall and Devon both came from Mercian families, but had each married their predecessors' daughters at least five and ten years before their appointments, receiving lands in those localities from their respective fathers-in-law. *Anglo-Saxon Wills*, ed. Whitelock, no. 3; S.D. Keynes, 'Cnut's earls', in *The Reign of Cnut: King of England, Denmark and Norway*, ed. A.R. Rumble (Leicester, 1994), p. 68.

[19] *Memorials of Saint Dunstan, Archbishop of Canterbury, Edited from Various Sources*, ed. W. Stubbs (London, 1874), p. 356; *Gesetze der Angelsachsen*, ed. Liebermann, I, 442–44; P. Wormald, 'Aethelred the Lawmaker', in *Ethelred the Unready: Papers from the Millenary Conference*, ed. D. Hill, BAR, British ser. 59 (Oxford, 1978), pp. 57–80 at p. 74.

[20] In Frankish law codes and Carolingian orders to *missi* the dower was only fixed at a third share of the husband's property. J.L. Nelson, 'The Wary Widow', in *Property and Power in the Early Middle Ages*, eds. W. Davies and P. Fouracre (Cambridge, 1995), pp. 82–113 at p. 87.

three words for wedding and marriage, but no word for engagement.[21] Marriage was particularly associated with peacemaking in Anglo-Saxon England, and women were not usually promised to men long before their marriages, which is a feature of many exagamous unions. Among the high nobility in late-Saxon England serial exogamy played an important role in creating extended kinship networks, with both the historical and the linguistic evidence suggesting a more limited role for endogamy.

Some of the functions often associated with endogamous marriages may have been fulfilled in Uhtred's family by the prosecution of a feud. *De obsessione* describes four sets of murders perpetrated between the families of Ealdorman Uhtred and Thurbrand Hold c. 1016–72. Kapelle has argued that those deaths were judicial murders instigated by Danish and English royal families in order to control the north, but they are portrayed in *De obsessione* as the results of a family rivalry.[22] After Earl Ealdred had killed Thurbrand, he was reconciled with Thurbrand's son Karl, and after they had become blood-brothers they planned a joint pilgrimage to Rome. That apparent amity was destroyed when Karl murdered Earl Ealdred after entertaining him at his house near Rise, in Holderness. The feud then remained dormant until c. 1072–75, when Earl Waltheof, grandson of Ealdred, ordered the killing of the sons and grandsons of Karl while they were feasting at Settrington, in Holderness. Vengeance for the death of Ealdred had not been taken for forty years, but that delay was fully redeemed by that massacre.

The significant point about that family feud is that it was confined in a direct line from Uhtred to his son Ealdred, and then to his grandson, but it did not involve Ealdred's half-brothers, cousins, and in-laws. It has to be considered what considerations led Earl Waltheof four decades after the most recent murder within the framework of this feud to avenge his maternal grandfather. The sons of Karl had opposed the rule of William I, and it has been argued that Earl Waltheof ordered that blood-bath in order to ingratiate himself with the king, but there may also have been a personal dimension.[23] *De obsessione* records that Earl Siward had designated his

---

[21] J. Fischer and T.N. Toller, *An Old English Dictionary* (London, 1882), s.v.; A. Fischer, *Engagement, Wedding, and Marriage in Old English*, Anglistische Forschungen 176 (Heidelberg, 1986).

[22] W.E. Kapelle, *The Norman Conquest of the North: The Region and Its Transformation, 1000–1135* (London, 1979), pp. 17–24; cf. Morris, *Marriage and Murder*; Keynes, 'Cnut's Earls', p. 86 n. 228.

[23] A. Williams, *The English and the Norman Conquest* (Woodbridge, 1995), p. 59.

son Waltheof as earl of Northumbria because Waltheof's maternal grandfather Earl Ealdred had held the earldom. After Waltheof was appointed as earl of Northumbria in 1072 he may have wished to re-establish the importance of his maternal descent, but devolution of property, the most obvious means by which lines of descent were invested with social value, did not establish the importance of his maternal line. The dowry estates held by his mother Ælfflæd had passed to another branch of the family, and there is no other evidence of the matrilineal descent of property to Earl Waltheof. By crippling the family which was remembered as the murderers of his maternal grandfather and great-grandfather he established the primacy of his Anglo-Saxon origins, dramatically reminding other families of the importance of his maternal descent.

Bilateral kinship and serial exogamy provided Ealdorman Uhtred and his sons with political power during the first half of the eleventh century, and influenced appointments during the second half. Earl Siward appointed Gospatric, brother of Earl Eadulf, to rule over Cumberland.[24] Following the death of Siward in 1055, his successor Earl Tostig removed that Gospatric, and favoured another Gospatric, grandson of Uhtred and great-grandson of Æthelred II.[25] There were apparently good relations among the three more closely inter-related branches of Uhtred's kindred, descended solely from northern families, but less so with the fourth more distant branch, descended from King Æthelred's daughter Ælfgifu. In 1064–65 Earl Tostig and his sister Queen Edith sought to crush the power of those three inter-linked branches of Uhtred's family by ordering the murder of the first Gospatric and two of his cognatic kinsmen.[26] In 1065, however, Earl Tostig was driven into exile because of those murders, and Osulf, son of Earl Eadulf, was appointed to rule the Bamburgh region under Earl Morcar of Northumbria.[27] Between 1041 and 1065 members of Uhtred's kindred belonged to the innermost circles of power in northern England.

In the Durham tradition exogamy was portrayed as the norm, and marriage to women of royal birth as the ideal. Serial exogamy enabled local earls and ealdormen to extend their power so that they became figures of regional and national importance, but there were also additional benefits.

---

[24] *Anglo-Saxon Writs*, ed. Harmer, no. 121.

[25] *The Life of King Edward Who Rests at Westminster, Attributed to a Monk of Saint-Bertin*, ed. and trans. F. Barlow (London, 2nd ed. 1992), pp. 54–56.

[26] *The Chronicle of John of Worcester*, eds. McGurk et al., p. 599.

[27] Symeon of Durham, *Historia regum*, ed. Arnold, II, 198.

Three intertwined branches of Ealdorman Uhtred's family provided each other with mutual support against the hostility of Earls Erik and Tostig, and the circulation of the Tees estates as dowry wealth may have enhanced that kinship solidarity. Property and feud respectively contributed towards horizontal and vertical kinship ties, facilitating a century of almost continuous rule and influence by Ealdorman Uhtred's family over Northumbria and its surrounding regions.

Endogamy in Normandy c. 996–1066

Roger of Tosny succeeded to the family's estates concentrated around the forest of Conches in south-east Normandy in 1024, and between 1023 and 1026 he arranged an exogamous marriage between his elder daughter Berthe and Guy, lord of Laval castle in north-west Maine.[28] Roger himself died in 1040, and was succeeded by his son Ralph (d. 1102), who first appears in the ducal charter witness lists in 1050.[29] Between 1040 and 1050 Roger's widow Godehildis married her husband's kinsman, Count Richard of Évreux, while Adelaide, daughter of Roger and Godehildis, married another kinsman, William FitzOsbern, the ducal steward.[30] The principal estates of the Tosny, FitzOsbern and Évreux families were within sixty km of each other, clustered around the Iton and Risle valleys, and were assessed at roughly equal rates of military service to be rendered.[31] The Tosny women were married to neighbours of comparable rank when their kinsmen succeeded to the family estates, but there was a divergence in the dowries of Berthe of Tosny and her half-sister Adelaide.

The exogamously married Berthe was able to give two estates in the Norman Vexin from her dowry to Marmoutier abbey in 1055, when her son became a monk there.[32] Those estates were peripheral to the main territorial interests of the Tosny family. The endogamously married Adelaide was able to grant not only two estates near the forest of Conches, and one in the

---

[28] L. Musset, 'Aux origines d'une classe dirigeante: les Tosny, grands barons normands du Xe au XIIIe siècle', *Francia* 5 (1977), 45–80 at p. 54.

[29] Musset, 'Aux origines', p. 55; *Recueil des Actes des Ducs de Normandie de 911 à 1066*, ed. M. Farroux (Caen, 1961), no. 122.

[30] Musset, 'Aux origines', pp. 54–55.

[31] *Scriptores Rerum Gestarum Willelmi Conquestoris*, ed. J.A. Giles (London, 1845), pp. 21–22; *Red Book of the Exchequer*, ed. H. Hall, 3 vols. (London, 1896), II, 627, 643, 645.

[32] *Cartulaire Manceau de Marmoutier*, ed. E. Laurain, 2 vols. (Laval, 1911), I, no. 2.

Pays de Caux, but churches, tithes and mills from four estates in the Andelle valley, to her husband's monastic foundation at Lyre, where she was buried in 1065.[33] Her estates lay in the heartlands of the Tosny power, and gifts from her dowry were both qualitatively and quantitatively superior to those made by Berthe.

Female inheritance customs probably also resulted in a larger dowry for an endogamous marriage in the family of Adelaide of Tosny's husband. His father Osbern and his mother, Emma, daughter of Count Ralph, were first cousins. Emma's dowry probably included Lyre and Glos, which subsequently became the ecclesiastical and administrative centres of the FitzOsbern honour of Bréteuil.[34] Emma's half-sister made an exogamous marriage to Ralph of Beaufour, but none of the major estates which had been held by her father Count Ralph were subsequently held by members of the Beaufour family.[35] In both families a woman who married a kinsman seems to have received a much more generous dowry than her half-sister who married exogamously. As Adelaide was the younger half-sister, and Emma was the elder half-sister, order of birth was an insignificant factor. The key connection was the one between their fathers and their husbands.

Duby has suggested that endogamy enabled estates which had been dispersed through earlier marriages to be reunited with the patrimony, and that families in eleventh-century France focused their attention upon vertical ties of descent between fathers and eldest sons at the expense of horizontal connections.[36] It is hard to find examples of the reintegration of estates into patrimonies as a result of endogamy, and it has been argued that endogamy stems from the need to strengthen kinship solidarity between close male relatives.[37] Approbation of those unions is symbolized by low bride-price payments from grooms to brides' families. Generous dowries and low bride-price payments provide economic incentives for men to marry their kinswomen, the objective being to reinforce lateral kinship ties. Such con-

---

[33] *Recueil des Actes des Ducs de Normandie*, ed. Farroux, no. 120.

[34] D.C. Douglas, 'The Ancestors of William FitzOsbern', *EHR* 59 (1944), 62–79 at p. 69; D. Bates, 'Notes sur l'Aristocratie Normande', *Annales de Normandie* 23 (1973), 7–39 at p. 11.

[35] William of Jumièges, *Gesta Normannorum ducum*, ed. and trans. E. van Houts, 2 vols. (Oxford, 1995), II, 174; *Recueil des Actes des Ducs de Normandie*, ed. Farroux, no. 13.

[36] Duby, *Medieval Marriage*, p. 8; idem, *The Chivalrous Society*, trans. C. Postan (Berkeley, 1977), pp. 59–60.

[37] L. Holy, *Kinship, Honour, and Solidarity* (London, 1979), pp. 63–65, 77–78, 102–03.

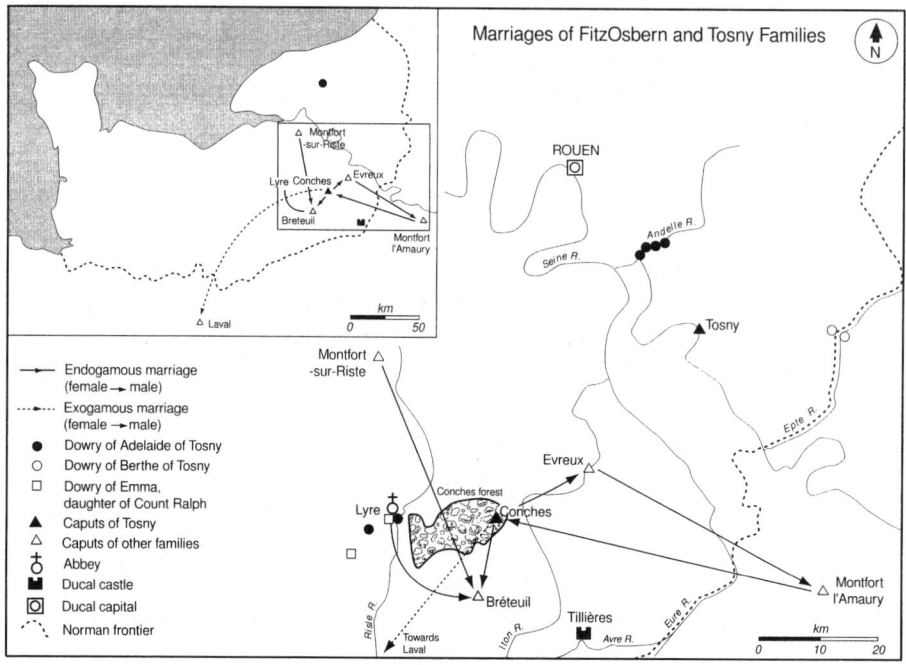

Map 2: Marriages of FitzOsbern and Tosny Families

Kinship and the Social Order in England and Normandy 119

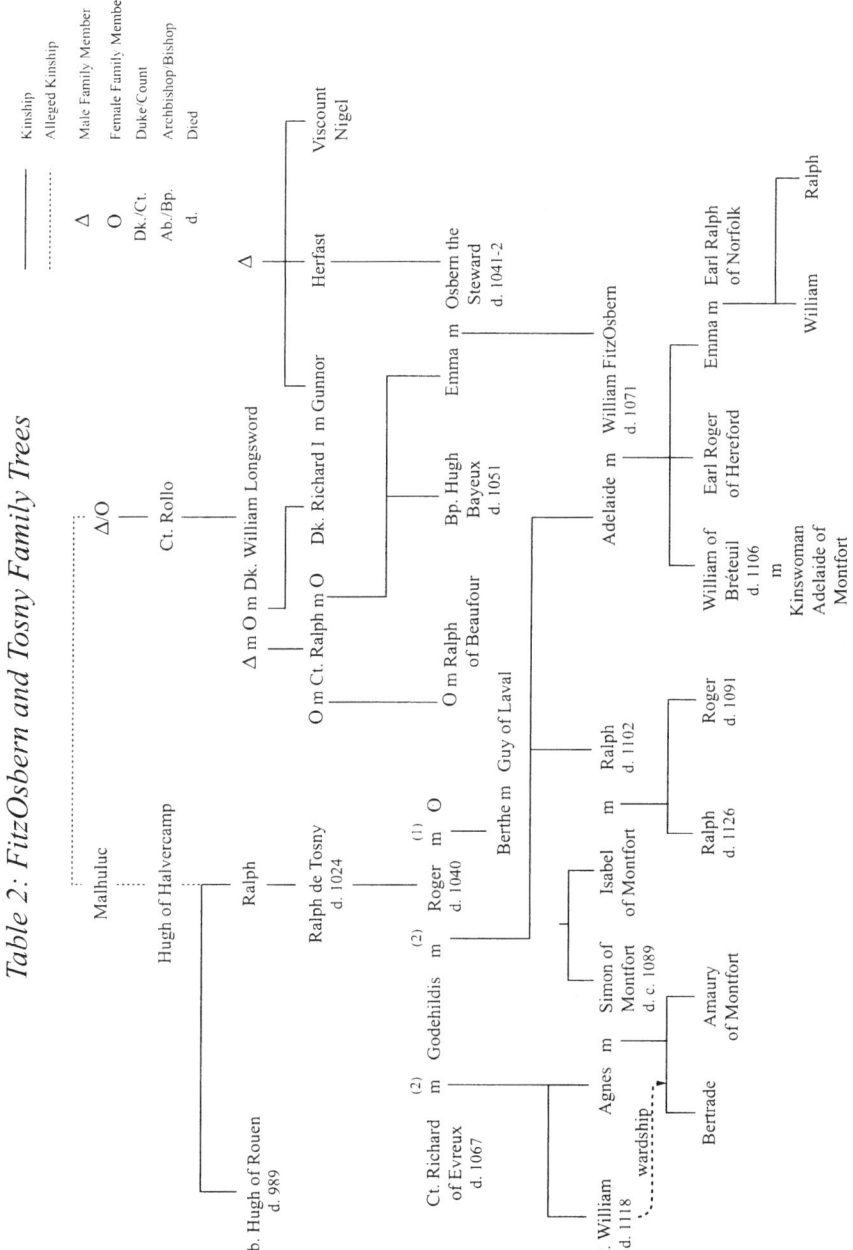

Table 2: FitzOsbern and Tosny Family Trees

siderations may have influenced the generous dowries in the endogamous marriages arranged by the Tosny and FitzOsbern families. If the motivation behind generous dowries is to be evaluated in terms of kinship strategies, the interaction between descent and alliance needs to be considered, by focusing upon the genealogies of the Tosny and FitzOsbern families.

The *Acts of the Archbishops of Rouen*, written at the end of the eleventh century, noted that the founder of the Tosny family, Ralph, was a son of Hugh of Halvercamp, and a brother of Archbishop Hugh of Rouen (949–89).[38] Paternal filiation and ties with a high ecclesiastic were emphasized in that genealogy. The first change in the family's identity was in the nomenclature of Ralph's son, also called Ralph. In 991 he followed his father in using a surname derived from a family relationship, 'Ralph filius Hugonis' (which here means nephew of Archbishop Hugh).[39] In 1014 he witnessed a charter as 'Ralph of Tosny'.[40] The adoption of a toponymic surname may have arisen from the circumstances that surrounded the issue of that 1014 charter. It documented reparations made to Chartres cathedral for damage caused to its property in Duke Richard II's war against the counts of Blois, Maine and Meulan, who had been defeated by Ralph of Tosny, his son Roger and Viscount Nigel of the Cotentin at the siege of Tillières c. 1010–13.[41] Besides Ralph of Tosny, that 1014 donation was witnessed by six of the duke's closest kinsfolk, also by six household officials and by three others. Ralph's reception into the ducal *familia* may have led Ralph to replace his patronymic surname with the toponymic surname, Tosny. Although Tosny was far from the family's main estates around Conches, it was only thirty km down the Seine from the ducal capital at Rouen, and hence may have drawn attention to connections with the ducal family.[42] The change in Tosny nomenclature may have prepared the ground for a shift of emphasis in the family's genealogy.

Orderic recorded an entirely different genealogy from that of the Rouen *Acta*: he noted c. 1109 that Roger of Tosny (d. 1040) was descended from Malhuluc who had helped his nephew, Count Rollo, to conquer Normandy

---

[38] Musset, 'Aux origines', p. 48.

[39] *Recueil des Actes des Ducs de Normandie*, ed. Farroux, p. 22 n. 15.

[40] Ibid., no. 15.

[41] Ibid.; William of Jumièges, *Gesta Normannorum*, ed. Van Houts, II, 22.

[42] A similar instance may be found with the Mortemer family. Roger, the ducal commander at the battle of Mortemer, and his descendants retained that toponymic surname from the late eleventh century, even though they no longer held Mortemer itself after 1054. Orderic, *Ecclesiastical History*, ed. Chibnall, IV, 86–88; *Complete Peerage*, eds. W. Doubleday et al., 12 vols. (London, 1910–59), IX, 266.

from the Franks.⁴³ The Tosny family were important benefactors of Orderic's abbey, and his version of the family's descent almost certainly reflects the message which they sought to convey about themselves.⁴⁴ The Rouen *Acta*, however, had a different purpose: by emphasizing kinship connections between Ralph of Tosny and Archbishop Hugh of Halvercamp it strengthened the claims which had been made by Archbishop Robert of Rouen c. 996–1006 to the archiepiscopal estates which had been granted to the Tosny family by their kinsman Archbishop Hugh.⁴⁵ A wish by the Tosny family to get rid of that ecclesiastical claim may have prompted an emphasis upon descent from Malhuluc, but that does not quite explain why he was identified as Rollo's uncle.

The generous dowry provision for the marriage between Adelaide of Tosny and William FitzOsbern suggests another influential factor in the equation. The Tosny family had been closely connected with the family of William FitzOsbern since at least the siege of Tillières. The other commander at Tillières, Viscount Nigel of the Cotentin, has been identified as a kinsman of William FitzOsbern's grandfather, Herfast, and the contacts between those two families were reinforced by gifts from Roger of Tosny to FitzOsbern's family abbey at Lyre before 1040.⁴⁶ For the Tosny family a next obvious step was for Adelaide to marry William FitzOsbern, but there may have been obstacles since William FitzOsbern was the son of the half-nephew and niece of Duke Richard II, and may well have been expected to marry a kinswoman. Osbern the steward, however, had died c. 1041–42, while William was still a bachelor, and that had a bearing too. An anthropological study suggests that men tend to marry their kinswomen if their fathers are still alive, but after their fathers' deaths they are more likely to marry exogamously.⁴⁷ Such freedom may have enabled William FitzOsbern to marry Adelaide. He was able to reinforce bonds of friendship with the Tosny family, and to receive a large dowry.

That link may also provide a rationale for the alleged relationship between Duke Rollo and the Tosny's ancestor, Malhuluc. It created a

---

⁴³ William of Jumièges, *Gesta Normannorum*, ed. Van Houts, II, 94.

⁴⁴ Orderic, *Ecclesiastical History*, ed. Chibnall, III, 124–26.

⁴⁵ *Recueil des Actes des Ducs de Normandie*, ed. Farroux, no. 10.

⁴⁶ E. Searle, *Predatory Kinship and the Creation of Norman Power, 840–1066* (Berkeley, 1988), p. 103; *Recueil des actes de Henri II: roi d'Angleterre et duc de Normandie*, ed. L. Delisle, 4 vols. (Paris, 1909), I, 552.

⁴⁷ Holy, *Kinship and Honour*, p. 66.

family tie between the Tosny dynasty and William FitzOsbern's lineage, as well as with the dukes of Normandy. Details suggest that FitzOsbern's family history influenced the modification of the Tosny genealogy. Herfast, founder of the FitzOsbern lineage, was the uncle of Duke Richard II, on whose behalf the Tosny family had fought at Tillières. It was Herfast's putative kinsman, Viscount Nigel, who defeated a fleet dispatched by King Æthelred II from England in 1005 in order to humiliate Duke Richard II.[48] Both families could thus look back to ducal uncles as founders, and also to kinsmen who had helped their ducal nephews to overcome threats from foreign rulers. The development of a new Tosny genealogy arose from the combination of ducal military service, a desire to distance themselves from the archbishopric of Rouen, and most importantly from wishing to strengthen the bonds of kinship with the FitzOsbern family.

The five Norman families who claimed kinship with the ducal family through the sisters and nieces of Countess Gunnor used toponymic surnames before 1066, but the five dynasties who were descended from ducal agnates either used patronymic surnames or comital titles.[49] Osbern the steward witnessed two charters as 'filius Herfast'.[50] His son witnessed sixty charters as William FitzOsbern, and in the remaining six charters he only used his Christian name.[51] During the late tenth and early eleventh centuries male descendants of Count Gilbert of Brionne (grandson of Duke Richard I) used the patronyms FitzGilbert and FitzRichard, and surnames derived from other family relationships.[52] In neither surnames nor genealogies of the FitzGilbert and FitzOsbern families was there any recognition of female ancestors. William FitzOsbern received Bréteuil castle from his maternal uncle, Bishop Hugh of Bayeux in 1051, and the estates that Richard and Baldwin FitzGilbert inherited from their father in the early 1050s were insubstantial.[53] Although devolution of property did not link

---

[48] William of Jumièges, *Gesta Normannorum*, ed. Van Houts, II, 12.

[49] D. Bates, *Normandy before 1066* (London, 1982), pp. 113–14; *Recueil des Actes des Ducs de Normandie*, ed. Farroux, no. 106.

[50] *Recueil des Actes des Ducs de Normandie*, ed. Farroux, p. 525.

[51] Ibid., p. 559; *Regesta Regum Anglo-Normannorum 1066–1100*, ed. H.W.C. Davis (London, 1913), p. 148.

[52] *Recueil des Actes des Ducs de Normandie*, ed. Farroux, p. 532; *Regesta Regum Anglo-Normannorum 1066–1100*, ed. Davis, p. 146; *Regesta Regum Anglo-Normannorum 1100–1135*, eds. C. Johnson and H.A. Cronne (London, 1956), pp. 420–21.

[53] Bates, 'Notes sur l'Aristocratie Normande', p. 11; J.C. Ward, 'Royal Service and Reward: the Clare family and the Crown, 1066–1154', *ANS* 11 (1988), 261–78 at p. 261.

fathers and sons with their earlier male relatives there was a remarkably strong recognition of agnatic kinship in those two families.

The marriage strategy of those two families may have played a significant role in the creation of agnatic attitudes. Both Osbern and his grandson, William of Bréteuil married close kinswomen, and FitzOsbern's marriage was regarded as an endogamous match.[54] Where wives' names are given, three of the four marriages arranged by the sons and grandsons of Count Gilbert were endogamous.[55] Marriage to kinswomen enabled men to honour family achievements to a much greater extent than when they married exogamously, and generous dowries symbolized the social significance of those unions. If the key change to family structure was a new emphasis upon vertical ties between fathers and sons, then endogamy could be viewed as part of that process. Fathers pushed their sons and daughters into marriages which emphasized links with their own kin. This left a much reduced role for maternal descent and other kinship ties, thereby contributing to the creation of agnatic lineages.

For the Tosny family the principal cause of a new emphasis upon an ancient agnatic founder was its alliance strategy with the FitzOsbern family. In the border region between Anjou, the Ile-de-France, Maine and Normandy, horizontal kinship ties had an important role in politics. In the 1050s Ralph of Tosny (d. 1102) married Isabel, sister of Simon of Montfort, who in turn married Agnes, Ralph's half-sister.[56] After that double marriage the FitzOsbern, Tosny, Montfort and Évreux families were linked through a series of overlapping kinship ties, which resulted in the creation of a network of mutual protection. In 1061 Ralph of Tosny was exiled, but Simon of Montfort, and Waleran of Bréteuil (a dependant of William FitzOsbern) were prominent among those who persuaded Duke William to pardon Ralph in 1063.[57] In 1087 Count William of Évreux agreed to Duke Robert Curthose's request that William's niece, Bertrade of Montfort should marry the count of Anjou.[58] One of the conditions was that Count William's nephew, William of Bréteuil should receive from Duke Robert estates in the Andelle valley. William of Bréteuil's mother and

---

[54] William of Jumièges, *Gesta Normannorum*, ed. Van Houts, II, 174–76; Orderic, *Ecclesiastical History*, ed. Chibnall, VI, 40.

[55] Ward, 'Royal Service and Reward', p. 262.

[56] Orderic, *Ecclesiastical History*, ed. Chibnall, III, 126–28.

[57] Ibid., II, 90, 104–06.

[58] Ibid., IV, 184–86.

maternal grandfather had both held rights there, but the decisive factor was Count William's willingness to use his authority over his niece to benefit his half-nephew William.[59]

The kinsmen supported each other during a series of rebellions and succession crises in 1078, 1088, 1100, 1118 and 1124, but there was a conflict between the families c. 1090–91 over the inheritance of the honours of Bréteuil and Évreux.[60] Both Count William of Évreux and William of Bréteuil were without legitimate male issue, and Roger of Tosny, younger son of Ralph, and Amaury of Montfort, nephew of Count William, were rival claimants.[61] Peace was quickly established between the families without arbitration by feudal superiors, following the death in battle of a kinsman of both sides. Roger of Tosny was recognized as heir to both honours, but died almost immediately. On Count William of Évreux's death in 1118 Amaury of Montfort was prevented from taking possession of the honour of Évreux by King Henry I, because Amaury was a vassal of King Louis VI of France.[62] The royal custodian, however, believed that Amaury had been unjustly deprived of his inheritance, and unexpectedly surrendered Évreux to him. Endogamous ties established in the 1040s and 1050s created a lasting political framework which enabled those families to negotiate with neighbouring rulers from the 1060s until the 1120s, and strengthened their rights to property.

Endogamy brought considerable social and political benefits, but it was not very effective in maintaining the social peace during the minority of Duke William I. In 1040–42 there were three murders: Osbern FitzHerfast was killed by William of Montgomery, Roger of Tosny by Roger of Beaumont, and Count Gilbert of Brionne by Count Richard of Évreux's brother.[63] All six families traced descent from different members of the ducal family, but single bonds of kinship were not highly valued. No other kinship ties were established between the families of the killers and their victims in the late eleventh and early twelfth centuries, and between 1090 and 1136 their subsequent political encounters oscillated between co-operation and conflict.[64] Single bonds of kinship were not invested with as

---

[59] *Recueil des Actes des Ducs de Normandie*, ed. Farroux, nos. 13, 120.

[60] Orderic, *Ecclesiastical History*, ed. Chibnall, II, 358; III, 100; IV, 155; V, 300; VI, 188.

[61] Ibid., IV, 213–17.

[62] Ibid., VI, 188, 204, 244.

[63] William of Jumièges, *Gesta Normannorum*, ed. Van Houts, II, 90–98.

[64] Orderic, *Ecclesiastical History*, ed. Chibnall, IV, 288–90; V, 300; VI, 456–58, 464.

much value as in *De obsessione*, but there was no feud between those families.

De obsessione dwelled upon the prestige of marriage to King Æthelred II's daughter, but such hypergamous unions were occasionally depicted in negative terms in Anglo-Norman sources. Thus the marriage of Robert of Giroie to a cousin of Duke William appeared to be a good match until the Duke besieged Robert, who was given a poisoned apple to eat by his wife.[65] It was remembered at Fountains abbey that after Drogo of Beuvrière accidentally killed his wife, a kinswoman of William I, he fled England c. 1071–86.[66] King William II ordered and commanded the obscure knight Humphrey of Bohun to marry the daughter of the baronial sheriff, Edward of Salisbury, according to the traditions of Llanthony abbey.[67] There is a hint that Bohun did not wish to marry her. Moreover, such unequal unions did not necessarily bring happiness to the women involved. Agnes, daughter and heiress of Count Guy of Ponthieu, was treated by her husband, Robert of Bellême, as if she were worse than 'a hateful slave girl'.[68] After the death of her brother, the high-born wife of Nigel d'Aubigny received no kindness from her husband, who repudiated her in 1118, and deprived her of her dower from her first marriage to the earl of Northumberland.[69] Memories of such incidents warned noblemen that the advantages of hypergamy were offset by wives' continued loyalty to their own fathers and brothers. Even women who were of a higher social rank than their husbands had to fear maltreatment more from non-kinsmen spouses, than when their brothers and uncles were the cousins of their husbands. The nature of the negative framing of hypergamy points to a secular ideology of kinship which favoured endogamy and monogamy.

There is no surviving information on rites of marriage, but two charters provide a hint of the differing attitudes towards monogamy in England and Normandy. In King Edgar's grant of dower lands in 975 to his wife it stated that the royal couple should be 'two in one flesh'.[70] In Duke Richard II's grant of dower to his wife, drawn up c. 996–1006, the relationship

---

[65] Ibid., II, 29.

[66] B. English, *The Lords of Holderness, 1086–1260: A Study in Feudal Society* (Oxford, 1979), p. 7.

[67] *Monasticon Anglicanum*, VI (London, 1830), p. 134.

[68] Orderic, *Ecclesiastical History*, ed. Chibnall, IV, pp. 282–84, 300.

[69] Ibid., V, 40.

[70] *Anglo-Saxon Charters*, ed. Sawyer, no. 725.

between men and women was discussed since the Garden of Eden.[71] There was an insistence that those who were joined in marriage were not to be separated. The difference in the extent to which the sanctity of marriage was emphasized can be linked to preferences towards exogamy in England and endogamy in Normandy. The Norman nobility's predilection for endogamy did not, however, result in any surviving objections from the duchy's episcopate. The archbishopric of Rouen was reserved for ducal kinsmen, and the bishoprics of Bayeux, Coutances, Le Mans, Lisieux and Sées drew their incumbents from the leading local families.[72] It made little sense for bishops to break up the social cohesion of families through hostility towards endogamy, because donations to monasteries were often tied up with strong family identities during the tenth and eleventh centuries. A putative link between monogamy and endogamy may have provided a spiritual justification for their stance.

There were, however, tough negotiations over the endogamous marriages of eleventh-century rulers and their courtiers. The endogamous marriages of Count Geoffrey of Anjou in 1038, Duke William of Normandy in 1049, Count Baldwin of Flanders in 1051 and the daughter of King Henry I in 1101 met with the opposition of pontiffs and prelates.[73] Pope Urban II's refusal to allow King Philip I of France to divorce his kinswoman in order to marry another kinswoman in the 1090s was linked to the 'Wars of the Investitures'.[74] There was an investigation c. 1106–07 into whether the marriage of the imprisoned earl of Northumberland to Gundreda of Gournay was endogamous before she was allowed to marry Nigel d'Aubigny, a 'new man' of King Henry I.[75] The archbishop of Rouen's claim that Anselm, archbishop of Canterbury (1093–1109), had agreed to the endogamous marriage of the royal chamberlain as long as alms were paid by the couple, was refuted by Anselm, but the marriage was not annulled.[76] The reactions of prelates to the marriages of secular rulers and

---

[71] *Recueil des Actes des Ducs de Normandie*, ed. Farroux, no. 11.

[72] Bates, *Normandy before 1066*, pp. 209–14.

[73] O. Guillot, *Le Comte de Anjou et son entourage au XIe siècle* (Paris, 1972), I, 46 n. 225; Bates, *Normandy before 1066*, p. 199; Herman of Tournai, *The Restoration of the Monastery of Saint Martin of Tournai*, trans. L.H. Nelson (Washington D.C., 1996), p. 27; *The Letters of Saint Anselm of Canterbury*, ed. and trans. W. Fröhlich, 3 vols. (Kalamazoo, 1990–94), III, no. 424.

[74] Duby, *The Knight, the Lady, and the Priest*, pp. 5–13 at p. 13.

[75] *The Letters of Saint Anselm*, ed. and trans. Fröhlich, III, no. 423.

[76] Ibid., III, no. 419.

their courtiers can perhaps be distinguished from local relations between bishops and barons. The vigour with which the Anglo-Saxon episcopate tackled some of the problems that arose from serial exogamy contrasts with the seemingly conservative response of their Norman counterparts towards endogamy. The conduct of both groups, however, arose from ecclesiastical adjustments to secular behaviour.

The Trial and Punishment of Earl Waltheof

Earl Waltheof, son of Earl Siward, married William I's niece, Judith, in 1070. In 1075, at the celebration of the wedding of Ralph of Gael, lord of Gael in Brittany and earl of Norfolk, to Emma, daughter of William FitzOsbern and sister of Earl Roger of Hereford, the brothers-in-law Ralph and Roger sought to persuade their guest Earl Waltheof to join their revolt.[77] The campaign was a military fiasco. Waltheof subsequently admitted to knowledge of the rebellion, seeking royal clemency, but on the deposition of his wife was summoned to trial for treason.[78] The debate between Anglo-Norman historians over whether Earl Waltheof was forced to rebel by the French earls, or joined the revolt of his own volition had a bearing upon punishment, as he was judged according to English law.[79] *II Cnut 68.2* entitled a defendant to clemency if his crime was an involuntary act, but treason was punished by the death penalty in *III Edgar 7.3*.[80] After a year of deliberation the judges were unable to agree on a verdict, and in 1076 on William I's orders Earl Waltheof was executed.[81] Modern historians have focused upon the short-term causes of Earl Waltheof's presumed participation in the revolt, ranging from putative opposition to state taxation in northern England to persuading the Danes to invade in

---

[77] Orderic, *Ecclesiastical History*, ed. Chibnall, II, 312–18; William of Malmesbury, *De gestis regum*, ed. Stubbs, II, 313; *The Anglo-Saxon Chronicle*, eds. Whitelock et al., pp. 156–58.

[78] *The Anglo-Saxon Chronicle*, eds. Whitelock et al., p. 157; Orderic, *Ecclesiastical History*, ed. Chibnall, II, 320–22.

[79] Orderic, *Ecclesiastical History*, ed. Chibnall, II, 132; Florence (John) of Worcester, *Chronicon ex chronicis*, ed. B. Thorpe, 2 vols. (London, 1859), II, 10–11; William of Malmesbury, *De gestis regum*, ed. Stubbs, II, 313–14.

[80] *Gesetze der Angelsachsen*, ed. Liebermann, I, pp. 204, 354. The distinction is absent from the *Leges Willelmi*, but reappears in the *Leges Henrici Primi*.

[81] Orderic, *Ecclesiastical History*, ed. Chibnall, II, 320–22.

1075–76, but the origins of his estrangement lay in the circumstances surrounding his marriage in 1070.[82]

According to Anglo-Norman sources, after the 1069 northern revolt had collapsed, Waltheof surrendered to William I and swore an oath of homage, and shortly afterwards married Judith, receiving the earldom of Northampton.[83] From this perspective the marriage was bound up with ties of vassalage and subordination. In fact Waltheof had held the earldom of Northampton since 1065, and it was probably regranted in 1070.[84] The *Anglo-Saxon Chronicle*'s version of those events differs substantially from the Anglo-Norman sources: it records the exchange of pledges of peace between Earl Waltheof and King William I, closer to a relationship between equals.[85] The contrast between Anglo-Saxon and Anglo-Norman sources arose from contemporary differences of opinion, and William I and Earl Waltheof may not have seen eye to eye on the obligations that arose from the peace ceremonies and marriage alliance of 1070.

The family traditions of Earl Waltheof's kindred may have led him to assume that an important alliance would follow from marriage to the king's niece, just as his great-grandfather's marriage to Æthelred II's daughter had, but from a Norman perspective that hypergamous and exogamous bond was less valuable.[86] Shortly after 1070 the king granted Waltheof fifty hides of land in Northamptonshire and Huntingdonshire, and in 1072 the earldom of Northumbria.[87] Earldoms and wealth were not, however, linked to power at court. Earl Waltheof had attended the royal court in 1067–68, but he does not appear in any charter witness lists c. 1070–75.[88] In the early 970s and 1050s Waltheof's predecessors had been responsible for accompanying Scottish monarchs to the English royal courts, but in

---

[82] Kapelle, *The Norman Conquest of the North*, pp. 134–35; *Dictionary of National Biography*, eds. L.S. Stephen and S. Lee (Oxford, 1917 and later edns.), XX, 722–24 at p. 724.

[83] Orderic, *Ecclesiastical History*, ed. Chibnall, II, 262; *Life of Waltheof*, in *The Itinerary of John Leland*, ed. L.T. Smith, 5 vols. (London, 1908), II, 130–42 at p. 130.

[84] Kapelle, *The Norman Conquest of the North*, p. 101.

[85] *The Anglo-Saxon Chronicle*, eds. Whitelock et al., p. 150.

[86] Although Earl Waltheof was the step-great-grandson of the step-daughter of the great-aunt of William I, they probably did not regard each other as kin before the 1070 marriage.

[87] *The Early Charters of Eastern England*, ed. Hart, pp. 236–37; Symeon of Durham, *Historia regum*, ed. Arnold, II, 199.

[88] *Regesta regum Anglo-Normannorum*, ed. Davis, nos. 21–23.

1074 the sheriff of York escorted Edgar Ætheling from Durham, after his departure from Scotland, to William I's court in Normandy, providing the party with hospitality at every castle.[89] The sheriff stood in a preeminent position to Earl Waltheof in his own earldom, and he appears to have been excluded from the royal court, household, and family.

In 1075–76 Countess Judith made two depositions to the royal court, which suggests that she was skilled in court negotiations. Her second petition secured the burial of Earl Waltheof's body at Crowland abbey, two weeks after his execution.[90] It ensured that rumours of his treachery were more easily quashed, and led to the development of the cult of St Waltheof. Stafford has argued that although royal kinswomen and æthelings could exercise powerful roles at court in particular circumstances, leading to periodic appearances in witness lists, they were usually omitted because they held no official rank.[91] Countess Judith could have exercised a powerful influence at William I's court without appearing in the witness lists. She perhaps used her influence to secure privileges for Earl Waltheof, but in a conflict of interests was bound to side with her uncle against her husband.

Earl Roger of Hereford was also summoned to trial in 1075.[92] Archbishop Lanfranc in his letters of 1075 addressed Earl Roger as his 'dearest son and friend', and reminded him never to forget that he was the son of William FitzOsbern.[93] He shared kinship with William I through several lines, providing him with more security than Earl Waltheof, but clemency was not granted: he forfeited his estates and offices, and was condemned to life imprisonment.[94] According to Orderic, when William I was dying he refused to release Roger, and after 1086 he disappears from the historical record.[95] The earls who shared kinship with William I, whether through marriage or descent, were punished harshly. The

---

[89] Symeon of Durham, *Historia regum*, ed. Arnold, II, 382; *Annales Dunelmenses*, ed. G.H. Pertz, *MGH SS* 19 (Hannover, 1866), 507–08 at p. 508; *The Anglo-Saxon Chronicle*, eds. Whitelock et al., pp. 155–56.

[90] Orderic, *Ecclesiastical History*, ed. Chibnall, II, 320–322.

[91] P. Stafford, *Queen Emma and Queen Edith: Queenship and Womens' Power in 11th-century England* (London, 1997), pp. 193–206.

[92] Orderic, *Ecclesiastical History*, ed. Chibnall, II, 318.

[93] *Letters of Lanfranc, Archbishop of Canterbury*, eds. H. Clover and M. Gibson (London, 1979), nos. 31–33a.

[94] Orderic, *Ecclesiastical History*, ed. Chibnall, II, 318.

[95] Ibid., III, 96.

rebellions of the close kinsmen of the first three Anglo-Norman kings were generally punished more severely than the revolts of baronial families, who were either not related to the royal family, or who only shared distant bonds of kinship.[96] That differentiation was the reverse of Anglo-Saxon customs of royal punishment: traitors who were not the kinsmen of kings were on occasion executed and mutilated, but the defections and revolts of ealdormen and earls, who were connected through marriage to Kings Æthelred II and Edward the Confessor, were forgiven.[97] The differentiation in Anglo-Norman customs of punishment contrasted with ducal practices before 1066, when both kinsmen of dukes and non-kinsmen forfeited estates and were exiled for rebellion, but neither category was deprived of life or limb.[98] The harsh punishment of Earls Roger and Waltheof may have in turn affected their families' kinship strategies.

After 1076 close bonds of friendship developed between the rebel families. In 1106 the brother of Earl Roger, William of Bréteuil, designated his sister's son, William of Gael, as his heir, and after her younger son Ralph of Gael took possession of the honour, he granted the Andelle valley estates to Ralph of Tosny (d. 1126).[99] Mathilda, elder daughter of Earl Waltheof, married in succession Simon of Senlis, and secondly her kinsman

---

[96] For execution and mutilation of close kinsmen and kinswomen of Kings William II and Henry I in 1096, 1106, and 1119, *The Anglo-Saxon Chronicle*, eds. Whitelock et al., p. 173; Henry of Huntingdon, *Historia Anglorum*, ed. and trans. D. Greenway (Oxford, 1996), p. 698; William of Malmesbury, *De gestis regum*, ed. Stubbs, II, 372–73; Orderic, *Ecclesiastical History*, ed. Chibnall, VI, 211. William of Aldera, executed in 1096, has stood as either godfather to William II, or as a joint godfather with him to another child, and was a ritual kinsman.

[97] For killing of Ealdorman Ælfhelm and the blinding of his sons in 1006, *The Anglo-Saxon Chronicle*, eds. Whitelock et al., p. 87; killings of Siferth and Morcar in 1015, ibid., p. 94; blinding and killing of Ælfred ætheling in 1036, ibid., pp. 103–04; *Encomium Emmae reginae*, Campbell, p. lxv; for toleration of the defections of Ealdormen Uhtred and Eadric Streona (married to Æthelred II's daughters, Ælfgifu and Ealdgyth), S.D. Keynes, 'A Tale of Two Kings: Alfred the Great and Æthelred the Unready', *TRHS* 36 (1986), pp. 195–217 at pp. 213–16; and P. Stafford, 'The Reign of Æthelred II, A Study in the Limitations of Royal Policy and Action', in *Ethelred the Unready*, ed. Hill, pp. 15–46 at pp. 33–34. The case should not be overstated, as Earl Ælfgar, son of Leofric of Mercia (d. 1057), was not recognized as a royal kinsman, but was forgiven for his treason.

[98] For an example of harsh punishment of ducal kinsman, William of Jumièges, *Gesta Normannorum*, ed. Van Houts, II, 126.

[99] William of Jumièges, *Gesta Normannorum*, ed. Van Houts, II, 230 n. 3; Orderic, *Ecclesiastical History*, ed. Chibnall, VI, 250.

David, youngest son of Malcolm III of Scotland. Her younger sister, Adelaide, married Ralph of Tosny (d. 1126).[100] Mathilda's husbands received the earldom and honour of Huntingdon, but Adelaide's dowry comprised 100 carucates, around one-fifth of the dower held by Countess Judith in 1086.[101] The younger daughter's dowry was generous, and was probably used to show that the Tosny dynasty and Waltheof's family regarded each other as kin. Aristocratic families that could call upon the support of close kinsmen based in different regions of the Anglo-Norman polity may have been better placed to resist the infliction of harsh punishments for rebellion, than lords who had to rely more exclusively upon kinship with rulers. That perhaps encouraged this group of families to establish bonds of endogamy over the types of distance usually associated with exogamy.

Conclusion

Endogamy and exogamy have been categorized as representing secular and ecclesiastical models of marriage, but in early eleventh-century England and Normandy there were regional distinctions in attitudes towards marriage that encompassed clergy and laity. In England male and female serial exogamy over long distances, regulated by royal and ecclesiastical authorities, led to the creation of extended kinship networks that outlasted the deaths of the original spouses. In Normandy secular preferences towards endogamy and monogamy strengthened agnatic ideologies of descent, and met with the tacit approval of the episcopate. Such descriptive differences, however, underestimate the subtleties of kinship as practised in the two regions. Variations in dowries and the conscious modification of the Tosny genealogy strengthened horizontal bonds between Norman dynasties, while memories of a blood feud helped to create vertical lines of descent in Ealdorman Uhtred's kindred. In both regions horizontal and vertical bonds achieved a certain equilibrium, with kinship fulfilling similar roles. The Winchester treason trials in 1076 were the outcome of the meeting of those two systems. Differences between English and Norman

---

[100] *Complete Peerage*, eds. Doubleday et al., VI, 640–41.

[101] *Life of Waltheof*, ed. Smith, p. 139; Countess Judith's estates in 1086, *DB*, ff. 130v (Middlesex), 160 (Oxfordshire), 182v (Buckinghamshire), 202–202v (Cambridgeshire), 206v–207 (Huntingdonshire), 217–217v (Bedfordshire), 228 (Northamptonshire), 238 (Leicestershire), 293v (Rutland), 366v–367 (Lincolnshire).

perceptions of hypergamy and exogamy led to Earl Waltheof's estrangement, and his punishment and that of Earl Roger were the first steps in a change in punishments for treason that separated the late Anglo-Saxon era from the Anglo-Norman. Duby and Goody have argued that marriage was one of the principal battlegrounds between the clergy and the laity for authority and wealth, but when kinship is viewed in a less universal framework it becomes clear that there was a close bond between kinship and the social order. In eleventh-century England and Normandy the regulation of that relationship by secular and ecclesiastical authorities may have been of far greater importance to both the clergy and the laity than a conflict between endogamy and exogamy.

Forging Unity between Monks and Laity in Anglo-Norman England: The Fraternity of Ramsey Abbey[1]

HIROKAZU TSURUSHIMA

Introduction

It is impossible to exaggerate the importance of the religious fraternity as an institution of intercession and its influence, direct or indirect, on European societies in the tenth, eleventh, and twelfth centuries.[2] The fraternity is not a convivial association, such as Anglo-Saxon drinking gilds or the confréries.[3] Nor is it an alliance between lay sovereigns, but a covenant (*conventio*) between a monastery and another monastery, monk, priest, gild, or lay person, for the salvation of one's soul through the monks' prayer. Its members covered ecclesiastical communities and indivi-

---

[1] This article owes much to the thoughtful and helpful comments of Ann Williams and Susan Reynolds. This research was supported by the 1997 grant-in-aid for scientific research (C) from the Japanese Ministry of Education.

[2] On this subject, H.E.J. Cowdrey, 'Unions and Confraternity with Cluny', *Journal of Ecclesiastical History* 16 (1965), 152–62; T. Sekiguchi, 'Confraternity with Cluny in the High Middle Ages', *Seiyo Shigaku* (Studies in Western History) 105 (1977), 1–20 (written in Japanese); idem, 'Über den Prekarienvertrag', *Socio-Economic History* 43–1 (1977), 1–24 (written in Japanese). On the Cluniac settlement in England, see B. Golding, 'The Coming of the Cluniacs', *ANS* 3 (1981), 65–77.

[3] G. Rosser, 'The Anglo-Saxon Gilds', in *Minsters and Parish Churches: The Local Church in Transition 950–1200*, ed. J. Blair (Oxford, 1988), pp. 31–34.

dual religious of other houses and chapters; ecclesiastical persons, including bishops and parish priests; and the laity, including royalty, great landowners, local worthies, and lay folks from the immediate neighbourhood of the monastery. Because the monks were regarded as intercessors, it was obvious that people wished to share as intimately as possible in the benefits of their prayers for the living and the dead. In particular, the benefactors of the monastery had a special claim to reception as *confratres*, who shared in the prayers and alms of the monks (*pars et societas in omnibus benefactis*).[4] A member of the fraternity might also enjoy such rights as that of taking the religious habit on his deathbed, or that of burial in the midst of the monks.[5]

Whereas on the continent numerous studies have been made of the fraternity, in England its study, particularly of the fraternity of lay people, has been neglected; even though, as the *Libri vitae* of Durham and New Minster show, the institution of the fraternity was common even before the Norman Conquest.[6] Many books concerning church history or the Anglo-Norman world devote only a few pages to this subject, and their main concern, if any, has been with the fraternity between the monasteries, rather than that between the monastery and the laity, even in the case of royal or baronial families, to say nothing of the local families.[7] However, considering the religious enthusiasm of lay people in the eleventh and twelfth centuries, this is a subject worthy of further consideration.[8] One of the reasons for this neglect may be that the peak period of the fraternity was

---

[4] Sekiguchi, 'Confraternity', p. 5.

[5] D. Knowles, *The Monastic Order in England: A History of Its Development from the Times of St. Dunstan to the Fourth Lateran Council 943–1216* (Cambridge, 1950; first edition 1940), pp. 472–79; J. Burton, *Monastic and Religious Orders in Britain 1000–1300* (Cambridge, 1994), pp. 216–17.

[6] *Liber vitæ Ecclesiæ Dunelmensis*, ed. J. Stevenson (London and Edinburgh, 1841); *Liber Vitae: Register and Martyrology of New Minster and Hyde Abbey, Winchester*, ed. W. de G. Birch (London and Winchester, 1892); *The Liber Vitae of the New Minster and Hyde Abbey Winchester: British Library Stowe 944, Together with Leaves from British Library Cotton Vespasian A. VIII and British Library Cotton Titus D. XXVI*, ed. S. Keynes (Copenhagen, 1996).

[7] F. Barlow, *The English Church: 1066–1154* (London, 1979), pp. 184–88. Cf. B. Golding, 'Anglo-Norman Knightly Burials', in *The Ideals and Practices of Medieval Knighthood. Papers from the First and Second Strawberry Hill Conferences*, eds. C. Harper-Bill and R. Harvey (Woodbridge, 1986), pp. 35–48; H. Tsurushima, 'The Fraternity of Rochester Cathedral Priory about 1100', *ANS* 14 (1991), 313–37.

[8] Sekiguchi, 'Confraternity', p. 5.

also the period of the Norman Conquest. Much attention has been paid to the Norman settlement and to the so-called 'feudalization' after the Conquest. But in such a time, when so much in English society was in a state of flux, is it not obvious to imagine that people, fearing the approach of death, should desire to enter into fraternity with the monks?[9] If so, how far was this agreement common and widespread throughout England? How did it relate to the reorganization of rural and local society? How did it relate to the grants of lands by the great Benedictine abbeys, resulting from the king's demand that such abbeys should provide him with soldiers?

Methodology

This article is concerned with the fraternity of laymen with monks after the Norman Conquest. The names of fraternity members, as recited by the deacon during Mass, were inscribed in a book, the *liber vitae*, which developed from marginal notes of the names in a missal. On their anniversaries, the members' names were read from the register of deaths, that is the *necrologium* or *martyrologium*, which developed from marginal recordings of the names in the *kalendarium*. Neither source, however, is suitable for my approach here, because in both cases it is difficult to identify the families of the individuals concerned.[10] The charters in the monastic cartulary, however, include the benefactor's whole family and the names of the local witnesses, as well as many references to the ceremony in the chapter-house. As for the terminology, I have translated 'fraternitas'

---

[9] In this article I will not discuss the influence of the Cluniac practice of fraternity upon the old-established English monasteries; this is a problem to be solved in the near future. On this point, Tsurushima, 'The Fraternity of Rochester', p. 324, n. 65. I would like to avoid such a misunderstanding as "Tsurushima equates fraternity with burial [...], but there is no conclusive evidence that fraternity conferred burial [...]' (D. Postles, 'Monastic Burials of Non-Patronal Lay Benefactors', *The Journal of Ecclesiastical History* 47 (1996), 620–37 at p. 625 n. 20). It may have been impossible for Rochester Cathedral Priory to offer graves in the priory to all the lay members of the fraternity. It is obvious that there were differences in membership qualification among them. Some were given graves in the cathedral; others were only accorded a part of the spiritual benefits. Probably many were not given graves in the monks' cemetery. But to die in the priory or as a monk may have been their final desire. This is why I stressed the function of the grave in the fraternity in the aforementioned paper, but I may have overstressed it.

[10] J.S. Moore, 'Family-Entries in English *Libri Vitae*, c. 1050–c. 1530', *Nomina* 16 (1993), 99–128; 18 (1995), 77–117.

literally as 'fraternity', rather than as 'confraternity'. In the following I limit the discussion to the relationship between fraternity and land-grants at Ramsey abbey, so that we may see here one aspect of local society. I have worked out twelve examples referring to fraternity from the cartulary and chronicle of Ramsey abbey, as shown in Table 1.[11] Nine of these twelve are concerned with the laity. A few examples will be discussed here in detail.[12]

1. Pleines of Slepe

In 1086 Ramsey abbey held twenty hides at St Ives or Slepe (Huntingdonshire), with all its appurtenances, including the neighbouring hamlets of Woodhurst and Old Hurst. Three of the abbot's men ('homines abbatis'), Everard, Ingelram, and Pleines, held four hides of these lands.[13] They perhaps were related. While two hides in Old Hurst may be traced to Ingelram, Woodhurst may be the land held by Pleines.[14] Between 1091 and 1102, Pleines of Slepe, with his two sons, William and Richard, made an agreement ('conventio') with Aldwin, abbot of Ramsey, and the whole chapter of the convent, concerning his fief ('feodum'), consisting of one hide and twenty-eight acres of land. Before this agreement the land had belonged to his property ('dominium'), but he probably gave it to the abbey, after which the abbot had returned it to him as his fief. He was now to hold one hide and eighteen acres in hereditary right, and the remaining ten acres from God and St Ives. For this reason he, his wife Beatrix, and his sons and daughters were accepted into fraternity with the monks. After his death, his heir was to hold the land with everything due to him, without all the reliefs (Table 1, no. 5).[15]

---

[11] The numbers in the Table and Map are synchronized.

[12] Full discussion of the fraternity of Ramsey abbey will be presented at another opportunity.

[13] *DB*, I, f. 204c.

[14] *VCH Huntingdonshire*, II, 250.

[15] 'Haec est conventio quam Pleines de Slepa, cum duobus filiis Willelmo et Ricardo, cum Aldwino abbate de Rameseia, totiusque capituli conventu, fecit de feudo suo, id est terra unius hidae, et terra viginti et octo agrorum, quos ipse ante hanc in suo possederat dominio, hic autem ex his decem cum praefata hida jure hereditario possidebit, agros reliquos vero Deo, et Sancto obtulit Yvoni. Quapropter ipse et ejus conjux Beatrix, cum filiis et filiabus suis, in nostra recepti sunt fraternitate. Post decessum vero ejus, filius quem sibi elegerit heredem, hanc, praefatam terram cum omni debita sibi, absque omni relevatione, possidebit substantiam. Hujus igitur conventionis hi descripti sunt testes,

This covenant reveals the social position of Pleines and his family. Their rights over the land of Woodhurst, located to the north of St Ives, were very strong. Although Domesday Book informs us that this land belonged to Slepe, a manor of Ramsey abbey, the charter, issued after 1086, holds that it was the property ('dominium') of Pleines at the time of Domesday Book. Old Hurst and Woodhurst were included in the soke of Slepe, and were chapelries of its church.[16] Both lands may have been part of the 'warland' of Slepe.[17]

The details of the agreement are also interesting. The donor (Pleines) transfers a piece of land to the property of the donee (the abbot), who then gives its usufruct back to the donor as a fief. In a broad sense, the land was converted into a free leasehold, although the condition of this holding still seems to be heritable.[18] There is no reference to military service or rent. Some scholars might regard this tenement in fief as being similar to tenure by knight-service in the thirteenth century. But it may be that the obligation to provide knight-service did not arise from the land ('feodum') but from the personal relationship between Pleines and the abbot, who, as lord, required such service as need arose. What is notable here, is that the fraternity agreement may have consolidated this man-lord relationship between the family of Pleines and the abbot.

Pleines of Slepe was a man of importance in the local community, one of a number of local worthies, some of whom appear as witnesses to the agreement. The first witness is Reginald the monk, who, between 1114 and 1130, was granted, with his sons, land at Barnwell (Northamptonshire) as an inheritance ('in haereditatem') in return for the service of one knight ('pro servitio unius militis') and a hundred shillings each year to the abbey

---

Reinaldus Monachus, Herveus Monachus, Rogerus de Castel, Hugo Interpres, et filii ejus Odo et Gumer, frater ejus Horulf, et Rogerus filius ejus, Ailfwardus de Riptuna' (*Cartularium monasterii de Rameseia*, eds. W.H. Hart and P.A. Lyons, 3 vols. (1884–93), I, p. 129).

[16] '[...[ecclesiam de Slepe, et de Wodehurst, et de Woldhurst, capellas ad eandem ecclesiam pertinentes [...]' (*Cartularium*, eds. Hart and Lyons, II, 165; *VCH Huntingdonshire*, II, 210).

[17] Such lands owed services to Ramsey's manor of Slepe, but did not belong to the church, but to the tenants who rendered the services. On warland, R. Faith, *The English Peasantry and the Growth of Lordship* (London, 1997), pp. 89–125.

[18] This agreement can be regarded as a *precaria* contract, particularly as a *precaria oblata*, which the continental historians have frequently discussed (Sekiguchi, 'Über den Prekarienvertrag', p. 6).

of Ramsey.¹⁹ Reginald, like Pleines, may also have had land at Woodhurst, for a tenement there was held in the thirteenth century by the Le Moyne family, who may have been Reginald's descendants. He had a son called Berengar, a name also popular in the Le Moyne family.²⁰ One of the witnesses to Reginald's charter was Hugh the interpreter.²¹ Hugh also attests the 'conventio' of Pleines, in company with his brother Heorunwulf, whose insular name might suggest that Hugh and Heorunwulf were native English.²² Another man who attested both charters is Alfward of Ripton, a place located within four miles of Woodhurst. The witnesses of Pleines's 'conventio' thus formed a close community, a group of neighbours, all local worthies in the lordship of Ramsey abbey.²³ They were free men, holding their own lands, who could also be responsible for military service if need be.

2. William Pecche

In 1086, William Pecche was a tenant of Aubrey de Vere, Roger Bigod, and especially Richard FitzGilbert for lands in Essex, Norfolk, Suffolk and Cambridgeshire.²⁴ In 1088, when he married an Englishwoman, Alfwen, both of them entered into fraternity with Ramsey abbey.²⁵ By their agreement, Abbot Herbert of Ramsey gave William the fraternity of the

---

[19] *Cartularium*, eds. Hart and Lyons, II, 259–60.

[20] *VCH Huntingdonshire*, II, 250.

[21] *Chronicon Abbatiæ Rameseiensis, a sæc. X. usque ad an. circiter 1200*, ed. W. Dunn Macray (London, 1886; rept. New York and Vaduz, 1964), p. 260 no. 288; H. Tsurushima, 'Domesday Interpreters', *ANS* 18 (1996), 215.

[22] O. von Feilitzen, *The Pre-Conquest Personal Names of Domesday Book* (Uppsala, 1937), p. 289.

[23] Only few studies have so far been made on independent freemen after the Norman Conquest, excluding some attempts to show local peculiarities. It should be noted that the Domesday account often fails to refer to them. Cf. A. Williams, 'The Abbey Tenants and Servants in the Twelfth Century', forthcoming.

[24] *DB*, II, ff. 39a, 77a, 105b, 175a, 390a, 396b.

[25] This case shows the intermixture of English and Norman, as demonstrated by A. Williams, *The English and the Norman Conquest* (Woodbridge, 1995), p. 198. Cf. J. Hudson, 'Life-Grants of Land and the Development of Inheritance in Anglo-Norman England', *ANS* 12 (1990), 67–80; idem, *The Formation of the English Common Law* (London, 1996), p. 119.

monastery and granted that he might have the land of Over (Cambridgeshire) in his custody for his own and the abbey's profit, on the following conditions: firstly, that he should immediately pay the community one mark of gold for their acceptance; secondly, that he should henceforth render them six pounds of silver pennies for the usufruct of the land ('pro usufructuario terrae') every year; thirdly, that he would be buried in the cemetery of the church of St Benedict after his death; fourthly, that a hundred shillings or a mark of gold should be given to the aforesaid church for the salvation of his soul; fifthly, that his wife Alfwen would hold this land on the same condition as her husband, if she survived him, as long as she lived; and sixthly, that certainly after her death it should revert to the hand of the abbot or his successor and that there should be no malicious action nor contradiction (Table 1, no. 3).[26]

This grant differs from the previous one in several respects. The grant describes a particularly onerous contract. The donee, William Pecche, at first had to pay one mark of gold, as a down-payment for the community's assent, and, secondly, would pay six pounds of silver annually for the usufruct of the land. It is important here to note that the term 'to hold the fief' was used both in respect of the usufruct of land and the payment of rent. The land at Over was a leasehold for life. In 1086 Ramsey's manor of Over comprised ten hides and three virgates of a fifteen-hide vill.[27] The manor belonged to the abbot's property, since it was assigned to the

---

[26] 'Herebertus, Dei gratia abbas Ramesensis ecclesiae, filiis fidei catholicae. Volo vos scire et veritati testimonium dare, quod Willelmo Pecche damus fraternitatem nostri et nostrae congregationis, et concedimus, ut sub sua custodia habeat terram de Ofra, ad proficuum suum et nostrum, sub hac conditione, ut ad praesens solvat nobis marcam auri pro nostra concessione, et singulis deinceps annis sex libras denariorum pro usufructuario terrae, et locum sepulturae habeat post decessum vitae suae in cymiterio ecclesiae Sancti Benedicti; et centum solidi dentur de suo proprio ad ipsam ecclesiam pro anima ejus, vel marca auri. Uxor vero ejus, quam hodie habet, scilicet Alffwen, si supervixerit ei, tenebit ipsam terram in vita sua sub hac eadem conditione, scilicet, post decessum vitae ejus recedet in manum abbatis, sive mei ipsius sive successoris mei, absque ulla calumnia et obloquio, et tam bene vestita, ut fuerit in die, qua ipsam Alfwen mortalis infirmitas praeoccupaverit. Testimonio nostri et totius congregationis, et Rodulfi et Ansgeri capellanorum regis Willelmi junioris, et Alfgari Praepositi, et Turkilli Dapiferi, et Folquini. Actum Rameseiae, anno Domini millesimo octogesimo octavo, indictione undecima, decima quinta kalendas Julii.' (Cartularium, eds. Hart and Lyons, I, 120–21).

[27] DB, I, ff. 192c-d, 193a, 199a, 201a, 202c; Inquisitio comitatus Cantabrigiensis, ed. N.E.S.A. Hamilton (London, 1876), pp. 91–92. The composition of manors in Over is shown in Table II. Before 1066, the abbot's manor had consisted of one inland and two warlands.

monks' food.[28] Therefore William Pecche held this land 'at fee-farm' for his and his wife's lives.[29] A charter of Henry I, confirming the grant, holds that 'it was witnessed [...] that William Pecche and Alfwen his wife were not to hold the land of Over from the fief of the abbot of Ramsey except in their own lives, by rendering six pounds every year, but after their deaths the land was to return to the property of the church and abbot without any claim'.[30] Nevertheless, the descendants of William continued to hold the land at Over, standing against the claims of successive abbots to restore it into the abbey's demesne. It was only in the time of Henry III that the land returned. However, this long-term tenure of Over does not mean that the fief had heritability as an attribute in the eleventh and early twelfth century. *De jure*, William held this manor only for his and his wife's lives. *De facto*, succession continued to play a role in the power relations between man and lord, and depended upon the abbot's goodwill. Hamo, the son of William Pecche, had the lease renewed, but after 1194, relations between the family and the abbots deteriorated, and in 1232, another Hamo, the great-grandson of William Pecche, abandoned his claims, and gave the estate up to Ramsey.[31]

We should not overlook, however, the fact that the fraternity was given to William Pecche at the same time that he was granted the usufruct of Over for life. He was accepted not only as a man of the abbot, but also as a member of the brothers, to share in their prayers, and to have his grave in the abbey's cemetery. The fraternityship could strengthen the relations between man and lord.[32] Sometimes human relationships were not established by worldly social bonds alone, but also with the help of more spiritual and mental relations, as well as pious mentalities. The abbey

---

[28] *VCH Cambridgeshire*, IX, 343.

[29] H. Tsurushima, 'Feodum in Kent c. 1066–1215', *Journal of Medieval History* 21 (1995), 97–115.

[30] 'Willelmus Peccatum et Elfwenna uxor sua non debuerunt tenere terram de Oura de feudo abbatis Ram[esiae] nisi tantummodo in vita sua, per vi. libras inde reddendo per annum, sed post decessum eorum debuit terra illa redire in dominio ecclesiae et abbatis absque omni calumnia' (*Chronicon*, ed. Dunn Macray, p. 228 no. 224).

[31] Hudson, 'Life-grants of land', p. 69.

[32] Tsurushima, 'The Fraternity of Rochester', p. 322. This point is expressed best by B. Golding when he notes: 'feudal relationships intermesh with spiritual ones, the lord and his vassals are expected to be united in death as in life' ('Anglo-Norman Knightly Burials', p. 43; also C. Harper-Bill, 'The Struggle for Benefices in East Anglia', *ANS* 11 (1988), 114–15).

accepted the whole family, grandparents, the person himself, his wife and his children, as members in the fraternity. Sometimes hierarchical relations were also included. In 1081, for instance, when Nigel Fossard entered into fraternity with the monks, it included King William, Queen Mathilda, Earl Robert (Nigel's lord), Nigel himself, his wife and his elected heir, his son, and his parents (Table 1, no.1).[33]

Conclusion

In conclusion, it appears, firstly, that in the course of the ceremonial entrance into fraternity, land was granted to laymen. Pleines of Slepe was re-granted his fief; William Pecche was granted a fief by the abbot of Ramsey. The former had been the grantee's own property; therefore Pleines held it in hereditary right. On the other hand, the land which William held had once been part of a manor of the abbey, including six hides of demesne. Therefore his land was held for two lives at rent ('ad firmam'). Both charters used the same word, 'feodum', but the content of the grants was different. It seems reasonable to suppose that in the late eleventh and early twelfth centuries, the word 'feodum' does not mean a specific tenure, that is a particular kind of land with particular rights and services, but only a holding in general. In 1081, for instance, in return for 'full fraternity' ('plenam fraternitatem') with Ramsey, Nigel Fossard granted the abbey two plough-lands in Bromham (Bedfordshire), and its church with some tithes.[34] In 1086, there were several tenements in Bromham, including two hides held by Hugh from Countess Judith, which, according to Domesday Book, 'belong to the countess's "feodum" but do not lie in this land'.[35] 'Feodum' in this instance may mean no more than 'holding', in the sense of the countess's total holding or honour.[36]

---

[33] *Cartularium*, eds. Hart and Lyons, I, pp. 127–28.

[34] Above, n. 33.

[35] 'De feudo quidem comitissae est sed non jacet in hac terra' (*DB*, I, f. 217b).

[36] The entry for Judith's two hides at Bromham suggests a dispute, probably with Hugh of Beauchamp, who was almost certainly sheriff of Bedfordshire, and who held the main manor of Bromham. Indeed he is likely to be the Hugh named as Judith's tenant for the detached two hides, which may originally have been part of the 'warland' of Bromham; in 1066, Godwine, Earl Harold's man, held them, but he could sell the land, which means that he only rendered customary dues, presumably to the chief manor of Bromham, then held by Alsige, man of the earl's sister, Queen Edith (*DB*, I, f. 213c).

A second conclusion relates to the close relationship between the so-called feudal ties, that is the personal ties between abbot and man through the land-grant, and spiritual ties through the establishment of fraternity. The members of Ramsey abbey's fraternity covered a wide range of social classes (Table 1). They included members of noble families, like Eudo *dapifer*, minor noble families, like Nigel Fossard, Drew of Hastings and William Pecche himself, shrieval families, like Ralph, brother of Ilger, local worthies, such as Pleines of Slepe, members of local English families, like Wulfnoth and Alfhelm Facet of Wells, and even someone with a landed interest in London. The fraternity also included some local priests, and even a parish gild.[37] Their lands are geographically distributed within a fifty-kilometre radius from the abbey, with a concentration to the south-west of Ramsey (see Map). This range of distribution is larger than that of Rochester Cathedral Priory fraternity, for Ramsey abbey was more interregional than Rochester Priory, whose lands lay concentrated in Kent.[38]

The content of the fraternity granted to people by the monks differed according to their donations, status and power. In all cases, however, worldly ties and spiritual ties, or in other words, ties with the living and ties with the dead, came to be intermingled in the fraternity covenant (*conventio*). This 'marriage' seems to have contributed to the solidarity of the lordship with Ramsey abbey. We may also say that although the bond was vertical, as between lord and man, the sense of sharing in prayers or burial places also gave a sense of unity to the members of the fraternity within their local community.

---

[37] *Cartularium*, eds. Hart and Lyons, I, 131. Wistow used to be called Kingston before 969, and its church was the minster and mother church of the area of Ramsey. Table 1 nos. 10 and 12 may suggest the reorganization of parochial system under the control of the abbot (*VCH Huntingdonshire*, II, 247–48).

[38] On the geographical range of the fraternity of Rochester Cathedral Priory, H. Tsurushima, 'Bishop Gundulf and Rochester Cathedral Priory as an Intermediary between English and Normans in Anglo-Norman Local Society', in *State, Church and Society in Medieval England, Symposium in the Faculty of Education, Kumamoto University, 1992*, Studies in Western History 31 (Fukuoka (Japan), 1993), p. 49.

The Fraternity of Ramsey Abbey 143

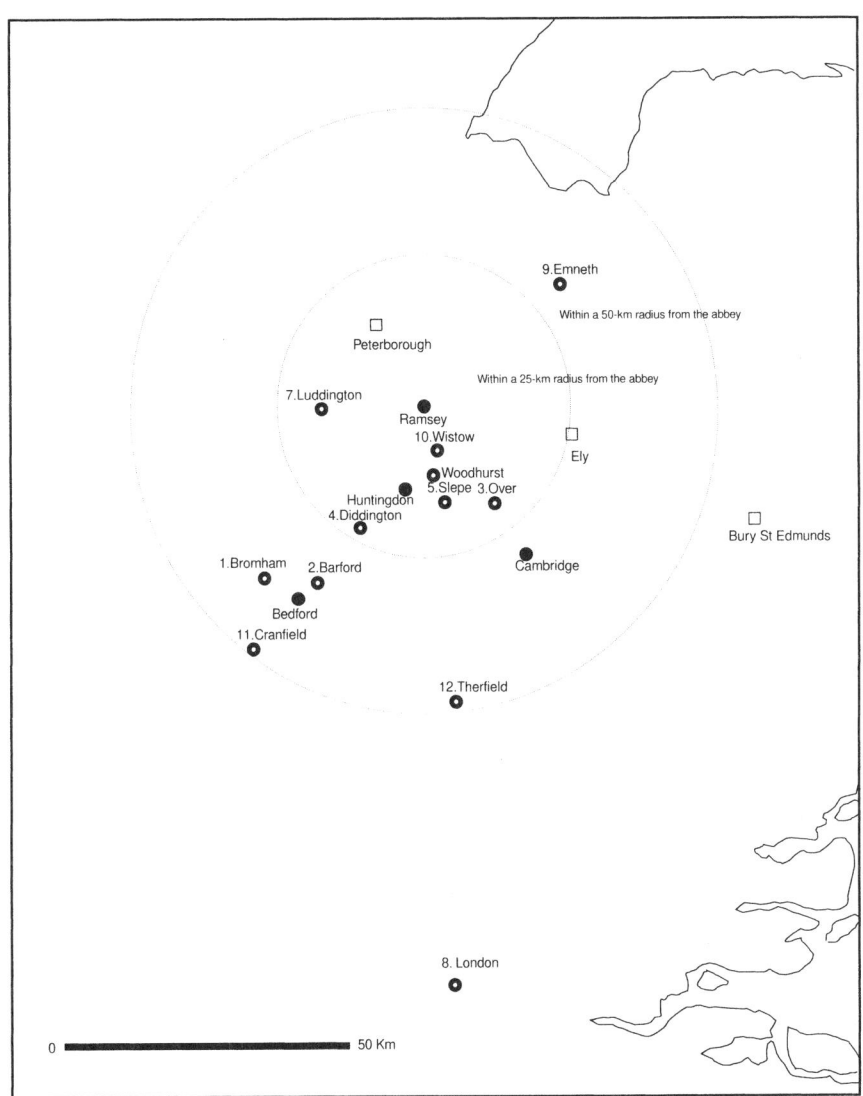

Laymen, Priests and a Parish Gild as Members of the Fraternity of Ramsey Abbey

Table 1: The Fraternity of Ramsey Abbey c. 1080–c. 1150[39]

	Members	Place	County
Laity	1 Nigel Fossard King William Queen Mathilda Earl Robert wife and son, the heir parents	Bromham	Beds.
	2 Eudo *dapifer* sister Muriel	Barford	Beds.
	3 William Pecche wife Alfwen	Over	Cambs.
	4 Ralph, king's *dapifer*, brother of Ilger wife	Diddington Stow	
	5 Pleines of Slepe wife Beatrix sons William and Richard daughters	Slepe (St Ives)	Hunts.
	6 Wulfnoth wife sons		
	7 Drew of Hastings wife Mathilda sons	Luddington	Hunts.
	8 Roger, son of Kumbold	land in London	
	9 Alfhelm Facet of Wells	Emneth	Norf.
Clergy	10 Siward the clerk of Wistow	Wistow	Hunts.
	11 Geoffrey the presbyter	Cranfield	Beds.
Gild	12 brothers of Therfield in gild	Therfield	Herts.

---

[39] Beds. = Bedfordshire; Cambs. = Cambridgeshire; Hunts. = Huntingdonshire; Herts. = Hertfordshire; Norf. = Norfolk.

The Fraternity of Ramsey Abbey

Cart. = *Cartularium*, eds. Hart and Lyons
Chr. = *Chronicon*, ed. Dunn Macray

Year	Words	*Cart.*	*Chr.*
1081	fraternity; prayer; all the benefits; society	I, 127–28	234
1080–87	fraternity	II, 257–58	207
1088	fraternity; grave; salvation; habit the service of half a knight	I, 120–21 II, 258	228
1091–1100	fraternity; grave *feodum*; the service of one knight	II, 259 cf. I, 128	234
1091–1102	fraternity *feodum*	I, 129	235–36
1114–33	fraternity	I, 128	235
1114–19	society of benefit *feodum*	I, 131	238
1114–33	fraternity	I, 132–33	240
1133–60	confrater (*homo*; *serviens*)	II, 268	272–73
	salvation; habit	I, 130	236–37
1133–66	fraternity	I, 152	272
1114–33	fraternity; communion of benefits	I, 131	

Table 2: The Manor of Over[40]

Lord	Tenant	Lord TRE	Tenant TRE	Hidage	Reference
1 The abbot of Ramsey				10 h. 3 v.	'in dominio aecclesiae'
2 The abbess of Chatteris				1 h.	'in dominio aecclesiae'
3 Hardwin of Scales	Ralph	the abbot of Ely	sokeman	2 h. 1 v. (0.5 h.)	He could not grant or sell outside the church without the abbot's permission
		the abbot of Ely	two sokemen	(3 v.)	The soke remained with the abbot of Ely
		the abbot of Ramsey	seven men	(1 h.)	They could sell without the soke
4 Picot of Cambridge	Swain	the abbot of Ramsey	Godric the hawker[41]	0.5 h.	He could sell
5 Countess Judith	Roger	Earl Waltheof	Godwine Cild[42]	0.5 h.	He could grant but the soke remained with the abbot of Ramsey
Total				15 h.	

---

[40] TRE = *Tempore Regis Edwardi*; h. = hide; v. = virgate.

[41] 'Godricus ancipitrarius homo abbatis de Rameseia' (*Inquisitio comitatus Cantabrigiensis*, ed. Hamilton, p. 92). This Swain may have been Swain of Over, who was one of witnesses on the abbot's side in an agreement made between Drew of Hastings and Abbot Reginald (*Cartularium*, eds. Hart and Lyons, I, 131). His land used to belong to the abbot's manor before the Norman Conquest. Godric the hawker held it, but he could sell it. It was what may have been called a sokeland, and after 1066 Picot occupied it. Swain may have been an Englishman and a son of Godric. If so, he kept his family land and remained a man of the abbot.

[42] 'Godeuuinus scild. homo comitis Walleui' (*Inquisitio comitatus Cantabrigiensis*, ed. Hamilton, p. 92).

Part Three

Conflict and Affirmation

———

Parchment and Power in Abbey and Cathedral: Chartres, Sherborne and Vézelay, c. 1000–1175

JOHN O. WARD

During the years covered by the present article, as is well known, the insertion of spiritual power into temporal arrangements and affairs, whether the result of monastic, episcopal or papal aggression, or of donors' zeal, produced conflicts over jurisdiction and property, tolls and commercial rights, protection and advocacy, tithes and other revenue questions. Not all these conflicts were clear-cut cases of lay versus clerical disputes: some of the most bitter conflicts, indeed, took place between abbots and local bishops.[1] In medieval conditions, such disputes were unavoidable. The paradoxical situation has been well put by Little:

> The religion of the age was thus presided over by a caste of specialists who professed poverty, spurned power, and, in the midst of an economy of utter misery, indulged in a spirituality founded upon conspicuous consumption.[2]

Elsewhere in the same book, he writes:

> More basic still were problems arising from the very nature of property and

---

[1] Hugh of Poitiers, *The Vézelay Chronicle and Other Documents from MS. Auxerre 227 and Elsewhere, Translated into English with Notes, Introduction, and Accompanying Material*, eds. and trans. J. Scott and J.O. Ward (Binghamton, NY, 1992); B.H. Rosenwein, T. Head and S. Farmer, 'Monks and Their Enemies: A Comparative Approach', *Speculum* 66 (1991), 764–96 at p. 774; Senecal, above.

[2] L.K. Little, *Benedictine Maledictions: Liturgical Cursing in Romanesque France* (Ithaca and London, 1993), pp. 194–95.

donations [...]. In the absence of a strong state and with the moribund condition of Roman property law, the norms governing land were basically [...] late Roman and early Germanic. [...] The relevant consequences of this included the lack of any absolute dominion and hence the impossibility of transmitting dominion with the gift of land. Besides, a donor could not impose his will through time upon his kin and heirs. In addition, it was standard practice for there to be overlapping claims on a terrain [...].[3]

Resultant disputes not infrequently provoked secular interests to violence, particularly when ecclesiastical attitudes were intransigent, and society lacked effective institutions of public authority.[4] Unable to meet violence directly, the church developed an impressive array of alternative strategies, including a final resort to interdict or excommunication.[5]

The basic position which the church found itself in is indicated by three illuminations taken from manuscripts that themselves played a role in dispute settlements at Chartres, Sherborne and Vézelay. This article focuses upon those three illuminations as evidence for secular and ecclesiastical relations, and then considers how they, and the manuscripts in which they are found, relate to broader perceptions of conflict and negotiation between churchmen and warriors during the Central Middle Ages.

The Sherborne Illumination of St John

The first illumination comes from a cartulary belonging to the Benedictine abbey of Sherborne (Dorset), a puzzling volume of disparate contents.[6] In

---

[3] Little, *Benedictine Maledictions*, p. 224.

[4] *The Letters and Poems of Fulbert of Chartres*, ed. and trans. F. Behrends (Oxford, 1976), pp. xiii-xiv; G. Duby, 'Recherches sur l'évolution des institutions judiciaires pendant le Xe et le XIe siècle dans le Sud de la Bourgogne', in idem, *Hommes et Structures du Moyen Age: recueil d'articles* (Paris, 1973), pp. 7–60; P.J. Geary, 'Living with Conflicts in Stateless France: A Typology of Conflict Management Mechanisms, 1050–1200', in idem, *Living with the Dead in the Middle Ages* (Ithaca and London, 1994), pp. 125–60; R. Landes, *Relics, Apocalypse and the Deceits of History: Ademar of Chabannes, 989–1034* (Cambridge, MA, 1995), p. 26.

[5] Rosenwein et al., 'Monks and Their Enemies', pp. 764–69; Geary, 'Living with Conflicts', pp. 145–60. Geary points out that excommunication and interdict were options not, of course, available to monks (P.J. Geary, 'Humiliation of Saints', in *Living with the Dead*, pp. 95–124 at pp. 95–96).

[6] BL Add. MS 46,487; F. Wormald, 'The Sherborne "Chartulary"', in *Fritz Saxl (1890–1948): A Volume of Memorial Essays from his Friends in England*, ed. D.J. Gordon

the first place, the collection contains dispute documents (charters, agreements, letters, and the like) dating from c. 998 onwards and compiled shortly after 1146, and relating to several issues that resulted in violent quarrels c. 1142–45 between the monks at Sherborne and Bishop Joscelin of Salisbury (c. 1142–84). In the second place, we find a substantial assemblage of basically liturgical documents, namely the passion of Christ according to the four evangelists, Gospel extracts and collects for various feasts, blessings, and other ceremonies, including Christmas Eve, the feast day of St Wesinus, bishop of Sherborne, Candlemas, Ash Wednesday, and Palm Sunday. The collection is unusual in that the dispute documents were not added to the liturgical sections of the manuscript, as was common at the time. In the present case, the documentary section precedes the liturgical pieces and forms part of the original plan for the volume. There are two miniatures in the volume, a half-page portrayal of St Mark, young and beardless, and a full-page illumination of St John, old and bearded, which is the subject of this paragraph.[7] The stiff, angular manner of this latter illumination is unusual in that there is no Evangelist's symbol and the figure is standing.[8] Wormald draws an analogy with the figure of an Old Testament priest-prophet, Huri, from a Bible manuscript of the Liège abbey of Saint-Laurent painted in the first half of the twelfth century.[9] The page seems meant to suggest the kind of fully-robed church elder who might have confronted secular offenders or would-be offenders. The left hand is held at chest height, with two forefingers extended in a manner suggestive of instruction or warning and common in Ottonian illuminations, yet in fact holding a stylus.[10] This latter is clearly related to the action of the right hand, which holds a scroll or banderole containing the first words of St John's Gospel: 'in principio erat verbum et verbum erat [...]'. The forefinger points, as if referring to the contents of the scroll. The point at

---

(London etc., 1957), pp. 101–19.

[7] Two more have been, apparently, lost.

[8] According to the BL microfilm description (the volume itself is normally in a display case).

[9] Wormald, 'The Sherborne "Chartulary"', pp. 110–11.

[10] H. Mayr-Harting, *Ottonian Book Illumination: An Historical Study*, 2 vols. (London, 1991), I, 115, 116, 118, 169, 170, 172, 177, 183, 185, 190 and plates XIX, XXIII, XXIV; II, 112, 121, 169 (etc.); most famously, perhaps, in MS Clm 4452, the Gospel or Pericope Book of Henry II (1007–14): A. Boeckler, *Deutsche Buchmalerei, vorgotischer Zeit* (Taunus, 1959), p. 31. The gesture is used by Christ, Mary Magdalene, and angels in these miniatures.

Plate 1. The Sherborne Illumination of St John: BL Add. MS 46,487
(reproduced by permission of The British Library)

which the quotation from the Gospel of St John breaks off is intentional. The next words ('apud Deum et Deus erat verbum') are appropriate because the major weapon of the church was the word, not just the Bible, but other texts too, which churches were keen to render as sacred and inviolate as possible. The St John illumination thus provides a powerful visual image of the monks' claim to exercise their authority against both laymen and episcopal power. Historically, it can perhaps be regarded as a continuation of the golden age of late Anglo-Saxon monastic art, and, in its contemporary framework, as part of a comprehensive attempt to render socially permanent the rights and privileges set out in the documents with which it was associated.

The Illumination of Fulbert of Chartres

The illumination of Fulbert of Chartres shows a churchman in his pastoral role: the right hand blessing, the left holding the bishop's crook, just as in the Sherborne illumination St John's left hand holds a pen, and his right the opening words of his Gospel. This illumination comes from a Chartres manuscript, relating to the years 1026–28, a time of local anarchy, the growth of private justice, monarchical recess and heightened religious zeal.[11] Many historians, including Geary, Duby, White, Landes and Head, have described the episcopal initiatives of this period, designed to establish order and salvational goals amid chaos.[12] This illumination shows a bishop

---

[11] Chartres, Bibliothèque Municipale, MS nouv. acq. 4, edited and discussed by R. Merlet and Abbé Clerval, *Un Manuscrit Chartrain du XIe Siècle: Fulbert, Évêque de Chartres, Martyrologe à l'usage de l'église de Chartres, Fulbert et sa Cathédrale, Nécrologe du Chapitre Notre-Dame de Chartres, chartes et pièces liturgiques*, Société Archéologique d'Eure-et-Loir (Chartres, 1893). Also *The Letters and Poems of Fulbert of Chartres*, ed. Behrends, p. xliii, n. 6.

[12] Geary, 'Living with Conflicts'; G. Duby, *The Knight, the Lady and the Priest: The Making of Modern Marriage in Medieval France*, trans. B. Bray (London, 1985), ch. 3, for example; S.D. White, '"*Pactum... legem vincit et amor judicium*". The Settlement of Disputes by Compromise in Eleventh-Century Western France', *American Journal of Legal History* 22 (1978), 281–308; idem, 'Proposing the Ordeal and Avoiding It: Strategy and Power in Western French Litigation, 1050–1110', in: *Cultures of Power: Lordship, Status, and Process in Twelfth-Century Europe*, ed. T.N. Bisson (Philadelphia, 1995), pp. 89–123; Landes, *Relics, Apocalypse and the Deceits of History*; *The Peace of God: Social Violence and Religious Response in France around the Year 1000*, eds. T. Head and R. Landes (Ithaca and London, 1992).

Plate 2. The Illumination of Fulbert of Chartres: Chartres, Bibliothèque Municipale, MS nouv. acq. 4
(Merlet & Clerval, between pp.46 & 47; reproduced by permission of The British Library)

Plate 3. Facsimile of Bibliothèque Municipale, MS nouv. acq. 4
(Merlet and Clerval, opposite p. 227; reproduced by permission of The British Library)

exercising his pre-eminent duty: Fulbert of Chartres, counselling his flock in the church which he laboured to rebuild after the fire of 1020.[13] The church is the sacred meeting place of the people gathered at the west end, and the clergy at the east end. Verses found in a manuscript from the neighbouring abbey of Saint-Père say of Fulbert:

> For twenty-one years and six months the venerable pastor nourished the Lord's sheep, striving to meet, clothe, feed and give drink to the weak, the naked, the thirsting and the starving.[14]

This illumination stresses the great mission of the church, its entitlement to be heard in dispute and obeyed when it confronted greed, violence, and arrogance.[15] It is likely that the leading citizen, with the golden braid on his shoes, is meant to represent Count Eudes II, one of the principal benefactors of the cathedral. If so, there is an analogy with the double portrait of count and countess in the abbey book from Vézelay to be mentioned shortly: harmony between secular and ecclesiastical powers is the message in both illuminations, the secular power donating, the spiritual instructing and preparing the laity for salvation. Fulbert is described in his obit as 'vir eloquentissimus tam in divinis quam in omnium liberalium artium libris'.[16]

It is significant that Fulbert, in the miniature under discussion, is dressed as a simple priest, that is, 'he is not clothed with the dalmatic, the vestment of the deacon, over the alb and stole'.[17] Merlet and Clerval point out that just as the bishop unites in his person all the aspects that confer the different degrees of the sacerdotal order, so his costume should reflect 'the characteristic vestments of the priest, deacon and subdeacon'. They see Fulbert's costume in the present illumination as an exception to the general

---

[13] *The Letters and Poems of Fulbert of Chartres*, ed. Behrends, p. xx; *Un Manuscrit Chartrain*, eds. Merlet and Clerval, colour plate opposite p. 227. No longer extant in the manuscript when Merlet and Clerval studied it were illustrations of Fulbert visiting the poor and succouring the sick.

[14] Two can be seen at the top of the present illustration and others probably accompanied lost miniatures; *The Letters and Poems of Fulbert of Chartres*, ed. Behrends, pp. xlii-xliii; also Fulbert's poem *The Joy of Peace*, ibid., pp. 262–63.

[15] The obit in the Chartres manuscript (*Un Manuscrit Chartrain*, eds. Merlet and Clerval, pp. 48–49) describes Fulbert as the ornament of the bishops of his day, the great light given by God to the world, 'pauperum sustentator, desolatorum consolator, predonum et latronum refrenator'.

[16] *Un Manuscrit Chartrain*, eds. Merlet and Clerval, pp. 48–49.

[17] *Un Manuscrit Chartrain*, eds. Merlet and Clerval, pp. 93–94.

medieval rule concerning the arrangements of episcopal dress. Only the cross or the shepherd's crook indicates his pontifical status. There is, perhaps, a message here. All persons in the picture (except the bishop, it seems) are dressed in their Sunday best, but precise indicators of station and rank are absent: we have a picture of a prosperous community in harmony, underneath the umbrella of the new church, each group or person with a role to play in the pattern of salvation. Thus Fulbert talks and blesses whilst his clergy behind him hold the authoritative books, the sacred repository of *verbum*. The women are placed in the porch, behind their menfolk, who are admitted to the nave proper. Their heads are covered but they are richly dressed and they hold out their hands in exactly the same gestures of acclamation, welcome, and acceptance as Christ's disciples in a celebrated Ottonian manuscript illumination.[18] The bishop protects all his flock, not simply the male feudal hierarchy.

The Auxerre Illumination of Girart and Bertha of Roussillon

The third illumination comes from Auxerre manuscript 227, a volume composed at the abbey of Vézelay c. 1167–70 to memorialize the outcome of a devastating series of tripartite conflicts between the abbey, the local bishops, and the local counts. The illumination forms the only historiated miniature in the volume and represents a peculiarly evocative piece of history.[19] The illuminator has presented us with an idealized portrait of the ninth-century donors upon whose lands the Vézelay convent was originally built, namely Girart of Roussillon, who is of *Chanson de geste* fame, and his wife Bertha. Together they seem to hold a branch-like sceptre symbolizing their gift of land and, with their free hand, they point to or acclaim the branch. This was an important gesture for the monks, because the foundation of their hard-fought battle against counts and bishops was the clause in the founders' charter, which immediately follows the illumination, providing for complete autonomy of local powers on the part of the endowed convent, and asserting the unique dominion of saints Peter and Paul.[20] The presentation of such a harmonious miniature, followed by the

---

[18] Boeckler, *Deutsche Buchmalerei*, p. 31.

[19] The frontispiece of *Monumenta Vizeliacensia: textes relatifs à l'histoire de l'abbaye de Vézelay*, ed. R.B.C. Huygens, CCCM 42 (Turnhout, 1976).

[20] Hugh of Poitiers, *The Vézelay Chronicle*, eds. Scott and Ward, pp. 97–104, 357–62 (by E.L. Cox), and for a description by F. Avril, ibid., pp. xvi-xvii.

Plate 4. The Auxerre Illumination of Girart and Bertha of Roussillon: Auxerre, Bibliothèque Municipale, MS 227, f. 22
(reproduced with permission)

details of the endowment, was the abbey's attempt to put forward an envisaged state of peace, in which secular donors ensure their salvation, the endowed church possesses pristine liberty and autonomy, as well as the wherewithal to exist and guarantee salvation for the donors and their dependants.[21] It is a harmonious and reciprocal situation, disturbed only to the peril of all.[22]

These illuminations, which portray vividly some of the means, justifications, and envisaged goals that accompanied the church's defence of its resources and autonomy against the greedy, short-term money-managers of the day. They come from and help to explain the compilation of complex—and to modern onlookers puzzling—manuscript volumes assembled by local churches to assist with the ever-burdensome task of inculcating the *verbum* amongst local populations. The volumes were intended, no doubt, to operate either directly by way of those who would see and could understand them (cathedral and parish clergy, monks), or through those (the lay community) who would—as in the Chartres miniature—listen to those who could see and understand. How else could the church tackle that basic shortcoming donors faced, the binding of future generations? Many scholars have lately pointed to these oddly assembled volumes, mixing sacred and profane with such perplexing zeal. Their labours have uncovered numerous monastic texts in which dispute and general chronicles, maledictions and ritual cursing formulas, charters, real and forged, and letters, have been sacralized as it were, by being written into bibles and other altar books.[23] Bijsterveld has shown how the Saint-Hubert chronicle

---

[21] Hugh of Poitiers, *The Vézelay Chronicle*, eds. Scott and Ward, pp. 131–32, 154–55.

[22] Indeed, were we better informed about Vézelay and its relations with its neighbours, we might have supposed that such gestures as the miniature under consideration could have been intended to form part of the development of *familiaritas* partnerships with the local nobility: Rosenwein et al., 'Monks and Their Enemies', pp. 772–77. At the very least, we have here, in the cartulary and *Brief History* of the Auxerre manuscript 227, an illustration of the monastic role 'in preserving, transmitting and forming [...] onomastic and thus familial memory' in a given locality (P.J. Geary, *Phantoms of Remembrance: Memory and Oblivion at the End of the First Millennium* (Princeton, 1994), pp. 76–77; see pp. 75–80 and ch. 3 (pp. 81–114) generally). The Vézelay situation seems to fit the picture described in Rosenwein et al., 'Monks and Their Enemies', pp. 768–69, and has elements of the Fleury (ibid., pp. 778–86) and the Marmoutier (ibid., pp. 791–93) patterns.

[23] In addition to works already mentioned by Geary, Landes, Little and Wormald, see *The Early History of Glastonbury: An Edition, Translation and Study of William of Malmesbury's* De antiquitate Glastonie Ecclesie, ed. and trans. J. Scott (Woodbridge, 1981), pp. 3–14, ch. 4, pp. 27ff; E. Searle, 'Battle Abbey and Exemption: The Forged Charters',

in Liège combines the functions of history with donation or gift record, in a context sacralized by the addition of chants for liturgical purposes.[24] I have myself recently attempted to show that the Auxerre manuscript 227 from Vézelay was not an arbitrary collection of disparate and unbalanced pieces, but an elaborate attempt to foster harmony by memorializing a dispute settlement designed to preserve the abbey's autonomous jurisdiction.[25] Sazama has lately shown this jurisdiction to have been inherent in the design and execution of the abbey church's decorative sculptural programme and in the architecture of the galilee or narthex, emphasizing as they do the pastoral, quasi-sacerdotal authority of the Vézelay abbot.[26] The apparent paradox that some parts of this manuscript display violent antipathy towards the 'viperous counts and bishops' (the major chronicle itself), whilst others (the cartulary, with its miniature, discussed above, and annals) are relatively neutral, and the *Brief History* is almost favourable, should occasion no surprise. Such contrasts, Little points out, were integral features of the medieval process of dispute settlement.[27] Infringement and violation led to ecclesiastical opposition and intransigence, which led to secular violence and 'the extreme rhetoric of malediction' on the part of the church. Yet, the resultant settlement is matter-of-fact in tone and quietly accepted by the very parties lately in conflict. There are even on record extreme acts of secular contrition and penance, with former enemies sometimes becoming 'participants and partners in the society and charity of the monks' as well as 'special friends of the monastery'.[28]

EHR 83 (1968), 449–80; also Hugh of Poitiers, *The Vézelay Chronicle*, eds. Scott and Ward, pp. 58–71.

[24] A.J.A. Bijsterveld, 'The Commemoration of Patrons and Gifts in Chronicles from the Diocese of Liège, Eleventh–Twelfth Centuries', *Revue Bénédictine* 109 (1999), forthcoming.

[25] J. Ward, 'Memorializing Dispute Resolution in the Twelfth-Century: Annal, History and Chronicle at Vézelay', in *Conference The Medieval Chronicle. Utrecht, 13–16 July 1996. Summaries* ([Utrecht, 1997]), pp. 123–24.

[26] K.M. Sazama, 'The Assertion of Monastic Spiritual and Temporal Authority in the Vézelay *Chronicle* and the Sculpture of Sainte-Madeleine', in *Conference The Medieval Chronicle. Utrecht, 13–16 July 1996. Summaries* ([Utrecht, 1997]) 94–95. At the 1997 International Medieval Congress at Leeds K.M. Sazama delivered a paper on 'Monastic Engagement with the Laity and the Romanesque Galilee' [at Vézelay].

[27] Little, *Benedictine Maledictions*, p. 226.

[28] Rosenwein et al., 'Monks and Their Enemies', p. 772; Geary, 'Living with Conflicts', pp. 155–57, 'Humiliation of Saints', pp. 106–14.

Of the three ecclesiastical institutions discussed here only Chartres merits further consideration in the present context, because the contents of the Chartres manuscript throw into sharper relief our understanding of the changing nature of ecclesiastical strategies of power and control over the laity of the period. The volume contains liturgical texts, offices, music and rules for establishing the liturgical celebration of key dates in the ecclesiastical calendar, a martyrology, and litanies for saints. The latter should not surprise us as we have lately learned how important the 'humiliation', that is placing on the ground of saints' relics, was in the coercing of local opinion.[29] The manuscript also includes a necrology, which functions as a list of benefactions and contains mini-chronicles recounting the benefactions of local bishops. The longest of these is the twenty-eight-line notice on Ivo of Chartres, whose death in 1115 concludes the document. Bijsterveld has commented on the similar use of necrologies at Saint-Hubert abbey in the Ardennes.[30] Not only does the Chartres necrology record few counts—because they were so often associated with attacks on the vast and far-flung possessions of the Chartres diocese[31]—but it specifically condemns the secular attacks on the 'pristina tranquillitas' of the church, a phrase which recalls the persistent emphasis upon 'pristina libertas' in the Auxerre manuscript.[32] Other charters in the Chartres manuscript serve to bind local counts to their agreements not to exact tolls from 'the Virgin Mary's rustics' or from the common property of the canons. In others, chapter officials in their turn promise to refrain from uncustomary exactions or the pressing of claims against local lords: harmony is a two-sided coin and the Chartres manuscript was clearly meant to be a comprehensive dossier designed to reinforce the collective memory which alone could guarantee fragile negotiated oral agreements.

Perhaps the most interesting item in the manuscript, however, is a precise record of the ultimate ecclesiastical sanction in the event of

---

[29] Geary, 'Humiliation of Saints'; Little, *Benedictine Maledictions*, pp. 26–44; *Un Manuscrit Chartrain*, eds. Merlet and Clerval, pp. 231–32.

[30] Bijsterveld, 'The Commemoration of Patrons and Gifts'.

[31] Cf. 'per violentiam Carnotensium comitum', *Un Manuscrit Chartrain*, eds. Merlet and Clerval, pp. 185–86. The Chartres diocese was perhaps the largest in France before 1697 and certainly one of the richest: *Dictionnaire d'histoire et de géographie écclesiastique*, eds. A. Baudrillart, A. de Meyer and É. Van Cauwenbergh (Paris, 1953),ı XII, 563.

[32] *Un Manuscrit Chartrain*, eds. Merlet and Clerval, p. 186; Hugh of Poitiers, *The Vézelay Chronicle*, eds. Scott and Ward, pp. 131–34, 151–57, etc.

uncontrollable secular hostility: the *clamor* or clamour.[33] In this ritual, the deacon and subdeacon, on bended knee before the altar—with the eucharist still upon it—and no doubt before a large crowd of the faithful, and with the clergy prostrate, make a specially solemn appeal or clamour 'ad te Domine Jesu', to whom 'suppliciter clamamus' because

> iniquitous and proud men relying on their own strength and not God, have risen up against us, and invaded the lands which have been entrusted by the faithful to you. They have afflicted your poor with grief, hunger and nakedness.

The clamour text calls upon Christ to bring the usurpers to heel and begins with the words 'in spiritu humilitatis et in animo contrito'. It is followed in the ceremony as a whole by psalms, collects, and other forms of devotion. This clamour ceremony represented an intensification of—or, in the case of monks, perhaps, an alternative to—the ceremony of anathema and excommunication, which followed the breakdown of negotiations between a church and its secular violator. To accompany the ceremony of anathema itself, all the altar ornaments and reliquaries, and even the crucifix itself, were placed on the choir floor.[34] All the bells of all the nearby churches and of the church in question were set ringing for the promulgation of the sentence.[35] The clamour ceremony represented an addition to this anathema ceremony. Following the day when the anathema was pronounced, each morning, at mass, the long clamour prayer was made by the priest in a high voice, with the choir boys lying down on their stomachs before the denuded altar, all the clergy prostrate on the sanctuary floor and the bells continuously ringing. The clamour ceremony, a kind of repeat of the anathema ceremony, with the clamour prayer coming instead of the formula of excommunication, was itself repeated each day until composition was arrived at with the offending secular body. According to Merlet and Clerval, several charters from the eleventh and twelfth centuries make clear

---

[33] Little, *Benedictine Maledictions*, pp. 25–26, 44–46; Geary, 'Humiliation of Saints', pp. 98, 100–03, 105; *Un Manuscrit Chartrain*, eds. Merlet and Clerval, pp. 231–38; *The Letters and Poems of Fulbert of Chartres*, ed. Behrends, p. xix, n. 10.

[34] On 'a piece of coarse cloth such as would be used for a hair shirt': Geary, 'Humiliation of Saints', p. 98; *Un Manuscrit Chartrain*, eds. Merlet and Clerval, pp. 233–34 uses the word *cilice*, which means either a hair-shirt or a rough cloth, for the cloth which covered the steps up to the altar during the 'humiliation' of the relics.

[35] *Un Manuscrit Chartrain*, eds. Merlet and Clerval, p. 232 for a description from a document of 1210.

that this simple but powerful community ceremony was enough to compel the local lords to restore to the churches what they had taken.[36] Merlet and Clerval associate the clamour text in the Chartres manuscript with the persecution of the lands of Notre-Dame of Chartres by Geoffrey, viscount of Châteaudun, to whom Fulbert refers in a letter to King Robert the Pious of France, and they date it to c. 1020.[37] They follow Dunod in his *Histoire de Besançon* (1750) in claiming that Fulbert himself composed the clamour prayer, and saw it as a kind of last resort, following excommunication and appeal to count, duke, and king. Little in turn follows Merlet and Clerval in seeing Fulbert's clamour text as the earliest example of a type that spread rapidly throughout France, and, according to them, via Cluny, to Italy.[38]

We know of some thirty churches having had such documents.[39] The geography and chronology of these clamour and closely related curse texts have been analyzed by Little, and are significant. The texts are found in areas where monarchy and sub-monarchical structures were ultimately to become powerful, but at a time when those structures were in recess, and local anarchy was at its height. By 1255, Little argues, when monarchy had emerged as the key body able to enforce order, these texts disappear from our records. They do not, it seems, occur where monarchy was proverbially weak, for example in southern France. It is no accident that all three of the texts used as illustrative in the present article, are associated with shrill appeals by the ecclesiastical bodies in question to the monarchs of the day, and to the new, quasi-monarchical authority of the time, the pope, in order to restore and guarantee order in their regions. Little argues further that the clamour never appeared where there was no feudal devolution of public

---

[36] *Un Manuscrit Chartrain*, eds. Merlet and Clerval, p. 234; Geary, 'Humiliation of Saints', pp. 106–54 discusses the efficacy of the custom and why it was efficacious.

[37] *Un Manuscrit Chartrain*, eds. Merlet and Clerval, pp. 235–36; *The Letters and Poems of Fulbert of Chartres*, ed. Behrends, pp. 103, 179–81 (1021–25); Little, *Benedictine Maledictions*, p. 45. R. Kaiser, *Bischofsherrschaft zwischen Königtum und Fürstenmacht* (Bonn, 1981), pp. 415–20 discusses the Chartres power situation: Fulbert himself was a royal candidate for the episcopacy and Chartres, though in the royal domain, was one of those dioceses in which king and count struggled for possession of the see (*The Letters and Poems of Fulbert of Chartres*, ed. Behrends, p. xviii). The clamour could also have arisen in connection with the depredations of Count Ralph, against whom, following excommunication, Fulbert appealed to the pope (ibid., p. 15 (1006–08), p. 107 (after 1021)).

[38] *Un Manuscrit Chartrain*, eds. Merlet and Clerval, pp. 235–36.

[39] Little, *Benedictine Maledictions*, pp. 25–26. For Cluny, Rosenwein et al., 'Monks and Their Enemies', p. 771.

authority such as had occurred in France between late Carolingian times and the later twelfth century.[40] Little's maps of 'Churches with clamors' and 'Places where liturgical curses were used' do not include Vézelay, though the region in which Vézelay found itself is well represented.[41] More specifically, at exactly that moment in Vézelay history at which a clamour ceremony might have been expected, none was enacted, even though there was a kind of humiliation of relics.[42] Why was there no clamour at Vézelay? Because the tearful moment in question was in fact the prelude to an abandonment of the process by the abbey in favour of a direct appeal to the crown.[43] The authority of the crown—and of legally attested documentation—was coming to supplant the emotional attempt to manipulate the local community by way of the clamour ceremony.[44] Indeed, so profound were the economic changes of the day at Vézelay that the common foundation of sentiment that might in former times have united the monks to their community had weakened in favour of an antagonism sometimes called the 'communal revolution'.[45] At the same time, internal monastic factions, promoted, it seems, both by the local count and by the rivalry of Cluny, arise to characterize the years immediately following the compilation of the Auxerre manuscript, resulting ultimately in its mutilation.[46] This manuscript is, in fact, a monument to a new age, in which law, document and constituted public authority would triumph over community

---

[40] That is, the British Isles, German territories, or the Italian and Iberian peninsulas: Little, *Benedictine Maledictions*, pp. 45, 207, 218.

[41] Little, *Benedictine Maledictions*, pp. 49 and 148, maps 1 and 2.

[42] Hugh of Poitiers, *The Vézelay Chronicle*, eds. Scott and Ward, pp. 289–91 no. 55; *Monumenta Vizeliacensia*, ed. Huygens, p. 572, lines 2355ff. Hugh of Poitiers even records a 'clamor ululantium' and 'commixtus clamor et promiscuus fletus' on the part of the tearful clergy and people, but no clamour ceremony.

[43] Hugh of Poitiers, *The Vézelay Chronicle*, ed. Scott and Ward, pp. 294–97 nos. 57–59.

[44] Little, *Benedictine Maledictions*, pp. 207, 230–39; Hugh of Poitiers, *The Vézelay Chronicle*, eds. Scott and Ward, pp. 10–11.

[45] Hugh of Poitiers, *The Vézelay Chronicle*, eds. Scott and Ward, pp. 29–42, though note the curious unity of townsmen and abbot when confronted by alien 'heresy' (ibid., pp. 314–15). Indeed, we may see the Auxerre manuscript as fulfilling the need to address 'the problems of lost intimacy and brotherhood through works of history', as at Marmoutier in the first quarter of the twelfth century (Rosenwein et al., 'Monks and Their Enemies', pp. 794, 796).

[46] Hugh of Poitiers, *The Vézelay Chronicle*, eds. Scott and Ward, book IV and p. 195, and note Little, *Benedictine Maledictions*, p. 23 (mutilation by scraping).

sentiment and ritualistic cursing as modes of ecclesiastical enforcement against lay aggression. Yet it is at the same time a monument to a passing age because the monastery as a hegemonic social institution has passed its prime and Vézelay's shrill plaints of aggression against ecclesiastical liberty recall the age of the investiture rather than the age of royal and bureaucratic government.

Thus it is that the three volumes from the three institutions selected for attention in the present article compass an age. From the first clamour embedded in a predominantly liturgical volume (Chartres), through an approximately balanced collection of dispute and liturgical documents (Sherborne), to a volume of primarily dispute-related texts (Vézelay), to the eve, that is, of the reign of law and public authority, ecclesiastical and especially monastic bodies sought to manipulate common memory and the communal textual reference archive in the interests of their own views of right order in the world. The volumes that survive as witnesses on parchment to this effort to circumscribe power have presented historians with a puzzle by reason of the very heterogeneity of their contents. It is only when they are viewed in the broader context of dispute resolution and memorialization, as is made increasingly clear from the studies of recent historians, that the rationale behind them can be properly appreciated.

Conflict and Compromise: The Premonstratensians of Ninove (Flanders) and the Laity in the Twelfth Century[1]

ARNOUD-JAN A. BIJSTERVELD

In hagiography, miraculous chastisements of those who offend the church or its properties are a frequent phenomenon.[2] Often these offenders, in their attempts to damage the monastery, not only tried to steal or ruin its property, but also acted violently against members of the monastery's *familia*. Between 1188/1189 and 1199 a Premonstratensian canon of the abbey of Ninove wrote the following, regarding 'a sinful man':

---

[1] This paper summarizes some results of a course on this theme, given by J.J. van Moolenbroek and myself, at the Vrije Universiteit at Amsterdam, from March to July 1997. I wish to thank the following students for their stimulating collaboration during this course: Marianne E. Foncke, Frans Hoving, Edwin Kok, Raymond de Lannoy, Aart Noordzij, and Gertram Schaeffer. Frans Hoving's paper 'Een kwestie van lange adem: Conflictstrategieën van het Ninoofse kapittel in de 12e eeuw' was of particular help to me. I also wish to thank Albert Derolez of the University of Gent, who drew my attention to the *Liber miraculorum* and the foundation history of Ninove abbey, Dirk Van de Perre, who provided me with all kinds of useful information regarding Ninove and critically read a previous version, and Dirk Heirbaut and Godfried Croenen for their relevant comments. My research project 'Gift exchange as an agent of social integration and political power in the Meuse-Demer-Scheldt area, c. 950–c. 1250' was supported by the Foundation for History, Archaeology and Art History, which is subsidized by the Netherlands Organization for Scientific Research (NWO).

[2] B. de Gaiffier, 'Les revendications de biens dans quelques documents hagiographiques', *Analecta Bollandiana* 50 (1932), 124–38; H. Platelle, 'Crime et châtiment à Marchiennes: Étude sur la conception et le fonctionnement de la justice d'après les Miracles de sainte Rictrude (XIIe s.)', *Sacris Erudiri* 24 (1980), 155–202; P.-A. Sigal, *L'homme et le miracle dans la France médiévale (XIe–XIIe siècle)* (Paris, 1985), pp. 276–82.

A heartless man from Rosegnies, named Alberic, who envied all who belonged to our estate at Renissart, one day arrived in anger in front of that estate's gate with a lance and took one of our hired labourers, tied his hands behind his back and carried him off to hang him. On hearing this, our brothers, intensely shocked and worried, ran after him and with great effort, and especially by order of the lady of that village, they succeeded in freeing the innocent from the sinner's hands. But the loving Lord, who said 'whoever it is who is unsettling your minds must bear God's judgement' [Galatians 5. 10], subsequently passed His judgement on him. As certain enemies by force of arms entered the village where he lived to fight their foes, this adversary of ours with his usual audacity [and] on his own with his lance pursued most of them a long way on their departure, although they had not done him any harm. [Then he] was seized by them with a spear, and dying in his sins he for good ceased envying our estate.[3]

This is chapter IV from the *Liber miraculorum s. Cornelii Ninivensis*, the book of miracles of St Cornelius, main patron saint of the Premonstratensian abbey of Ninove in Flanders. This abbey originated from a secular chapter founded in the Ninove parish church under the patronage of the local lord around 1119. This chapter was transformed into a Premonstratensian abbey in 1137 by Gerald I, lord of Ninove, in remembrance of his wife Gisla and himself.[4] As the parish church in all probability already possessed relics of the holy pope St Cornelius (d. 253), the abbey was dedicated not only to Our Lady, as was common Premonstratensian practice, but also to St Cornelius and St Cyprian.[5] St Cornelius's strong cult

---

[3] *Liber Miraculorum Ninivensium Sancti Cornelii Papae: Ein Beitrag zur Flandrischen Kirchengeschichte*, ed. W.W. Rockwell (Göttingen and New York, 1925; first edition Göttingen, 1914), p. 60 (ch. IV).

[4] *Liber miraculorum*, ed. Rockwell, pp. 72–73 (chs. XVI–XVII), pp. 87–91 (chs. XXXIII–XXXIV). On the lords of Ninove, the development of the town and the abbey's first century, H. Vangassen, *Geschiedenis van Ninove*, 2 vols. (Ninove, 1948–59), I, 11–13, 35–64; G. Mersch and J. Wauthoz-Glade, 'Abbaye de Ninove', in *Monasticon Belge. Tome VII. Province de Flandre Orientale*, eds. U. Berlière et al., 4 vols. (Liège, 1977–89), III, 485–535 at pp. 496–504; G. Vande Winkel, 'De Abdij van Sint-Cornelius en Sint-Cyprianus te Ninove: 1. Stichting en eerste bloei (1137–1300)', in *De premonstratenzerabdij van Ninove (1137–1796)*, eds. idem et al. (Ninove, 1985), pp. 5–13.

[5] *Liber miraculorum*, ed. Rockwell, pp. 72–73 (ch. XVI) relates how Amaury I (mentioned in 1078) and his son Amaury II (mentioned between 1078 and 1118/1119), successive lords of Ninove, adorned the church of Ninove with relics and designated three canons; E. Warlop, *The Flemish Nobility before 1300*, 4 vols. (Kortrijk, 1975–76), IV, 1017; Mersch and Wauthoz-Glade, 'Abbaye de Ninove', p. 497.

rapidly overshadowed both other patron saints. To enhance the veneration of St Cornelius and to commemorate his many miracles, a *liber miraculorum* or book of miracles was composed by an anonymous canon some time between 1188/1189 and 1199.[6] Fifty-eight chapters describe about as many miracles performed by St Cornelius, arranged in chastisement miracles (chs. I–XIV), protection miracles (chs. XV–XXI) and miraculous recoveries (chs. XXII–XXXI and L–LXXVI). The number of miraculous punishments, namely some eighteen, about one third of the miracles, is exceptional compared with the many other *libri miraculorum* from the eleventh and twelfth centuries.[7] The divine correction of laymen offending St Cornelius by attacking his abbey at Ninove, takes up such a big part of the *LM*, that a nineteenth-century editor published some of these miracles under the title *De persecutione ecclesiae Ninovensis*.[8] Our theme is what these miracle stories teach us about the relations between the Premonstratensians of Ninove and the laity in the second half of the twelfth century, and especially about the way they dealt with the laity in conflicts.

---

[6] The original manuscript containing the *Liber miraculorum* (henceforth: *LM*) is a compilation of the *LM* together with a foundation history of the abbey, *De fundatione Ninivensis abbatie* (henceforth: *DFNA*). The latter was written by a second hand after 1199, with additions by four hands writing after 1199, after 1221, after 1232, and around 1252 respectively. *DFNA* has been inserted into the *LM*, so that chs. I to XXXI and L to LXXVI (prologue (ff. 0–0v), ff. 1 to 15v, and 22r to 29v) constitute the *LM*, and chs. XXXII to XLIX (ff. 16r to 21v, and two loose sheets) constitute the *DFNA*. The manuscript is preserved at the library of the Union Theological Seminary at New York (MS 11) and was edited in 1914 and 1925 by W.W. Rockwell. For a description, Mersch and Wauthoz-Glade, 'Abbaye de Ninove', pp. 485–86; W. Van der Kelen, 'Het Liber Miraculorum Ninivensium Sancti Cornelii Papae', in *De abdij van Sint-Cornelius en Sint-Cyprianus: 700 Jaar premonstratenzers te Ninove*, eds. J. Van der Speeten et al. (Ninove, 1989), pp. 33–40; and the electronic database with the narrative sources from the Southern Low Countries, 600–1500, called *Narrative Sources* (at http://allserv.rug.ac.be/~jdploige/ sources) version 2.2 (1999), nos. ID D013 and L024. The composition's *datum post quem* is the death of Gerald II of Grimbergen, which occurred in 1188 or 1189 (see n. 20), and not in 1184, as Rockwell in his introduction to the *Liber miraculorum*, p. 29 n. 2, holds.

[7] In his analysis of over 3,300 posthumous miracle stories from this period, Sigal observes 61.4% miraculous recoveries and 12.6% chastisements; in the Ninove *LM* it is 57% and 32% respectively (Sigal, *L'homme et le miracle*, p. 290). The divine punishments can be found in chs. I to XIV (with ch. X relating two punishments, and ch. XIII three), and in ch. XX (collective punishment of the inhabitants of Ninove).

[8] *Balduini Ninovensis Chronicon*, ed. O. Holder-Egger, *MGH SS* 25 (Hannover, 1880), 515–56 at pp. 554–56. His excerpt is constituted of passages from *LM*, ed. Rockwell, pp. 72–79 (chs. XVI to XXI). See *Narrative Sources* version 2.2 (1999), no. ID D021.

Manuscript of the Liber miraculorum *and the* De fundatione Ninivensis abbatie: *New York, Union Theological Seminary, MS 11, f. 22ʳ*
(reproduced with permission)

The Abbey and Its Miracles

The abbey of Ninove was situated in the easternmost part of the county of Flanders, on the border with the duchy of Brabant. In this region many powerful noble families competed for superiority. These lords all promoted their own ecclesiastical foundations and looked with envy at each other's religious institutions, castles, and possessions. The abbey was founded in a time of radical social upheaval, near a small town which participated in the rapid economic development of Flanders in the second half of the twelfth century.[9] In this age of political, social, and economic transformation, the expanding and rich abbey of Ninove often incurred the violent envy of its noble, urban, and peasant neighbours. The abbey's *familia* (consisting of canons, lay brothers, lay sisters, and servants) as well as its possessions were frequently attacked because of jealousy or economic competition. The offenders were noblemen and their servants, as well as knights, peasants, and citizens of Ninove living close to the abbey and its estates. However, if we believe the Ninove *LM*, the abbey's *familia* never sought St Cornelius's protection in vain. As the prologue has it:

> If someone from the secular people, be it princes through their power, raiders through violence, or lesser people through dark cunning, took something which belonged to him [St Cornelius] or did injustice to his servants, he profoundly threatened their power, or made them perish quickly, but he did not tolerate himself to remain unrevenged. Indeed, in this way he governed his servants in every tempest of persecution and led them to tranquillity, so that they were always superior to their persecutors and after tribulation always turned up more numerous and richer.[10]

It is thus through St Cornelius's intervention that we can see the avenging hand of God, who acted with the full and merciless power of Old Testament vindictiveness, as the God of vengeance of Psalm 94. 1.[11] Of course, a *liber miraculorum*, which served to celebrate the saint's and God's almighty protection, allowed no shading in depicting enemies and

---

[9] About the urban development of Ninove until the thirteenth century, G. Vande Winkel, 'Over de oorsprong van de stad Ninove (tot ca. 1100): Een hypothese geherformuleerd', *Het Land van Aalst* 48 (1996), 203–24.

[10] *LM*, ed. Rockwell, p. 55 (prologue).

[11] Platelle, 'Crime et châtiment', p. 181; Sigal, *L'homme et le miracle*, pp. 276–82.

friends. In the rhetorical stance of hagiography, to which *libri miraculorum* belong, the underlying conflicts between laymen and canons could only be described in terms of winners and losers.[12] Nevertheless, the chastisement miracles do shed some light on the relationship between the Ninove canons and the surrounding lay world, and so do the other miracles where disputes are described. This also applies to the inserted foundation history of the abbey. Also, we get an idea of the ways in which conflicts between canons and laymen were settled. In a seminal article Platelle analyzed the conception and functioning of justice, conflict settlement and the relations between an abbey and lay lords as depicted in the *Miracula* of St Rictrud, main patron saint of the abbey of Marchiennes (county of Hainault).[13] The same can be done with the Ninove miracle stories, but this article only deals with conflicts which have an economic background, resulting from lay attacks on the abbey's property or its *familia*. The long-standing dispute that the abbey of Ninove had with its sister abbey of Dieleghem-Jette over the possession of the collegiate church of Liedekerke, as related in the foundation history, is not considered here because of our focus on the laity.[14]

According to the *LM*, St Cornelius's and God's vengeance struck seventeen individuals. In one separate miracle the townsmen of Ninove were collectively punished. Among the individuals, we encounter four lords, mentioned by name, a servant of one of these lords, two knights (*milites*), three anonymous men, two peasants, a citizen of Seneffe in Brabant, and two parishioners of Ninove, one anonymous and one called Erlebald, whose servant was divinely chastised as well (and possibly Erlebald's son too). The lay opponents of the abbey clearly stemmed from all levels of society. Their punishments mostly consisted of a sudden and sometimes violent death (eleven instances), sometimes preceded by insanity (twice), but also of a shameful and maddening stroke (once), ruination (twice), and paralysis (once). In the case of the citizens of Ninove, who had, together with the lord of Ninove and his wife, tried to appropriate the abbey's lands, their punishment consisted of the complete destruction of their town through fire. As a rule, acts of violence or slander against a

---

[12] B.H. Rosenwein, T. Head and S. Farmer, 'Monks and Their Enemies: A Comparative Approach', *Speculum* 66 (1991), 764–96 at p. 786.

[13] Platelle, 'Crime et châtiment'.

[14] On this conflict, D. Van de Perre, 'De abdijen van Ninove en Jette (Dielegem) en hun geschil over de kerk en het kapittel van Liedekerke (1092–1180)', *Analecta Praemonstratensia* 71 (1995), 264–99.

member of the *familia* and blasphemy were punished by a violent or miserable death. Theft and immorality were punished with illness.[15] The saint's revenge knew little mercy. Only once was an offender allowed to repent. This man, who had mockingly questioned the saints' intervention in worldly affairs, had consequently publicly befouled himself and had been struck with madness and a speech impediment. No longer daring to insult St Cornelius, he entered a Premonstratensian abbey, where he ended his days in peace.[16]

The Background of the Conflicts

The miracle stories only give scanty information about the real backgrounds of the conflicts between laymen and the abbey. As has been stated before, the underlying conflicts could only be described in terms of clear-cut winners and losers, and this did not allow for a nuanced account of what really brought about these disputes. In the *LM*, the reasons for the divine revenge striking adversaries are mostly phrased in terms of envy, intimidation, theft, plunder, maltreatment, devastation, refusal to pay oblations and levies, and the like. In fact in the *LM*, no distinction is made between possible underlying causes of the hostility and acts which can be regarded as elements of lay strategy in the process of conflict resolution, such as violence and plunder.

First of all, contended possession of land was of course a source of long-standing disputes everywhere. Conflicts arose from a donor or his heirs raising claims to land donated earlier, or from a donor's lord or a donor's dependants refusing to consent to an alienation. This must also have been a frequent cause of disagreement between Ninove, its noble benefactors, neighbouring peasants, and other people in its vicinity. It is mainly the abbey's estates lying outside Ninove which figure in the stories relating miraculous chastisements as a result of property conflicts. Ninove's estate at Renissart (in the duchy of Brabant, today's province of Hainault), some 40 km from Ninove, acquired in 1140 and 1142, was the site of no fewer than six of these miracles. It was probably its considerable distance from the abbey and its economic importance which caused this recurrent

---

[15] J. Jansen, 'Vroegmiddeleeuwse strafwonderen als bron van kennis over een orale samenleving', *Archief voor de Geschiedenis van de Katholieke Kerk in Nederland* 31 (1989), 163–91.

[16] *LM*, ed. Rockwell, pp. 62–63 (ch. VIII); Sigal, *L'homme et le miracle*, p. 213.

hostility.[17] Presumably, the abbey's advocates, i.e. the count of Flanders and the lord of Ninove as his vassal, were capable of protecting most of Ninove's twelve estates, which were situated in the immediate vicinity of Ninove, for the most part within the county of Flanders. The advocates' effective protection did not reach as far as Renissart, which was situated in the southernmost part of the duchy of Brabant.

In three famous cases, described in chapters I, II, and IV of the *LM*, three neighbouring lords—Giles of Trazegnies, Siger du Rœulx, and Alberic of Rosegnies—damaged and attacked the estate of Renissart, its brothers, personnel, and livestock. All three acted as fairly independent lords within the duchy of Brabant, in the border region with Hainault. Other sources record that over many years these lords had challenged the gifts made by their parents and relatives of parts of the Renissart estate to Ninove abbey, with the dispute continuing from the 1140s until 1185.[18] These lords opposed the diminishment of their inheritance through these gifts and continued to see the abbey as an intruder and a rival.[19]

The same must have been true for the lords of Ninove after 1144. After the death of Gerald I of Ninove, the abbey's founder, in that year, his successor and son-in-law Gerald of Grimbergen and his wife Mathilda for a long time challenged the donations made by their respective father and

---

[17] *LM*, ed. Rockwell, pp. 32–33, pp. 37–38 n. 5, p. 38 n. 4. Sigal, *L'homme et le miracle*, p. 208, has a map showing the occurrence of both miraculous recoveries and chastisements at Ninove: the former mostly happened to people originating from the direct neighbourhood of Ninove, the latter around Renissart; see ibid., pp. 209–10. For the location of Renissart, D.R. Duncker and H. Weiss, *Het hertogdom Brabant in kaart en prent: Zijn vier kwartieren Leuven, Brussel, Antwerpen, 's-Hertogenbosch* (Tielt and Bussum, 1983), pp. 92–93.

[18] *LM*, ed. Rockwell, pp. 32–39, who quotes from the chronicle called *Chronotaxis*, written in 1652 by the Ninove canon Godfrey van Elshoudt (d. 1666). This chronicle contains a year-by-year history of the abbey and its domain in the form of a calendar listing its acquisitions and dispute settlements between 1137 and 1197. Besides charters, the *LM*, the *DFNA*, and the twelfth-century necrology, Elshoudt perhaps used a kind of *liber traditionum*, now lost, which must have contained *notitiae* recording the abbey's acquisitions and agreements (*LM*, ed. Rockwell, pp. 17–18, p. 33 n. 3, p. 37 n. 5; Mersch and Wauthoz-Glade, 'Abbaye de Ninove', p. 488; this unedited chronicle is kept at Beveren, Rijksarchief, Abdij Ninove, no. 5).

[19] *LM*, ed. Rockwell, p. 65 (ch. X, about a *miles* fighting against the abbey, and about a lord who refused to consent in his subject's pious gift of a piece of land), and pp. 69–70 (ch. XIV, about a farmer promising to give money to lord Raso of Gavere to chase the brothers from their territory) can be interpreted in this light too.

father-in-law.[20] 'Led by avarice they (the heirs of Gerald I) attempted to take from the church what had been given by their father', the *LM* tells us.[21] After having taken some of the abbey's furniture, they pillaged its fields and harvest. They subsequently threatened to demolish two of the abbey's water mills, and, together with the citizens of Ninove, tried to turn the abbey's lands near Ninove into common pasture.[22] When the rumour spread that count Philip of Alsace, count of Flanders (1157–1191; co-regent until 1168) and the abbey's advocate, had been murdered, the lords of Grimbergen immediately came to Ninove and started to plunder the abbey, apparently with the preconceived plan to bring the abbey to an end once and for all.[23] The same day, however, news came through that the count was still alive. The lord of Grimbergen was forced to restore everything and had to promise the count to leave the abbey in peace. According to the *LM*, Gerald of Grimbergen became reconciled with the abbey and repented for his evil deeds by giving alms only just before his death in 1188 or 1189. At that point, he urged his friends and sons not to harm the abbey any more. He withdrew into the abbey of Grimbergen as a lay brother and died. The *LM* thus presents it as if the Grimbergen family established normal relations with the abbey only after forty years of struggle: when the *LM* was written, the abbey finally enjoyed bonds of friendship (*amicitia*) with Gerald's sons. In fact, however, from a charter dating from 1167, we know that animosity between Gerald II and the abbey had already officially

---

[20] For Gerald I of Ninove, *LM*, ed. Rockwell, p. 43 and n. 1; cf. Warlop, *The Flemish Nobility*, IV, 1017, who calls him Gerald II. Gerald II of Grimbergen as Gerald II was lord of Ninove from c. 1144 until 1188/1189. He is mentioned between 1149 and 1188 and died in 1188 or 1189. He married Mathilda, daughter of the abbey's founder, Gerald I of Ninove. She is mentioned between 1137 and 1175 and died before 1189 (*LM*, ed. Rockwell, pp. 43–44); J. Baerten, 'De Berthouts in de XIIe eeuw', *Handelingen van de Koninklijke Kring voor Oudheidkunde, Letteren en Kunst van Mechelen* 63 (1959), 17–29; Warlop, *The Flemish Nobility*, IV, 1017; J. Verbesselt, 'De oudste Brabantse adel en feodaliteit', in *De adel in het hertogdom Brabant*, eds. idem et al. (Brussel, 1985), pp. 9–43 at pp. 30–33). G. Croenen, *Familie en macht: de familie Berthout en de Brabantse adel, 12de – midden 14de eeuw* (unpublished Ph.D. thesis University of Gent, 1996) proposes a completely revised genealogy of the Berthout and Grimbergen families.

[21] *LM*, ed. Rockwell, p. 74 (ch. XVIII).

[22] *LM*, ed. Rockwell, p. 74 (ch. XVIII), pp. 75–77 (ch. XX).

[23] *LM*, ed. Rockwell, pp. 78–79 (ch. XXI). On Philip's advocacy, *De Oorkonden der Graven van Vlaanderen (Juli 1128 – September 1191). II. Uitgave. Band I: Regering van Diederik van de Elzas (Juli 1128 – 17 Januari 1168)*, eds. T. de Hemptinne and A. Verhulst (Brussel, 1988), no. 276 dated [25 Dec. 1166–24 Dec.] 1167.

ended in that year, in which the lord, his wife, and two sons promised to safeguard the abbey and confirmed its possessions, including the aforementioned two mills and common pasture.[24]

In the second place, conflicts could result from disagreement on joint use of land as a public road or as common meadows, or on collectively used woods, especially when the abbey claimed exclusive rights on land formerly in joint use. This may have been the case when a farmer near Renissart continued to use the abbey's arable land as a road, and when subjects of lord Walter Hawel of Ledeberg continued to steal wood from the abbey's forest near Kattem.[25] In the conflict between the abbey and the lord and the citizens of Ninove, the abbey's best meadows were turned into common pasture.[26]

A third cause of tension was refusal to hand over customary contributions, such as oblations in church and levies to be paid by the serfs of St Cornelius. This only concerned the humbler people, such as the Ninove parishioners, the abbey's serfs, and pilgrims. The *LM* makes it very clear that by such acts as these they incurred St Cornelius's wrath, i.e. (recurrence of) illness, or even death.[27]

Other causes of hostility mentioned in the *LM*, that is theft and plunder of crops and cattle, violence against the abbey's canons, lay brothers, and personnel, and the damaging of the abbey's property, such as mills and farms, may in fact be interpreted as parts of lay strategy in the process of conflict resolution rather than as the real causes of underlying conflict.[28] In

---

[24] This charter is inserted in the charter issued by Count Philip of Flanders, as in n. 23.

[25] *LM*, ed. Rockwell, p. 62 (ch. VIII); *DFNA*, ed. Rockwell, p. 96 (ch. XXXVIII).

[26] *LM* ed. Rockwell, pp. 75–77 (ch. XX).

[27] *LM*, ed. Rockwell, p. 64 (ch. IX), pp. 103–04 (chs. LII to LIV); Sigal, *L'homme et le miracle*, pp. 111–16.

[28] Instances of theft of corn or of cattle are related in *LM*, ed. Rockwell, pp. 57–59 (ch. I), pp. 59–60 (ch. III), pp. 65–66 (ch. XI), 68–69 (ch. XIII), p. 74 (ch. XVIII), pp. 78–79 (ch. XXI). *LM*, ed. Rockwell, pp. 57–59 (ch. I), pp. 60–61 (chs. IV, V, and VI) as well as *DFNA*, pp. 95–96 (ch. XXXVIII) all relate instances of lay maltreatment or even murder of the abbey's brothers and servants. Damage to the abbey's possessions is reported in *LM*, ed. Rockwell, pp. 66–68 (ch. XII), pp. 75–77 (ch. XX). On brief, small-scale military ventures as weapons deployed to support legal claims, R. Künzel, *Beelden en zelfbeelden van middeleeuwse mensen: Historisch-antropologische studies over groepsculturen in de Nederlanden, 7de-13de eeuw* (Nijmegen, 1997), p. 124, and S.D. White's contribution to 'Debate. The "Feudal Revolution"', *Past and Present*, no. 152 (1996), 196–223 at p. 212: 'Violence served not only as a method of expropriation, domination and intimidation, but also as a way of symbolically asserting rights, pressuring enemies to

several cases we can be quite sure of this.[29] In my introduction I related Alberic of Rosegnies's divine punishment, which arose from the seizure of one of the abbey's servants. From other sources we know that Alberic in 1172 proved that a part of the abbey's land at Renissart, which had earlier been sold to the abbey, in fact belonged to him, as his fief. After that, the canons, behind Alberic's back, succeeded in convincing his liege lords to grant that land to the abbey.[30] Only in 1179 did Alberic's brother Gerald recognize Ninove's rights to the land. Alberic, who must have died before 1179, thus had just cause to be angry with the abbey and to envy their possessions at Renissart. But no word about this in the *LM*!

Conflict Strategies

According to the *LM*, laymen in their conflicts with the abbey only resorted to violence: plunder, assault on lay brothers, public intimidation, devastation of the abbey's land, demolition of property, and theft of cattle. None of the more civilized strategies of settling conflicts seems to have been used by them. Nevertheless, looking at the canons' conflict strategies on the other hand, one observes that they did use negotiation, calling upon worldly or heavenly authorities, and excommunication as ways to fight their foes. The canons could only match lay violence by calling upon their advocate, the count of Flanders, but his close support could not always be relied upon, especially for the estates lying in Brabant, outside Flanders. The only sure answer for the canons was to invoke revenge from the world beyond. If we believe the *LM*, conflicts with laymen were most often solved through divine elimination of the enemy. But we can be fairly sure that more peaceful ways were tried as well. From many recent studies about medieval dispute settlement we know the importance of negotiation and mediation in

---

settle by distraining property, recovering rights and expressing righteous anger and justifiable enmity.'

[29] Plunder, theft, and violence as part of a conflict strategy are recorded in *LM*, ed. Rockwell, pp. 57–59 (ch. I), p. 60 (ch. IV), pp. 66–68 (ch. XII), p. 74 (ch. XVIII), pp. 75–79 (chs. XX and XXI).

[30] 'Partem terrae, quam nobis Hugo pauper, de quo ad annos 1140, 1142, vendiderat et inde warandiam promiserat, Albericus de Rosenis suum feodum esse probavit. Tenuit autem hanc a Marcilio castellano de Visvila; Marcilius autem a domino Wilhelmo de Birbais.' Cited by Rockwell in his introduction to *LM*, p. 38 n. 4, from the Elshoudt chronicle written in 1652 (see n. 18).

reaching a compromise.[31] In the miracle stories these strategies are also being employed by the canons of Ninove, and consequently, they must have been understood and used by the hostile laity as well.

Lord Giles of Trazegnies castle, a powerful lord in the border region between Brabant and Hainault, was Ninove's 'first and worst persecutor' ('primus et maximus Ninivensis ecclesie persecutor in curia nostra Reinirsart extitit').[32] The abbeys of Floreffe and Cambron, which had been endowed by Giles's parents and brother, also had long-standing disputes with him, because he challenged his relatives' donations to these abbeys.[33] Probably he also claimed hereditary rights to the estate of Renissart. After he had maltreated brothers of Ninove at Renissart, and plundered the estate time and again, the canons of Ninove with a gift induced him to go to the church of St Gertrud at Nivelles to swear an oath on the altar never to violate the abbey's property again. But soon he arrived with his henchmen and took with him almost the entire livestock of the estate. On this, the canons of Ninove had him excommunicated by the bishops of Cambrai and Liège. But he did not repent and this 'wild beast'—as the *LM* calls him— soon died a violent death. So the abbey of Ninove at first did follow the usual procedure of appeasement, consisting of gift-giving, negotiation, ceremonial agreement, and ritual reconciliation. When this did not work, they appealed to higher ecclesiastical authorities, who excommunicated him, and in the end they had no other choice but to appeal to God.

The same negotiating and mediating approach was used in other cases as well. In chapter VIII of the *LM*, mention is made of the frequent complaints the inhabitants of Seneffe used to make against the canons at Renissart. A

---

[31] For a short review article, with all relevant literature, P. Geary, 'Moral Obligations and Peer Pressure. Conflict Resolution in the Medieval Aristocracy', in *Georges Duby. L'écriture de l'Histoire*, eds. C. Duhamel-Amado and G. Lobrichon (Bruxelles, 1996), pp. 217–22.

[32] *LM*, ed. Rockwell, pp. 57–59 (ch. I).

[33] *LM*, ed. Rockwell, pp. 57–59 (ch. I). As lord of the Hainault seigniory of Silly (8 km south-west of Enghien) he was a *pair* of Mons. He also was a brave crusader (*LM*, ed. Rockwell, pp. 33–35; D. Van de Perre and R. Van Hauwe, 'De geschiedenis van Denderwindeke. Deel II: De middeleeuwse heren (ca. 1100–1487)', *Het Land van Aalst* 44 (1992), 1–62 at pp. 4–6). His parents were Osto I of Trazegnies (d. before 1138) and Helvida. In 1155 he confirmed and renewed a gift made by his parents to the abbey of Floreffe (*Histoire de l'abbaye de Floreffe de l'ordre de Prémontré*, ed. V. Barbier, 2 vols. (Namur, 1892), I, no. 30 dated 1155). Giles died in 1162 or 1163, after having been excommunicated due to a conflict with the abbey of Floreffe (ibid., no. 40 dated [c. 1163]).

somewhat more powerful townsman among the Seneffe inhabitants acted as their advocate and intermediary ('causidicus et mediator'), in which position he accepted gifts from both parties. In the end, however, he revealed himself as a false friend ('simulatus amicus') of the abbey and derided St Cornelius, for which he was punished.

In the ongoing conflict with Gerald of Grimbergen as lord of Ninove, the abbey also resorted to mediation and a judgement by the bishop.[34] In this same dispute the canons tried to buy peace by giving money to their enemy. In another chapter, it is stated that the lord and citizens of Ninove, acting together against the abbey, expected to receive money as a result of their threats.[35] The canons of Ninove frequently appealed to the ecclesiastical and worldly authorities to punish offenders. We already mentioned the excommunication of Giles of Trazegnies by the bishops of Cambrai and Liège. Also, charges against two thieves of the abbey's property were brought before the relevant worldly judges, but this did not always have the desired result.[36]

Another form of settling disputes was the so-called *deditio*, i.e. a ritual submission through prostration by one of the parties to the other.[37] It was most often used in conflict settlement between lay lords, but also appears in disputes in which ecclesiastical and religious leaders were involved. It was a radical way of solving a dispute which crippled all parties implicated and threatened to cause general loss of face. According to the diplomatic mores of the time, the party receiving the submission thereupon was supposed to show mercy, to raise the submitting party up from the ground, and to reach a compromise with which both parties could live and save face. The *deditio*, in fact a ritual through which both parties' positions were redefined, served as a noble privilege to reach mutual atonement. At one moment in the conflict with the lord of Ninove, the abbot, accompanied by the older canons, went to the castle. There he found the lord, his wife, and

---

[34] *LM*, ed. Rockwell, p. 74 (ch. XVIII).

[35] *LM*, ed. Rockwell, pp. 75–77 (ch. XX).

[36] *LM*, ed. Rockwell, pp. 59–60 (ch. III, charge against a servant of lord Siger du Rœulx, for stealing corn from a field at Renissart, brought before his lord, who did not punish this sacrilege); *DFNA*, pp. 94–96 (ch. XXXVIII, charges brought before lord Walther Hawel of Ledeberg against some of his subjects for daily thefts of wood).

[37] G. Althoff, 'Das Privileg der deditio. Formen gütlicher Konfliktbeendung in der mittelalterlichen Adelsgesellschaft', in idem, *Spielregeln der Politik im Mittelalter: Kommunikation in Frieden und Fehde* (Darmstadt, 1997), pp. 99–125; A.J.A. Bijsterveld, 'Eergevoel en conflictbeheersing in aristocratische en geestelijke kringen in de twaalfde-eeuwse Nederlanden', *Millennium* 11 (1997), 99–112.

his followers, and with his brothers and priests strikingly prostrated himself at their feet. As soon as the lord and his retinue perceived this wordless complaint, they fled and left the prostrated priests behind. Then, the abbot rose, returned to the abbey, and commended his case to Christ, His mother, and St Cornelius.[38] Apparently, the lord of Ninove and his retinue recognized this prostration to be a formal *deditio*, but did not want to grant due mercy to the abbot, and therefore fled the room. The abbot's attempt to reach a compromise and a settlement had failed.

Next to these standard conflict resolution mechanisms, also available to laymen, the canons of Ninove of course could resort to divine power. For this, they had at their disposal an extensive arsenal of religious weapons, i.e. prayers, the public ban, excommunication, malediction, ritual complaint, and even the carrying around and humiliation of their patron saint's relics.[39] By praying to St Cornelius, and invoking him as their 'mighty vindicator', they asked for his protection and avenging intercession. In times of misery, they would raise a clamour to God and St Cornelius, as when a servant of the abbey was shot at with an arrow.[40] In addition to prayers and invocations, the canons had St Cornelius's relics and therefore his actual physical presence to protect and to avenge them.[41] When the lords of Ninove carried off to their castle the abbey's wagons, filled with the fruits of harvest, the canons placed St Cornelius's shrine in the road in front of the wagons, to block their way.[42] But this did not stop the thieves:

---

[38] *LM*, ed. Rockwell, pp. 75–77 (ch. XX).

[39] Sigal, *L'homme et le miracle*, pp. 279–81; Künzel, *Beelden en zelfbeelden*, pp. 111–48 at pp. 114–20; L.K. Little, *Benedictine Maledictions: Liturgical Cursing in Romanesque France* (Ithaca and London, 1993); E. Bozoky, 'Voyage de reliques et démonstration du pouvoir aux temps féodaux', in *Voyages et voyageurs au Moyen Age. XXVIe Congrès de la S.H.M.E.S. (Limoges-Aubazine, mai 1995)* (Paris, 1996), pp. 267–80; L. Morelle, 'Les chartes dans la gestion des conflits (France du Nord, XIe–début du XIIe siècle)', *Bibliothèque de l'École des chartes* 155 (1997), 267–98 at pp. 294–96.

[40] *LM*, ed. Rockwell, pp. 66–68 (ch. XII): 'fit querimonia ad Deum et sanctum Cornelium pro tanto scelere.'

[41] In *LM*, ed. Rockwell, p. 64 (ch. IX) St Cornelius is described as 'quasi carne presente', 'seemingly present in the flesh' in the church of Ninove. The *LM* contains many examples of St Cornelius being invoked as the powerful vindicator, that is as '(potens) vindex' (*LM*, ed. Rockwell, p. 62 (ch. VII); p. 64 (ch. IX)) and 'ultor' (ibid., pp. 62–63 (ch. VIII)). Words expressing the 'just revenge' abound in the *LM*.

[42] *LM*, ed. Rockwell, p. 74 (ch. XVIII); Sigal, *L'homme et le miracle*, p. 162. The placing of relics in front of an offender's feet was a frequent strategy (Künzel, *Beelden en zelfbeelden*, p. 54). On the forcing of, and the challenges put to, saints, ibid., pp. 119, 129, 134, 139.

one of the lord's servants with his foot pushed the shrine out of the way, for which he, of course, had to pay with his life. By humiliating St Cornelius's relics, that is by putting his shrine in the road, the canons challenged him to do his protective and avenging work, which in this case failed. But the only thing that counted was the final victory, which was of course gained by the canons.

In a later stage of the same conflict, the lord of Ninove and the townsmen of Ninove made common cause and in a procession moved against the abbey and its workshops.[43] The canons expected the worst, and, unshod and dressed in their surplices, prepared St Cornelius's shrine. As soon as the lay intruders came within the walls of the cloister (*claustrum*), they would meet them and ask for mercy. But the intruders changed their minds, passed around the cloister, and returned to the town, while pulling down the fences around the abbey's meadows and letting in their cattle. By circling the abbey, the citizens of Ninove imitated the familiar ecclesiastical ritual of circling altars, churches, and recalcitrant feuders, to symbolically isolate the encircled object or persons from the world and to get them into their power.[44] The canons, however, had used St Cornelius's relics to symbolically demarcate the abbey's property and exclusive, sacred space, the cloister. On other occasions too, St Cornelius's relics proved to be trustworthy, as when the first lords of Ninove went out to fight a battle taking along relics.[45] Many ailing pilgrims recovered by touching the relics, by drinking the water in which the relics had been immersed,[46] or by just approaching them.[47] When a fire threatened houses near the abbey church, the shrine of St Cornelius was carried around and the fire miraculously went out.[48]

The canons of Ninove used all worldly and spiritual ways of fighting their battles with laymen, from common dispute settlement mechanisms to divine power in order to reach again the desired state of peace and

---

[43] *LM*, ed. Rockwell, pp. 75–77 (ch. XX).

[44] G. Koziol, *Begging Pardon and Favor: Ritual and Political Order in Early Medieval France* (Ithaca and London, 1992), pp. 142–43; Künzel, *Beelden en zelfbeelden*, p. 142. This ritual is reminiscent of the Old Testament encircling of the town of Jericho (Joshua 6. 1–16).

[45] *LM*, ed. Rockwell, pp. 72–73 (ch. XVI); Sigal, *L'homme et le miracle*, p. 48.

[46] *LM*, ed. Rockwell, p. 80 (ch. XXV), p. 110 (ch. LXIV).

[47] *LM*, ed. Rockwell, pp. 105–07 (ch. LVII).

[48] *LM*, ed. Rockwell, p. 105 (ch. LVI).

friendship, *pax et amicitia*. From the accounts in the *LM*, it is clear that the canons always played for high stakes, that is, in many instances they aimed to defeat their lay opponents without having to make any compromise. The canons of Ninove apparently not only counted on St Cornelius and God to stand on their side, but also on eternity. Even the most powerful lord would meet his death in due time, whereas the abbey's community and St Cornelius would live forever.[49] In the canons' belief of being God's elect and of being part of God's timeless redemptive scheme, the transient violence and hostility of laymen, fickle and mortal as they are, could not be taken seriously after all. In eternity's shadow the canons of Ninove could afford to await their enemies' death, after which they triumphantly recorded their downfall and death in the *LM*.

Conclusion

From the canons' point of view, good relations with the laity were based on reciprocal obligations. As long as noblemen with their arms protected the abbey and its *familia*, and respected its property and privileges, they could count on St Cornelius's protection and intercession. Reciprocal respect resulted in mutual goodwill. The relations with lesser people, knights, farmers, citizens of Ninove and even pilgrims, were based on the same contractual principle. In return for their veneration and gifts, St Cornelius would extend his protection over them as well.[50] Non-observance of their duties resulted in St Cornelius's intercession with God to punish the offenders. It was the canons who claimed to be the exclusive intermediaries between lay people and their patron saint. In their *LM* they make it very clear, that, although St Cornelius could even be invoked at home, the miraculously healed always needed to fulfil their part of the contract with the saint at the abbey, where his shrine was located.

For their part too, the canons' relation with St Cornelius took the shape of a tacit contract, involving the fulfilment of mutual obligations. The canons would venerate and honour St Cornelius as long as he fulfilled his part of the contract, i.e. protect the abbey, its *familia*, and its property. The canons could not only humbly invoke St Cornelius, but could also raise a clamour for justice against him, humiliate his relics, and even challenge

---

[49] On the different conceptions of conflict settlement held by laymen and clerics, Platelle, 'Crime et châtiment', p. 197; Künzel, *Beelden en zelfbeelden*, p. 146.

[50] Sigal, *L'homme et le miracle*, p. 280.

him to do a miracle.[51] The canons threatened that if he did not comply, they would not venerate him as fervently as they had done before.[52]

When a conflict with laymen arose, the canons used the usual ways to deal with it, namely negotiation and mediation, and appeals to the competent worldly and ecclesiastical authorities In contrast to their lay enemies, however, the canons had access to an arsenal of divine conflict strategies. That is why in the *LM* the sudden and violent deaths of opponents are described as miraculous chastisements, divine punishments for breaking the mutual contract and not fulfilling the reciprocal obligations. Those who broke the contract with worldly violence could expect this to be reciprocated with violence from beyond.

---

[51] As when a servant of the abbey was shot at with an arrow, and the canons raised a 'querimonia' to God and St Cornelius (*LM*, ed. Rockwell, pp. 66–68 (ch. XII)), and when a fire threatened to damage the abbey church, and a priest challenged St Cornelius by exclaiming: 'Holy Cornelius, if you tolerate your house to burn down, I swear all relics of the saints, and yours as well, will not be carried away, but be left inside and burn together' (*LM*, ed. Rockwell, p. 102 (ch. L)).

[52] When a parishioner of Ninove refused to pay his oblation in church, the parish priest—a canon of the abbey—burst out in tears and complained to St Cornelius 'O holy Cornelius, if you do not revenge me today because of this man, I will never serve you with a happy heart', whereupon the parishioner was struck with madness and died soon after (*LM*, ed. Rockwell, p. 64 (ch. IX); Sigal, *L'homme et le miracle*, p. 280).

Index of Persons

Adalbero, bishop of Laon, 12, 42, 44
Adela, countess of Flanders, 70
Adelaide of Tosny, wife of William FitzOsbern, 116, 117, 121
Adelaide, daughter of Earl Waltheof, 131
Adrevald of Fleury, 54, 58, 63
Ælfflæd, daughter of Earl Ealdred, 112, 115
Ælfgar, earl, son of Leofric of Mercia, 130
Ælfgifu, third wife of Ealdorman Uhtred, 109, 115, 130
Ælfhelm, Ealdorman, 130
Ælfred Ætheling, 130
Ælfric, bishop of East Anglia, 94
Ælfric Modercope, thegn, 94, 96
Ælfric, father of Wihtgar, 105
Æthelmær, brother of archbishop Stigand, 91, 95, 96, 97, 100, 101, 102, 104, 105
Æthelred II, king of England, 109, 115, 122, 125, 128, 130
Æthelthryth, daughter of Earl Ealdred, 109
Æthelweard of Cornwall and Devon, 113
Agnes, wife of Robert of Bellême, 125
Agnes, wife of Simon of Montfort, 123
Alan, abbot-elect of Saint-Wandrille, 79
Alberic of Rosegnies, 168, 174, 177
Albert, monk of Bec, 81
Aldwin, abbot of Ramsey, 136

Alfhelm Facet of Wells, 142, 144
Alfward of Ripton, 138
Alfwen, wife of William Pecche, 138, 139, 140, 144
Amann, E., 7
Amaury of Montfort, 124
Amaury I, lord of Ninove, 168
Amaury II, lord of Ninove, 168
Anand, thegn, 100
Ansbert, St, 55, 56
Anselm, abbot of Bec, archbishop of Canterbury, 7–11, 75, 77, 78, 80, 81, 83, 127
Arnulf I, count of Flanders, 52, 55
Arnulf III, count of Flanders, 29
Atto of Vercelli, 6
Aubrey de Vere, 138
Augustine, St, 37
Avitus, priest, 63
Baldric II, bishop of Liège, 30
Baldwin FitzGilbert, 123
Baldwin IV, count of Flanders, 65
Baldwin V, count of Flanders, 29, 70, 71, 126
Baldwin VII, count of Flanders, 27, 31
Baldwin I, count of Hainault, 32
Baldwin II, count of Hainault, 32, 33
Baldwin III, count of Hainault, 33
Baldwin IV, count of Hainault, 29, 33
Baldwin V, count of Hainault, 20, 32
Bartholomew of Jur, bishop of Laon, 49
Beatrix, wife of Pleines of Slepe, 136, 144
Beaufour family, 117

Beaumont family, 75, 83
Benedict, St, 54, 58, 63, 68, 74
Berengar, son of Reginald the monk, 138
Bertha, wife of Girart of Roussillon, 157
Berthe, wife of Guy of Laval, 116
Berthout family, 175
Bertin, St, 55, 51–72
Bertrade of Montfort, 124
Bertulf, St, 55
Bijsterveld, A.J.A., 159, 161
Bismarck, O. von, 3
Bloch, M., 11–12, 14
Boso, abbot of Bec, 76, 77–80
Bovo, abbot of Saint-Bertin, 51–72
Bresslau, H., 1–4
Brooke, Z.N., 9
Brungar, freeman, 96
Byrhtnoth of Essex, ealdorman, 113
Charlemagne, emperor, 3, 19, 26
Charles of Lotharingia, pretender to the French throne, 42
Charles VII, king of France, 26
Charles the Good, count of Flanders, 27, 29
Chédeville, A., 7
Clares, the, family, 75
Clerval, Abbé, 156, 162
Cnut, king of England, Denmark, and Norway, 109, 112
Conrad II, emperor, 2, 3
Cornelius, St, 167–83, 179
Crispins, the, noble family, 75
Cyprian, St, 168
David, son of Malcolm III of Scotland, 131
Desiderius, bishop of Thérouanne, 25, 26
Didier, bishop of Thérouanne, 23
Drew of Hastings, 142, 144, 146
Drogo, bishop of Thérouanne, 63, 67
Drogo, count of Vexin, 26
Drogo of Beuvrière, 125
Duby, G., 12–13, 117, 132, 153
Dumas, A., 7

Dunod, 163
Durkheim, E., 11
Eadric of Laxfield, 100, 101, 104, 105
Eadric Streona, ealdorman, 130
Eadulf, earl, brother of Earl Ealdred, 112
Ealdgyth, wife of Eadric Streona, 130
Ealdhun, bishop of Durham, 108, 109
Ealdred, earl, son of Ealdorman Uhtred, 109, 112, 114
Ecgfrida, first wife of Ealdorman Uhtred, 108, 109, 112, 113
Edgar, king of England, 113, 126
Edgar Ætheling, 129
Edith, queen of England, 115
Edward the Confessor, king of England, 100, 115, 130
Edward of Salisbury, sheriff of Wiltshire, 125
Emma, daughter of Count Ralph, 117
Emma, daughter of William FitzOsbern, 127
Enguerrand, bishop of Laon, 42
Erik, earl, 109
Erlebald, parishioner of Ninove, 172
Eudes II, count, 156
Eudo *dapifer*, 142, 144
Eugene, St, 54, 56
Eustace, monk of Bec, 81
Everard, abbot's man, 136
Farman the cellarer, monk of Bec, 81
FitzGilbert family, 122
FitzRichard family, 122
Fliche, A., 4–7
Folcuin, St, bishop of Thérouanne, 60, 66
Folcuin, monk of Saint-Bertin, abbot of Lobbes, 57, 60
Fridugis, abbot of Saint-Bertin, 60, 65
Fulbert of Chartres, 153–57
Fustel de Coulanges, N.D., 11
Galbert of Bruges, 29
Gaudric, bishop of Laon, 40, 42, 48
Geary, P.J., 153
Geoffrey, archbishop of Rouen, 78
Geoffrey, count of Anjou, 126

Index of Persons

Geoffrey, viscount of Châteaudun, 163
Geoffrey the presbyter, 144
Gerald, bishop of Cambrai, 12, 62
Gerald I, lord of Ninove, 168, 174, 175
Gerald II, lord of Grimbergen and Ninove, 169, 174, 175
Gerald of Brogne, 52, 53, 57
Gerald of Quierzy, 43, 48
Gerald, brother of Alberic of Rosegnies, 177
Ghislain, St, 53, 56, 68
Gilbert, bishop of Évreux, 77
Gilbert, count of Brionne, 74, 75, 82, 122, 124
Giles of Trazegnies, 174, 178, 179
Girart of Roussillon, 157
Gisla, wife of Gerald I of Ninove, 168
Gislebert, duke of Lotharingia, 53, 68
Godehildis, widow of Roger of Tosny, 116
Godescalc, bishop of Arras, 29
Godfrey van Elshoudt, canon of Ninove, 174
Godiva, wife of Earl Siward, 112
Godric the hawker, 146
Godwine, Earl Harold's man, 141
Godwine Cild, 146
Goody, J., 132
Goscelin of Canterbury, monk of Saint-Bertin, 67, 68
Gospatric, brother of Earl Eadulf, 115
Gospatric, grandson of Ealdorman Uhtred, 115
Gournay, lords of, 75
Gregory I, the Great, pope, 48
Gregory VII, pope, 3, 6
Grimbergen family, 175, 179
Gudwald, St, 55
Guibert of Nogent, 37–50
Gundreda of Gournay, wife of Nigel d'Aubigny, 126
Gunnor, countess, 122
Guy, count of Ponthieu, 125
Guy of Burgundy, 80
Guy, lord of Laval castle, 116

Gyrth, earl of East Anglia, 100, 104, 105
Hákon, son of earl Erik, 112
Hamo, great-grandson of William Pecche, 140
Hamo, son of William Pecche, 140
Hardwin of Scales, 146
Hariulf of Saint-Riquier, 56
Harold Godwineson, earl of Wessex, king of England, 100, 104, 105
Hauck, K., 4
Head, T., 153
Helinand, bishop of Laon, 42
Helvétius, A.-M., 68
Helvida, wife of Osto I, lord of Trazegnies, 178
Henry II, emperor, 151
Henry III, emperor, 3
Henry IV, emperor, 3, 71
Henry I, king of England, 8, 9, 74, 78, 107, 124, 126, 130, 140
Henry I, king of France, 2
Henry of France, archbishop of Reims, 24
Heorunwulf, brother of Hugh the interpreter, 138
Herbert, abbot of Ramsey, 138
Herfast, grandfather of William FitzOsbern, 121, 122
Herluin, abbot of Bec, 74, 77
Hugh Capet, king of France, 42
Hugh of Halvercamp, archbishop of Rouen, 120, 121
Hugh, bishop of Amiens, archbishop of Rouen, 74, 78
Hugh, bishop of Bayeux, 122
Hugh, abbot of Saint-Bertin and Saint-Quentin, 66
Hugh of Beauchamp, 141
Hugh of Poitiers, 164
Hugh the interpreter, 138
Humbert of Moyenmoutier, 6
Humphrey of Bohun, knight, 125
Huri, priest-prophet, 151
Huyghebaert, N., 57
Ingelram, abbot's man, 136

Innocent II, pope, 78
Isabel, sister of Simon of Montfort, 123
Ivo of Chartres, 161
Ivo, St, 68
John the Baptist, St, 68
John the Evangelist, St, 150–53
John, bishop of Thérouanne, 23, 25
John of Ypres, abbot of Saint-Bertin, 59
John IV, count of Armagnac, 26
John, count of Ponthieu, 28
Jonas of Orleans, 20
Joscelin, bishop of Salisbury, 151
Judith, countess of Northampton, wife of Waltheof, 127, 128, 129, 131, 141, 146
Kapelle, W.E., 114
Karl, son of Thurbrand Hold, 114
Ketil, family of, 96
Kilvert, son of Ligulf, 109
Lambert, bishop of Thérouanne, 23
Lambert of Saint-Omer, 61, 66
Landes, R., 153
Lanfranc, abbot of Bec, archbishop of Canterbury, 8, 9, 75, 129
Le Moyne family, 138
Leo IX, pope, 3, 12
Leo XIII, pope, 5
Little, L.K., 149
Louis the Pious, emperor, 20
Louis VI, king of France, 124
Lucian, 61, 63
Maitland, F.W., 7–9, 95
Malcolm III, king of Scotland, 131
Malhuluc, ancestor of Roger of Tosny, 121, 122
Manasses I, archbishop of Reims, 30
Manasses II, archbishop of Reims, 24
Manuel Comnenus, emperor of Byzantium, 77
Mark, St, 151
Mary, St, 161
Mathilda, queen of England, 141, 144
Mathilda, countess of Tuscany, 4
Mathilda, daughter of earl Waltheof, 131

Mathilda, wife of Drew of Hastings, 144
Mathilda, wife of Gerald II of Grimbergen and Ninove, 174, 175
Merlet, R., 156, 162
Meyer von Knonau, G., 3
Milo I, bishop of Thérouanne, 23, 32
Milo II, bishop of Thérouanne, 23
Misonne, D., 54
Morcar, earl of Northumbria, 115
Mortemer, family, 120
Muriel, sister of Eudo *dapifer*, 144
Nigel, viscount of the Cotentin, 120, 121
Nigel d'Aubigny, 125, 126
Nigel Fossard, 141, 142, 144
Odbert, abbot of Saint-Bertin, 58
Odo, son of Robert the Pious of France, 70
Omer, St, 55, 60, 64, 66
Orderic Vitalis, 82, 130
Orm, son of Gamel, lord of Kirkdale, 109
Osbern FitzHerfast, father of William FitzOsbern, steward, 117, 123, 124
Osto I, lord of Trazegnies, 178
Osulf, son of Earl Eadulf, 115
Otter, M., 67
Paul Orosius, 64
Paul, St, 4, 157
Peter Damian, 6
Peter, St, 4, 157
Philip I, king of France, 126
Philip of Alsace, count of Flanders, 175, 176
Picot, sheriff of Cambridgeshire, 146
Platelle, H., 172
Pleines of Slepe, 136–38, 142, 144
Prester John, 76, 77, 82
Ralph of Beaufour, 117
Ralph of Gael, lord of Gael, 127, 131
Ralph the staller, earl, 100, 101, 104, 105
Ralph of Tosny, son of Ralph, 120, 131
Ralph of Tosny, son of Roger, 108, 116, 117, 120

Index of Persons

Ralph, brother of Ilger, 142, 144
Ranulf Flambard, bishop of Durham, 8
Raoul, archbishop of Reims, 24
Raso, lord of Gavere, 174
Rather of Verona, 6
Reginald, abbot of Ramsey, 146
Reginald the monk, 137, 138
Renaud, archbishop of Reims, 24, 30
Richard I, duke of Normandy, 122
Richard II, duke of Normandy, 29, 120, 122, 126
Richard, count of Évreux, 28, 116, 124
Richard FitzGilbert, 123, 138
Richard of Saint-Vanne, 65
Richard, son of Pleines of Slepe, 136, 144
Richer, St, 56
Rictrud, St, 172
Riculfus, archbishop of Rouen, 24
Robert II the Pious, king of France, 70, 163
Robert I, duke of Normandy, 74
Robert Curthose, duke of Normandy, 23, 77, 80, 123
Robert, archbishop of Rouen, 121
Robert I, count of Flanders, 27, 29, 31
Robert II, count of Flanders, 27
Robert I, count of Meulan, 74, 80, 81, 82
Robert of Bellême, 125
Robert of Giroie, 125
Robert, earl, 141, 144
Robert, monk of Bec, 81
Roderic, abbot of Saint-Bertin, 65, 66, 69
Roger of Beaumont, 80, 82, 124
Roger of Bienfaite, 81, 82, 83
Roger Bigod, 138
Roger of Hereford, earl, son of William FitzOsbern, 127, 129
Roger of Tosny, son of Ralph, 116, 120, 121, 124
Roger, son of Kumbold, 144
Rollo, count, duke of Normandy, 121, 122
Rosenwein, B.H., 14

Saint-Bertin abbey, 51–72
Samson, archbishop of Reims, 24
Sazama, K.M., 160
Scholastica, St, 54, 58, 63
Sige, second wife of Ealdorman Uhtred, 108, 109
Siger du Rœulx, lord, 174, 179
Sigrid, widow of Earl Eadulf, 112, 113
Simon, monk of Saint-Bertin, 59, 66, 69
Simon of Montfort, 123
Simon of Senlis, 131
Siward, earl of York and Northampton, 112
Siward of Maldon, 101
Siward the clerk of Wistow, 144
Sophia, countess of Chiny, 29
Southern, R.W., 9
Stafford, P., 129
Steindorff, E., 3
Stephen, bishop of Noyon, 23
Stephen, St, 61, 63
Stigand, archbishop of Canterbury, 91, 96, 100, 104
Stubbs, W., 7–9
Styr of York, 108
Swain (of Over?), 146
Sweyn of Denmark, 109
Tellenbach, G., 4
Theobald, abbot of Bec, 78, 79
Theodred, bishop of London, 91
Thierry of Alsace, count of Flanders, 22, 27
Thierry, count of Flanders, 31
Thomas, lord of Marle castle, 41
Thorketil, freeman, 97
Thurbrand Hold, 109, 112, 114
Toli, freeman, 97
Tostig, earl of Northumbria, 115, 116
Uhtred, ealdorman of Northumbria, 108–9, 114, 115, 116
Urban II, pope, 78, 126
Vaughn, S., 10
Victor II, pope, 71
Virgin, Holy. *See* Mary, St
Vuicardus, donor, 25
Vulfran, St, 55, 56

Waitz, G., 2
Waleran II, count of Meulan, 83
Waleran of Bréteuil, 123
Walter Hawel, lord of Ledeberg, 176, 179
Waltheof, earl of Northampton and Northumbria, 114, 127–31, 146
Wandrille, St, 55, 56
Waudru, St, 53
Wesinus, St., bishop of Sherborne, 151
White, S.D., 14, 153
Wido, archbishop of Reims, 61, 63, 67
Wihtgar Algarson, 101
William the Bastard. *See* William the Conqueror
William the Conqueror, duke of Normandy, 8, 9, 74, 75, 77, 107, 114, 125, 126, 141, 144
William I, king of England *See* William the Conqueror, 183
William II, king of England, 8, 107, 125, 130
William, archbishop of Reims, 23
William of Beaumont, abbot of Bec, 77, 80
William, count of Évreux, 123, 124
William of Normandy, count of Flanders, 27
William I, count of Ponthieu, 27
William II, count of Ponthieu, 28
William of Aldera, 130
William of Bréteuil, 81, 83, 123, 124, 131
William Crispin, 81, 83
William FitzOsbern, ducal steward, 108, 116, 121, 122, 129
William of Gael, 131
William of Montgomery, 124
William Pecche, 138–41, 142, 144
William, son of Pleines of Slepe, 136, 144
Wormald, F., 151
Wulfnoth, 142, 144
Zachary, pope, 63

Index of Places

Abbeville priory, 34
Amiens, 78
Anchin abbey, 32
Andelle valley, 117, 124, 131
Anjou, 28, 123, 124, 126
Aquitaine, 68
Ardennes, 161
Arles, 24
Armagnac, 26
Arques, 28
Arras, 24, 26, 27, 29, 62, 65
Arrouaise abbey, 25
Artois, 21
Auchy abbey, 29
Aulne abbey, 32
Aumale, 28
Auxerre, 157–59, 160, 164
Bamburgh, 108, 115
Bar, 28
Barford, 144
Bari, 76
Barnwell, 137
Barsham, 105
Bastwick, 95
Bavaria, 2
Bayeux, 122, 126
Beaumont-sur-Oise, 28
Bec-Hellouin, Le, abbey, 23, 74
Bedfordshire, 131, 141, 144
Besançon, 163
Billockby, 105
Bishop's Hundred, 101
Blangy-en-Artois, 57
Blois, 120
Boulogne-sur-Mer, 55, 57
Brabant, duchy, 171, 173
Bradfield, 105
Bréteuil, 117, 122, 124
Brionne, 74, 80, 81, 84, 122
Brittany, 127
Brogne abbey, 52, 54, 68
Bromham, 141, 144
Bruges. *See* St Donatian's chapter
Brundall, 105
Buckinghamshire, 131
Burgundy, 14
Bury St Edmund's abbey, 91, 94, 96, 97, 101, 104
Caen, 75
Cambrai, 178, 179
Cambridgeshire, 94, 131, 138, 144
Cambron abbey, 178
Canossa, 4
Canterbury, 8, 10, 75, 91, 102, 127
Carpentras, 24
Cassel, 29
Catalonia, 32
Châlons-sur-Marne, 78
Champagne, 21, 28
Chartres, 120, 150, 153, 161, 163
Châteaudun, 163
Chatteris abbey, 146
Chickering, 106
Chiny, 29, 34
Chippenhall, 101, 105
Christ Church, cathedral at Canterbury, 67, 68
Clackclose Hundred, 97

Clermont, 78
Cluny, 2, 6, 14, 135, 163, 164
Conches, 116, 117, 120
Cornwall, 113
Cotentin, 120
Coutances, 126
Cranfield, 144
Crespin abbey, 33
Crowland abbey, 129
Cumberland, 115
Deuil, 54
Devon, 113
Diddington Stow, 144
Dieleghem-Jette abbey, 172
Dorset, 150
Durham, 108, 129, 134
East Anglia, 91, 103, 89–106
Elmham, 91, 102
Ely abbey, 91, 96, 97, 146
Emneth, 144
Enghien, 178
England, 7–11, 15, 60, 67, 75, 90, 107, 108–16, 125, 131, 134
Essex, 113, 138
Eu, 28
Évreux, 28, 77, 79, 116, 124
Eye, 101
Flanders, 21, 22, 23, 27, 29, 31, 35, 52, 68, 168, 171, 175
Fleury abbey, 54, 58, 63, 68, 159
Floreffe abbey, 178
Fontenelle abbey, 55, 56. *See also* Saint-Wandrille
Fountains abbey, 125
France, 4–7, 15, 20, 21, 35, 45, 51, 63, 68, 75, 117, 163
Furnes. *See* Veurne
Gael, 127
Gavere, 174
Gent, 55, 56
Germany, 1–4, 6, 27
Ghent. *See* Gent
Glos, 117
Grimbergen, abbey, 175
Grimbergen, lordship, 169, 175

Hainault, 20, 27, 29, 32, 35, 53, 68, 172, 173
Hasnon abbey, 32, 33
Hemblington, 105
Hemsby, 103
Hertfordshire, 144
Holderness, 112, 114
Horham, 106
Hoxne, 91
Huntingdonshire, 94, 97, 128, 131, 136, 144
Ile-de-France, 45, 123
Italy, 2, 163
Iton valley, 116
Jerusalem, 63
Jumièges abbey, 78
Kattem, 176
Kent, 142
Kingston. *See* Wistow
Kirkdale, 109
Langley, 100, 105
Laon, 37–50, 41, 50
Launditch Hundred, 100
Laval, 116
Le Mans, 126
Ledeberg, 176, 179
Leicestershire, 131
Liedekerke, 172
Liège, 30, 151, 160, 178, 179
Lincolnshire, 131
Lisieux, 77, 126
Llanthony abbey, 125
Lobbes abbey, 60
Loire valley, 58
London, 91, 142, 144
Lorraine, 28
Lotharingia, 2, 20, 21, 42, 52, 68
Low Countries, 15
Luddington, 144
Lyre abbey, 117, 121
Maine, 116, 120, 123
Marchiennes abbey, 32, 172
Marle castle, 41
Marmoutier abbey, 28, 116, 159
Melrose abbey, 32
Mercia, 113, 130

Index of Places

Meulan, 10, 28, 74, 80, 83, 120
Middlesex, 131
Midlands, 94, 109, 112
Mintlyn, 106
Mons, 53, 178
Monte Cassino abbey, 54, 58, 63, 68
Montreuil-sur-Mer, 55, 56
Mont-Saint-Quentin abbey, 25
Mortain, 28
Mortemer, 120
Namur, 27, 30, 34, 35, 54
Nancy, 22
New Minster, abbey at Winchester, 134
Ninove abbey, 167–83, 180
Nivelles, 178
Norfolk, 91, 95, 97, 127, 138, 144
Normandy, 21, 23, 24, 27, 29, 34, 35, 74, 75, 107, 116–27, 123, 131
North Elmham, 91, 105
Northamptonshire, 112, 128, 131, 137
Northumberland, 125, 126
Northumbria, 108–16, 108, 128
Notre-Dame cathedral, Chartres, 163
Notre-Dame cathedral, Laon, 43
Noyon, 23, 26, 31
Old Hurst, 136, 137
Orval abbey, 29
Over, 139, 144, 146
Oxonia, 131
Paris, 76
Pays de Caux, 117
Peterborough abbey, 112
Picardy, 21, 28
Poland, 2
Ponthieu, 23, 27, 33, 35
Ramsey abbey, 94, 97, 136, 146, 133–46
Reims, 23, 26, 30, 44, 61, 78, 79
Renissart, 168, 173, 174
Renty, 55
Rethel, 28
Rheims. *See* Reims
Ribemont, 28
Ripton, 138
Rise, 114
Risle valley, 83, 116

Rochester Cathedral Priory, 135, 142
Rollesby, 105
Rome, 3, 43, 114
Rosegnies, 168
Rouen, 77, 78, 120
Rutland, 131
Saint-Amand abbey, 31
Saint-André-en-Gouffern, 34
St Augustine's abbey, Canterbury, 67, 68, 78
St Benet's of Holme, abbey, 94, 97, 101, 104, 105
Saint-Benoit-sur-Loire. *See* Fleury
Saint-Bertin abbey, 31, 55, 57
Saint-Claude abbey, 25
Saint-Denis-en-Broqueroie abbey, 33, 54
St Donatian's chapter, Brugge, 31
Saint-Feuillien abbey, Le Rœulx, 33
St Gertrud abbey, Nivelles, 178
Saint-Ghislain abbey, 53, 68
Saint-Hubert abbey, 159, 161
St Ives. *See* Slepe
Saint-Josse-au-Bois abbey, 33
Saint-Laurent abbey, Liège, 151
St Mary's abbey, Nogent, 38, 50
Saint-Médard abbey, 78
Saint-Omer chapter, 57
Saint-Ouen abbey, 78
Saint-Père abbey, 156
St Peter's abbey, Gent, 55, 57
Saint-Pol, county, 71
Saint-Quentin abbey, 66
Saint-Quentin chapter, 29
Saint-Riquier (Centula), 56
Saint-Vaast abbey, Arras, 22
St Walburgis's chapter, Veurne, 29
Saint-Wandrille abbey, 55, 57, 78. *See also* Fontenelle abbey
Salisbury, 151
Scotland, 108, 129, 131
Scratby, 105
Sées, 126
Seine, 120
Seneffe, 172, 178
Senlis, 43

Settrington, 114
Sherborne abbey, 150–53
Silly, 178
Slepe, 136, 142, 144
Spain, 64
Stanningfield, 105
Strasbourg, 30
Suffolk, 91, 94, 96, 97, 138
Syleham, 105
Talou, 28
Tees valley, 108, 116
Therfield, 144
Thérouanne, 23, 25, 26, 32, 60, 61, 63
Thurleston, 105
Tillières, 120, 121, 122
Trazegnies, 178

Vendôme, 28
Vermandois, 28
Veurne, 29
Vexin, 26, 83, 116
Vézelay abbey, 150, 156, 157, 160
Vicoigne abbey, 20, 29
Welnetham, 105
Whitlingham, 105
Wickmere, 105
Winchester, 102, 132
Wistow, 142, 144
Woodhurst, 136, 137
Worcester, 89, 90, 94, 109
Worms, 6
York, 109, 113, 129
Yorkshire, 108, 112

Thematic Index

abbot's power, 52, 51–72, 97, 149, 160
advocacy, 31, 149, 174, 175
Anglican Church, 8
Anglo-Norman England, 10, 127, 130, 134
Anglo-Saxon England, 89–106, 130, 153
Annales, 7
annals. *See* historiography
aristocracy, 90
Benedictine restoration, 52
Benedictine rule, 53, 65, 74, 94
bishops. *See* episcopal power
canon law, 9, 107, 113
Carolingian empire, 5, 42, 164
Catholic Church. *See* Roman Catholic Church
chanceries, 20
charters. *See* diplomatic sources
chronicles. *See* historiography
clamour, 161–65, 180
cnihts, 94
comital power, 20, 52
commendation. *See* homage
commune, 39, 43, 164
conflict settlement, 171, 172
Council of Clermont, 78
counts. *See* comital power
Danes. *See* Vikings
deditio, 179
diplomatic sources, 19–35, 58, 71, 73, 90, 112, 151, 159, 175
dispute settlement, 14, 15, 39, 114, 124, 132, 149, 157, 160, 165, 177–82

Domesday Book, 91, 95, 96, 103, 137, 141
ducal power, 23, 75, 80, 81, 82, 130
dukes. *See* ducal power
endogamy, 107, 131
episcopal power, 21, 27, 37–50, 85, 89–106, 131, 149, 179
excommunication, 21, 30, 150, 162, 178, 179, 180
exemption, 75, 85
exogamy, 107, 131, 132
feud. *See* dispute settlement
fraternity, 133–46
freemen, 94
friendship, 75, 100, 122, 130, 175, 182
gesta (abbatum, episcoporum), 57, 59, 66, 77, 84
gift exchange, 12, 14, 73, 80, 90, 94, 120, 121, 134, 135, 137, 149, 173, 174, 178
Gregorian reform, 2, 10, 12, 13, 34, 44, 46
hagiography, 51–72, 54, 58, 59, 167, 172
historiography, 1, 58, 59, 65, 68, 159, 160, 169
homage, 77, 78, 91, 95, 128, 137, 142
humiliation, 161, 180
interaction of secular and ecclesiastical power. *See* negotiation
intitulatio, 20, 26–30
inventio. *See* relic narratives
investiture, 6, 9, 77, 78, 84
Investiture Contest, 126

invocation, 20, 22–26
kinship, 15, 108, 131, 107–32
knight-service, 137
Kulturkampf, 3
landownership, 13, 14, 15, 90, 95, 108, 112, 117, 123, 136, 173
De libertate Beccensis, 73–85
liturgical sources, 54, 56, 60, 135, 151, 160, 161, 165
lordship, 89–106
malediction, 159, 160
marriage, 107–32
Merovingian era, 5
miracles, 64, 167, 183
Monodiae, 37–50
negotiation, 150, 178, 183
Norman Conquest, 69, 94, 134, 135
Ottonian illumination, 151, 157

Peace of God, 45
peasantry, 90, 173
piety, 19–35
Premonstratensian order, 167
relic narratives, 51–72
Roman Catholic Church, 2, 3
royal power, 45, 79, 89, 164
sanctio, 20, 30–34
secular power, 34, 35, 73, 74, 83, 89
simony, 6, 42
soke, 95, 137
translatio. *See* relic narratives
Vikings, 51, 108, 128
violence, 11, 37, 39, 41, 44, 50, 150, 156, 160, 171, 172, 173, 176, 177, 182
wrath, God's, 34, 64, 171